EVIL MONEY

EVIL MONEY

Encounters Along the Money Trail

RACHEL EHRENFELD

A Division of Shapolsky Publishers

Evil Money

S.P.I. BOOKS
A division of Shapolsky Publishers, Inc.

Copyright © 1992, 1994 by Rachel Ehrenfeld

Previously published in hardcover
as by HarperCollins Publishers

ISBN 1-56171-333-3

For any additional information, contact:

S.P.I. BOOKS/Shapolsky Publishers, Inc.
136 West 22nd Street
New York, NY 10011
212/633-2022 / FAX 212/633-2123

Manufactured in Canada

10 9 8 7 6 5 4 3 2 1

To my family
and the fearless few

History suggests that capitalism is a necessary condition for political freedom. Clearly it is not a sufficient condition.

—MILTON FRIEDMAN,
Capitalism and Freedom (1962), Chapter I

Contents

FOREWORD TO THIS EDITION XI

ACKNOWLEDGMENTS XV

INTRODUCTION XIX

THE LANSKY LEGACY: "It's Better in The Bahamas" 1

THE TREASURE OF LA MINA 57

THE WHIP AT THE END OF THE POLAR CAP 123

BANK OF CREDIT AND COMMERCE INTERNATIONAL (BCCI):
   The Robin Hood of the Third World 159

THE COLOMBIZATION OF THE UNITED STATES:
   Abdicating to the Narcocracy 211

APPENDIX 249

NOTES 259

BIBLIOGRAPHY 279

INDEX 289

Foreword to this Edition

Dr. E is one of the most ubiquitous bloodhounds on the narco-dollar trail, and her work gives us possibly the best available roadmap of world-class criminality. She follows the illicit cash flows from Los Angeles to Switzerland, from Miami to Medellin. Her restless energy serves her well in following the constantly changing structure of this world financial underground. The multi-billion dollar drug money network can shift direction abruptly. When the heat is on Miami, the bundles of cocaine permeated bills begin to show up in Los Angeles. And Dr. E. turns up not much later, asking her audacious, impertinent questions.

Fickle as the cash trail may be, however, the global cast of characters remains remarkably stable. The notorious Bank of Credit and Commerce International served as central banker to the drug cartels for the better part of a decade. More respectable international banks continue the work without interruption.

It is no exaggeration to talk about a global Phantom Banking system, as the interface between the legitimate financial world and a variety of international criminal networks. The collapse of the BCCI brought some of the this demi-monde to light; its client base included drug lords from Columbia to southeast Asia, Palestinian terrorists and their multi-million dollar trade in munitions and covert intelligence operations, including the Central Intelligence Agency lifeline to the Afghan Mujaheen. But the BCCI was a Johnny-come-lately to this business. Elements of international finance have long been serving those who need to move large illicit sums, and this industry continues to flourish.

This system creates its own political economy. The indispensable elements for this kind of banking is the Fix, political prosecution against intrusive regulation. Some governments, such as the notorious offshore banking havens, provide it legally, through strict secrecy laws and a token supervisory apparatus. In others, mainly the world financial centers such as the United States, Phantom Banking has to purchase goodwill from the politicians, either legally through campaign contributions, or otherwise. The Savings and Loan debacle in the U.S. showed how easily this favor could be bought.

This political economy is so evident that one has to lose patience with the conspiracy theorists who trample the trail in their chase of red herrings, such as the CIA. The spooks in general rank low on the scale of those who understand and manipulate this world. Undoubtedly clients and probable incorporators of some of its institutions, they still come of as rather hapless stooges for the financial masterminds whose primary motive is greed.

It's Dr. E.'s great virtue that she keeps a sense of proportion in describing this system and portrays its more accurately than the sensational accounts in such wide circulation. "Evil Money" gives the reader a rare glimpse into this world of finance that considers itself beyond good and evil.

James Ring Adams
The Big Fix, Inside the S&L Scandal, and *A Full Service Bank: How Bill Stole Billions Around the World.*

Acknowledgments

IT WOULD be impossible to list all the many people and organizations who have assisted with the preparation of this manuscript, and some have requested anonymity. I wish to convey my sincerest gratitude to all of them wherever they may be and the following have my special thanks:

Floyd Abrams and his wife, Efrath
James Ring Adams, for friendship, a sharp pencil, and the title
David Asman, *The Wall Street Journal*
Pietro Banas, U.S. correspondent, *Il Mondo*, and his wife, Patrizia, for warmth and caring during a difficult moment
Christina Bennett, *Il Mondo*, the best research assistant
Paolo Bernasconi, Lugano
Frank Bierens, The Netherlands
Yossef Bodansky, Director, Task Force on Terrorism, Unconventional Warfare, House Republican Research Committee
Debbie Boughner, for keeping the light on
Charles (Chuck) Brooks, Senator Arlen Specter's office
Illa Brown, DEA

ACKNOWLEDGMENTS

Brian Bruh, Director, and Andy Flodin, FINCEN

James V. Capua, President, William H. Donner Foundation, whose confidence in my work and the project never faltered

Rico Carisch and Elisabeth Pura-Hann, SonntagsBlick, Zurich

Yigal Carmon, Israel's Prime Minister Adviser for Countering Terrorism

Don Congdon, my agent

George Craig, President and Chief Executive Officer, HarperCollins, for starting me off

Peter Djinis, Director, Office of Financial Enforcement, U.S. Treasury

William H. Donner Foundation

Dr. Peter Gasser, prosecutor, Zurich

Mark Greenberg, for his help with the manuscript and his insights

Dick Gregory, former U.S. Attorney, Miami

W. E. Gutman, for making good use of his special editorial talents

Rayburn Hess, INM, U.S. Department of State

Charles Intriago, Money Laundering Alert

Professor Raphael Israeli, Hebrew University, Jerusalem

Jeff Karsh, U.S. Treasury

Joel Kassiday, Senator Hank Brown's Office

Jane Kawhara, current Assistant U.S. Attorney, and Gordon Greenberg, former Assistant U.S. Attorney, Los Angeles

Dr. Mitchell Kline, for a refreshing outlook

Dan Kornstein, my lawyer, special thanks

Professor Ernest Kux, Zurich

Richard Larry and the Sara Scaife Foundation

Michael Levitas, Editor, Op-Ed Page, *New York Times*

Thomas Loreto, Special Agent, U.S. Customs

Paul McMullan, American Airlines captain for old-fashioned tlc (tender loving care), who probably saved my life on board Flight #107 London–New York

Dick Marty, the brave former prosecutor in Bellinzona, Ticino, Switzerland

Susan Moldow, Editor in Chief, HarperCollins

Pier Georgio Mordassini, Chief Magistrate, Bellinzona, Ticino, Switzerland

Hans G. Neilsson, Council of Europe, Strasbourg, France

Wilmer (Buddy) Parker III, U.S. Attorney, Atlanta, special thanks

Craig Passic, DEA

Mark Pieth, Head of Service on Organized Crime, Ministry of Justice, Berne, Switzerland

Thomas H. Roche, Associate U.S. Attorney, New York

Sydney Rotalinti, Swiss reporter from Bellinzona, Ticino, Switzerland, for friendship, integrity, support, and readiness to put himself in the line of fire

Sol Sanders, for keeping me informed and keeping my spirits from flagging

Charles Saphos, Legal Counsel for Interpol, Washington, D.C.

Brian Sargant, former member, RCMP

Stephen Schneider, Solicitor General's office, Canada

Mark Schulman, Jerusalem

Pam Schwarzer, for keeping me mobile

John Sexton, Dean, New York University School of Law

Abraham D. Sofaer, former legal counsel, Department of

State, who was also on Flight #107 London–New York and who became my guardian angel

Rod Stamler, former member, RCMP

Lynn Summers, Assistant U.S. Attorney, Florida

Professor Lewis Tambs, U.S. Ambassador to Colombia, 1983–85, for his friendship, time, and knowledge

Dr. Martin Tesher, for worrying

Ken Thompson, INM

Irving Tragen, OAS

Joseph B. Treaster, *New York Times*

Carlton Turner, former Presidential Assistant and Drug Abuse Policy Officer, the White House

Roger Urbanski, Special Agent, U.S. Customs

William von Raab, former Commissioner, U.S. Customs

Pat Wait, Administrative Assistant to Congresswoman Helen Bentley, for friendship

Benjamin Weiner, Probe International

Jane Wexton, Citibank

Michael Whibey, Washington, D.C.

Faith Whittlesey, former U.S. Ambassador to Switzerland, who generously shared her knowledge of Swiss culture, Swiss politics, and the Swiss banking system

Tim Wren, National Drug Information Unit (NDIU), London

Michael Zeldin, Department of Justice

Introduction

Evil Money was first published in the summer of 1992. My objective was to call attention to the threat illegal money, especially drug money, presents to the democratic institutions and free markets. Since Bill Clinton was inaugurated as President in 1993, the threat to the United States seems to have worsened. It is worse because the new president's financial, political, and personal ethics, as well as his associations, reflect all of the alarming trends described in *Evil Money*. It appears that in the group around the president willful blindness was common, and evil money bought political power.

A Little Rock friend and supporter of Bill Clinton is Dan Lasater. Lasater, a flamboyant businessman and convicted drug dealer, contributed heavily to Clinton's various campaigns. He made his private jet available for the Clintons' use, partied with them, entertainee them in his ski resort in New Mexico, and employed Clinton's half brother Roger, who is also a convicted drug dealer. The president was present at his brother's 1984 trial, in which there was testimony about Lasater's drug activities; the trial was widely covered in the Arkansas press. and yet Bill Clinton claims he knew nothing about Lasater's involvement with drugs. Apparently this ignorance was widespread in Little Rock, since even after being implicated in drug dealing at Roger Clinton's trial Lasater was awarded $664.8 million in Arkansas state bond contracts, making $1.7 million for himself. Lasater's own conviction came in October of 1986.

As early as 1983 there had been widespread talk in Little Rock about Lasater's lavish parties, at which cocaine was passed around on the hors d'ouvres trays. To Lasater, providing cocaine at these parties was no different than "paying for dinner and drinks for my friends." "I shared my success with them in that manner," he declared at his trial, where he admitted to such sharing in at least 180 instances. Lasater's cocaine distribution was not a matter of concern to the authorities until the Clinton trial testimony made it impossible to ignore. According to an Arkansas State Police investigator, Lasater's conduct "would not have led to a state police investigation, because it was not their practice then to conduct probes of recreational drug use. " This at a time when a much-publicized national "war on drugs" was supposedly being waged in the U.S.

The permissive Arkansas attitude towards drugs and drug money seems to have come with Clinton to Washington. We have Surgeon General Elders, whose son faces drug charges in Little Rock, publicly suggesting a study of "alternatives" to the present anti-drug laws. Meanwhile, *The Wall Street Journal* speculated editorially in February that one reason for the unprecedented number of Clinton White House personnel who have not as yet received permanent White House passes was their "recreational" drug use. In the same vein *Rolling Stone* in May's issue reports on "young administration aides," at a Washington party, dancing and chatting "as marijuana fumes wafted indiscreetly through the house."

Finally, Clinton has embraced the president of Colombia, Cesar Gaviria, successfully promoting him to be the next Secretary General of the Organization of American States, even though Columbia legalized drug use and there is plenty of evidence to suggest that during Gaviria's presidency Columbia was thoroughly taken over by the drug cartels, transforming the oldest democracy in Latin America to a genuine Narcocracy. Clearly, the Clinton Administration is not one from which we should expect a resolute war on drugs or any particular vigilance with respect to drug money laundering.

Senator John Kerry, (D. Mass.,) in the April 20, 1994 hearings of the Senate Foreign Relations Subcommittee on Terrorism, Narcotics and International Operations, declared that drugs, drug money laundering, and the crime they spread in their wake are "the most serious criminal threat in history, and perhaps the greatest national security threat of our time." This recognition may be too late; drug use is up. and drugs are available everywhere to anyone in the U.S. at low prices and in high quality. In Little Rock, Arkansas, crack cocaine can be bought for as low as $5 a vial, and cocaine sells for $100 a gram. In Burlington, Vermont, crack cocaine is a bit more expensive at $25 a rock, but heroin prices are among the cheapest in the U.S. at $24 per bag. In the U.S. the low prices and high quality of heroin are reflected in a 44% rise in heroin-related emergency room visits for the first half of 1993, according to Drug-Czar Lee Brown (May,11, 1994).

Drug money laundering is also up. The four major money laundering centers still are Los Angeles, Miami, Jacksonville, and San Antonio. In 1993 Los Angeles banks reported on $9.3 billion in surplus cash; Miami,

$5.4 billion; Jacksonville, $2.6 billion; and San Antonio, 2.5 billion. [source: Federal Reserve Board.] The signing of NAFTA at the end of 1993 will probably result in even larger amounts of surplus currency in American banks with the removal of trade barriers making it easier for both drugs and funds to cross the borders of North America.

Since *Evil Money* was first written, the evil aspects of drug trafficking and money laundering became more powerful and control more economies and peoples. On the heels of the independence of the eastern European states, came drug abuse and flourishing new centers of criminal organizations. New bonds of cooperation now link Nigerian, Russian, Italian, Colombian, Japanese, Pakistani, and Chinese criminal organizations, among others.

The continuing growth of radical Muslim fundamentalism carries with it escalation in drug trafficking to the West. Drugs are a double-edged sword for radical Islamic regimes; first, a tool to raise funds, second, a means to corrupt the West. This may be a partial explanation for the dramatic increase in heroin production allocated to the West, smuggled from Afganistan, Burma, Iran, and Pakistan, "the U.S. government estimates that opium yield...rose...from 24 metric tons in 1992 to 42 metric tons in 1993 [INM Strategy Report, pp. 9-12.] Political and economic turmoil in Africa further contributes to the growing traffic in drugs. The profits in turn fuel tribal warfare and factional disputes, further increasing the breakdown of law and order.

The "White Poison" of the Andes has spread throughout the world. The Colombian Cali and other cartels have expanded their base of operation and are now controlling the cocaine business in all South and Central America. In addition to cocaine, Latin American countries and Mexico are increasing their opium and hashish production for distribution in the U.S. As for the Caribbean Islands, they continue their role in providing transit and banking services for the booming business. The many treaties and agreements signed bilaterally and internationally with the U.S. has accomplished little to curb the flow of drugs and money. "Even in countries committed to controlling drug-related money laundering, criminal and civil laws permit only limited departure from bank secrecy laws in order to permit exchange of information. [GAO, 1993.] A comment by an ex-prosecutor in Switzerland, Paolo Bernasconi, sums up the post *Evil Money* reality. "Banks are too lenient in fighting money laundering, and government officials are doing too little...The efforts have failed." (*Schweizerische Handelszaltung*, April 22, 1994.)

Drug trafficking and especially money laundering have already become so pervasive, that the corruption of drug wealth has successfully penetrated business and government elites. Those not on the take are practicing passive tolerance. Drug money fuels the growing underground economy, which serves as a base for the continuing penetration of the legal economy and political institutions by criminal organizations. Calls from respected businessmen and Washington think-tanks to legalize drugs are growing. The dark reality of Narcocracy is about to replace expectations of a world enjoying universal blessings of personal and economic freedom that accompanied the fall of communism.

The Lansky Legacy:

"It's Better in The Bahamas"

You can buy an airstrip, or an island. You can buy citizenship. You can buy protection. You can buy justice. And should your drug cargo get seized by police, you can even buy it back.

—Carl Hiaasen and Jim McGee, "A Nation for Sale," *Miami Herald*, September 23, 1984

CAST OF CHARACTERS

Meyer Lansky—the "Godfather of money-laundering"
Lynden Oscar Pindling—Prime Minister of The Bahamas

Medellín cartel members:
Pablo Escobar-Gaviria
Jose Gonzalo Rodriguez Gacha
Jorge Ochoa Vasquez
Fabio Ochoa Vasquez
Carlos Lehder

Robert Merkle—former U.S. Attorney for Florida's Central District
Robert Vesco—American fugitive financier
Nigel Bowe—Bahamian lawyer
George Smith—cabinet official, Minister of Agriculture, Fisheries, and Local Government
John J. Roll—former Bahamian immigration officer
Everette Bannister—one of the most formidable wheeler-dealers in The Bahamas
Kendal Nottage—lawyer, cabinet minister, and member of the Bahamian Parliament and his wife, Rubie—also a lawyer
Eric Sawyer—manager of Bank of Nova Scotia branch in Nassau, The Bahamas
Howard Smith—the assistant commissioner of the Royal Bahamian Police Force
F. Lee Bailey—noted attorney who represented Lynden Pindling
Lev E. Dobriansky—former U.S. ambassador to The Bahamas

Carol Boyd Hallett—former U.S. ambassador to The Bahamas

Brian Ross—NBC reporter

Ira Silverman—NBC producer

William Marsden—investigative reporter, *Montreal Gazette*

Admiral Daniel Murphy—former chief of staff for Vice President George Bush

American drug traffickers:

Edward Ward

Barry Kane

Timothy Minnig

Robert L. Frappier

Arnold Katz

Bruce Griffin

George William Baron

Raymond Patriarca—head of New England crime family

Salvatore Michael Caruana—member of the Patriarca family

Members of the Royal Commission:

Sir Gerald Cash—Governor of The Bahamas

Sir James A. Smith—retired Bahamian Supreme Court Justice

Edwin Willes—retired Assistant Commissioner of the Royal Canadian Mounted Police (RCMP)

The Right Reverend Drexel W. Gomez—Bishop of Barbados

Robert J. Ellicott—chief counsel to the Royal Commission, former Attorney General of Australia

Anastasio Somoza—former dictator of Nicaragua

ALMOST SINCE their discovery by Christopher Columbus on his first expedition to the New World in 1492, the Bahamian islands have been a haven and a refuge to countless adventurers, rogues, and renegades. This sprawling archipelago has harbored eighteenth-century pirates, Prohibition-era liquor smugglers and rich, thirsty Americans, and modern drug runners.

The lure of The Bahamas is easy to understand. Comprised of barely 4,400 square miles of land over an area spanning in excess of 100,000 square miles of territorial waters, The Bahamas are sparsely populated. Some of the islands are uninhabited and most offer natural, well-protected anchorages amid coral reef outcroppings and shallow water lagoons. Hundreds of small boat marinas dot a jagged coastline that an impoverished constabulary finds difficult to patrol.

More than 700 islands and cays spread across 600 miles, 50 miles southeast of the Florida coast. A British possession for 300 years, until its independence in 1973, The Bahamas were jealously held by the Crown for their strategic rather than economic importance. Unlike its more profitable Caribbean sisters, The Bahamas have no vast plantations, just some timber, salt, tomatoes destined for export, and game fish for the occasional visitor. By the mid-twentieth century, however, with the dramatic growth in international travel, increasingly larger numbers of tourists began to pour into The Bahamas, lured by promises of sun and frolic.

When Fidel Castro took over Cuba and shut down the casinos in 1959, The Bahamas quickly became the new gambling center of the Caribbean. Unlike Sam Giancana, the American mobster who plotted Fidel Castro's murder in revenge for the Cuban dictator's seizure of organized crime assets, the far shrewder Meyer Lansky wrote off his loss of the Riviera Hotel in Havana and promptly moved his operations to Nassau, the capital of The Bahamas. Lansky was not really interested in running hotels. He saw the real money in the gaming business, so he set out to transform a sleepy island chain into a casino empire. After the experience of his once-profitable Cuban fiefdom, Lansky knew he could do even better in The Bahamas. After all, gambling offers the perfect cover for sanitizing money generated by national crime syndicates from activities such as drug trafficking and prostitution.[1]

No one disputes that Meyer Lansky developed, refined, and nearly perfected the techniques now used by the mob to protect and disguise their ill-gotten revenues. Lansky's larcenous genius must also be credited with developing the use of tax havens, such as The Bahamas, as a shelter against IRS scrutiny. The booming gaming business, which promoted the expansion of offshore banking in The Bahamas, made its role as tax haven even more efficient. Once a legitimate banking outlet was established for the cash-rich gaming business, it became a convenient cover to channel legitimate and illegal earnings through Bahamian, Swiss, and Panamanian banks. The disguised profits often found their way back to the United States—Miami banks in particular—as "clean" money. By masterfully maneuvering the illegal proceeds from criminal activities into the banking system where money was "filtered" back into mainstream economic activities, Lansky changed the face of organized crime. Lansky is also credited with having manipulated the U.S. political establishment into granting gambling legal status. But Lansky's single most enduring contribution to the underworld remains the stratagem of hiding behind and operating through otherwise legitimate enterprises, making crimes difficult to detect and virtually impossible to uproot.

The methods that Lansky invented are the very same methods employed today by modern drug money launderers and other criminals. Although some of the events described took place more than twenty-five years ago, they continue to have a direct impact on the activities of the financial, political, and criminal worlds today.

Lansky was not prone to strong-arm tactics. His genius was in understanding the power of money. Until he came along politicians had used the underworld to carry out their mandates. Bolstered by the vast illegal fortunes he and his confederates had amassed, Lansky succeeded in making the politicians work for organized crime. This model has served the mafia, the drug cartels, and drug money launderers all over the world. Lansky used The Bahamas as a major transshipment center for drug trafficking and drug money-laundering via Switzerland to the United States long before the Colombian cartels landed on the island's golden shores.

Lansky was unusually astute politically and understood, particularly after the Cuban debacle (1959), that his offshore operations would never be safe unless the government he dealt with had a longer life span than Castro's predecessor—President Fulgencio Batista—a man he had known personally and bought off. Since blacks were in the majority in The Bahamas, Lansky realized that political arrangements would be short-lived unless the ruling blacks were included. His intelligence and business acumen served him well. His ability to manipulate people and systems to his own benefit was not what the public generally expected from a gangster.

When Lansky first began to operate in The Bahamas, the islands were controlled by the Bay Street Boys, a motley crew of white Bahamian businessmen. But a disclosure of illegal kickbacks from Freeport casino interests to government officials during the election campaign led to their quick demise. Lansky wasted no time. He immediately helped install a government that would be responsive to his interests. He and his men quietly threw their support behind the opposition Progressive Liberal Party (PLP) and its leader Lynden Oscar Pindling, the self-styled "Black Moses of the people,"[2] a move that would ensure Lansky's legacy right up to the present.

In 1967 Pindling and the PLP won a close victory, ending the careers of the Bay Street Boys while ushering in an even more corrupt regime in The Bahamas, one that would last till today. Pindling and his followers had masterfully drawn their support from a new class of ethnically aware, politically active black Bahamians inspired and stirred by the black power movements emerging in the Caribbean and the United States. It did not take long for the new order and its newly elected officials to develop an unholy arrangement

7

with Lansky and his gang. Of course, generous payoffs oiled the wheels of the new government and favorably predisposed these officials to Lansky's activities.[3]

Little changed when The Bahamas achieved full independence in 1973. The die had been cast for the casual and corrupt style of Bahamian leadership, white or black.

Lynden Pindling had been Prime Minister during the six years that preceded Bahamian independence. He has since become firmly entrenched and has gained larger majorities in Parliament with each election. After six terms as Prime Minister, he shows no sign of political fatigue. The near-absolute certainty that the longer he endures politically the wealthier he becomes personally is a seductive incentive to remain in office.

In the 1970s after having long served as a way station for Colombian illegal aliens on their way to the United States, The Bahamas began to woo Colombian and other drug traffickers. If people could be smuggled in, why not drugs? It was an easier and far more profitable commodity.

The Bahamas offer an ideal transit point between Colombia and the United States. Loaded to the gunwales with cocaine and marijuana, light twin-engine aircraft slip away from numerous pirate Colombian airstrips and land, sometimes under the cover of darkness, on Bahamian runways. The Nassau airport on New Providence Island was frequently used in the early 1970s. In 1979 the Bahamian Government identified fourteen islands it claimed were heavily involved in drug trafficking. Among these were The Exumas, Andros, Grand Bahama, Bimini, Cat Island, Inagua, and Abaco. New Providence is located less than

200 miles from Fort Lauderdale; Bimini is only 50 miles from Miami and the Carolinas are also within easy range. On weekends, aircraft carrying cocaine blend in with recreational air traffic.

In Nassau, Bahamian airport officials turned a blind eye toward cocaine-laden airplanes and the false flight plans the pilots routinely filed to disguise their ties with Colombia. One of these pilots, Barry Kane, found that a Bahamian lawyer by the name of Nigel Bowe was very helpful to his business. For a fee Mr. Bowe helped to bribe corrupt airport officials. A Royal Commission convened in 1983 to investigate drug trafficking and drug money-laundering in The Bahamas found that "Mr. Bowe's involvement with drug traffickers far exceeded a lawyer/client relationship and that he benefitted materially from his numerous associations with them. We have concluded that he was aware of their activities and assisted them in their nefarious trade." The Royal Commission was highly critical of Bowe's manner and demeanor, referring to him as "vulgar" and "profane."[4]

In July 1976 when Barry Kane met the infamous Colombian drug trafficker Carlos Lehder in Toronto, both were already veteran drug runners. Lehder, a member of the Medellín cartel, had earned a reputation as an innovator, having devised new methods for shipping drugs from Colombia to the United States. At their meeting the two men drew up elaborate plans to intensify cocaine shipments into the United States. With the Bahamian connections in place, it did not take long for drug smuggling to become a major commerce generating hundreds of millions of tax-free dollars.

But there were problems. Drug trafficking was growing so

rapidly that the Nassau International Airport was no longer able to handle the traffic effectively. To complicate matters, DEA undercover agents from Miami were swooping down on Nassau and asking too many questions. Intent on expanding his drug-smuggling operation and anxious to evade official scrutiny—U.S. G-men in particular—Carlos Lehder purchased Norman's Cay, a fishhook-shaped islet forty miles southeast of Nassau. Appropriately named after an English buccaneer, the cay was within easy reach of Florida and came equipped with an airstrip capable of handling nighttime traffic.

Lehder's first act as proprietor was to evict about fifty residents from the cay and to replace them with a team of Colombian, U.S., and German hoodlums groomed to run his narcotics operation. Uninvited visitors, including yachtsman Walter Cronkite, the former CBS news anchor, were rudely discouraged from anchoring in the cay's turquoise waters. Some were shot at.

Carlos Lehder, as Lansky before him, chose The Bahamas as a major transshipment point to enhance and increase his business to the United States. Other Colombian drug lords found The Bahamas agreeable as well. Jorge Ochoa Vasquez and Pablo Escobar-Gaviria, the Medellín drug kingpins, even visited Lehder at Norman's Cay, congratulating him on his judicious choice of The Bahamas and the cay as the cartel's new stepping-stone to U.S. markets. They were particularly pleased with the discretion exercised by Bahamian banks. Ochoa and Escobar subsequently opened several bank accounts there into which Lehder made cash deposits generated by the cartel's narcotics sales in the United States. Once deposited, the money was wire-transferred to the cartel's bank accounts in Panama.

As reporter Paul Eddy wrote in his exposé of The Bahamas, "The close relationship between Ochoa, Escobar, and Lehder provided the nucleus of a coalition that would rule the cocaine trade during its period of greatest expansion."[5] But they could never have done it without Bahamian government cooperation.

The establishment of a Colombian drug empire in The Bahamas is largely the result of Bahamian politicians' insatiable appetite for bribes and kickbacks. The cloak of incorruptibility of Her Majesty's servants, evident in the ultimate English expression *take no one's shilling*, was shed in less than a decade. By the late 1970s The Bahamas was a nation for hire. Many Colombian racketeers bought cooperation and protection in The Bahamas. Dozens of marijuana and cocaine entrepreneurs from Colombia and elsewhere used the Bahamian pipeline.[6]

It did not take long for U.S. law enforcement agencies to pay closer attention. Stories began to circulate in the region about people who had been forced to leave the islands under threat of death from drug runners.

While U.S. officials were intent on cleaning up The Bahamas, the Bahamians had other ideas. The "raid" on Lehder's Norman's Cay headquarters on September 14, 1979, is a good example. The DEA had learned about Lehder's activities in Norman's Cay in 1978 and, for months, had urged Bahamian police to raid the place. Dubbed "Operation Raccoon," the planned raid had become a well-known secret in Nassau and Norman's Cay. Set for September 1, the raid was inexplicably delayed for two weeks, providing Lehder more than ample warning.

As expected, the raid was a farce. Thirty-three people were arrested but Carlos Lehder was not among them. The Bahamian police confiscated a small arsenal of weapons but found little cocaine. Members of the raiding party later claimed that they had been unable to identify Lehder and, incredibly, had not been told that he was the one who was in control of the cay. Within days all those arrested were released on a mere $2,000 bail each.[7]

How did Lehder manage to escape? He had bribed police officials. According to the 1983 Royal Commission of Inquiry investigating drug-related corruption in The Bahamas, it was Howard Smith, the assistant commissioner of the Royal Bahamian Police Force who decided not to arrest Lehder. Smith made a poor impression in his appearance before the Royal Commission. Its report noted, "On occasion [he] exhibited arrogance and hostility, and some of his answers appeared to be facetious."[8]

Smith cited a lack of evidence, contradicting the preraid briefing to his subordinates. The Royal Commission scrutinized Smith's bank accounts and found nearly $60,000 that Smith, the number-two man in the Bahamian police, could not account for. The commission concluded: ". . . Lehder did bribe the police to ensure his freedom, and we find that there must have been complicity on the part of [Assistant Commissioner of Police] Smith and other senior Police Officers."[9] Was Smith the only corrupt police officer in The Bahamas? U.S. law enforcement officials did not think so. Actually, as Jorge Ochoa discovered in the early eighties, not only were the Bahamian police accepting protection money from him but they were also in the habit of confiscating some of his cocaine. According to the *Miami Herald*, at least 2,000 kilos of cocaine were sold by Bahamian policemen in Miami.[10]

By 1985 Robert Merkle had enough. As U.S. Attorney for Florida's Central District, he had spent most of his professional career investigating the Medellín and Cali cartels, and probing their drug-trafficking activities in the United States.

Long convinced that the Colombian drug trade to the United States was aided and abetted by corrupt officials in Mexico, Central America, the Caribbean, and South America, Merkle, after numerous drug prosecutions, also began to notice the existence of a Bahamian connection. By the early 1980s, as much as 80 percent of the cocaine and marijuana entering the United States was estimated to come from The Bahamas. And by the mid-1980s at least 10 percent of the island's total economic activity was drug-related, thereby increasing Bahamian dependency on the illegal trade.[11] Merkle and his team of prosecutors, along with the DEA, had no difficulty connecting high-profile Carlos Lehder to his Norman's Cay operation.

The DEA soon began to hear reports that Lehder and other Medellín and Cali cartel members were receiving VIP treatment from members of the Bahamian Government. In little over a decade, the Pindling administration was barnacled with a layer of fixers, go-betweens, and bagmen who took the drug runner's money and passed it on to higher Bahamian officials.

It is not difficult to imagine the effect such money had on an otherwise impoverished Bahamas, where a good and honest living was difficult to secure even in the best of times. Unfortunately, for some time, stories about corruption, drug trafficking, and money-laundering were largely anecdotal. Documentation proved difficult. The Bahamas had no interest in initiating investigations and the locals were reluctant to talk to outsiders. Actually the Royal Commission criticized the Bahamian public's attitude toward the drug traffickers and its open antipathy for the efforts to control it. The commission commented, "this is a sad reflection on the attitude of the community towards police officers who carried out their duties honestly and to the best of their ability."

That false sense of security came to an abrupt end on September 5, 1983, when the National Broadcasting Company (NBC) in the United States produced a *Special Segment* during its "Nightly News" report. In "The Navy and The Bahamas," news correspondent Brian Ross told the story of American fugitive financier Robert Vesco, of his new drug-running career, of his base in Norman's Cay, and of his Colombian partner in crime Carlos Lehder. Vesco, who the U.S. Government charged, had swindled $224 million from his mutual fund Investors Overseas Services (IOS), sought asylum in The Bahamas. (The sum may have been no more than $60 million.) He had no problem paying for his Bahamian hospitality for nearly nine years, from 1972 until 1981, when he was forced to leave.

Vesco's involvement with Lehder provided enough dynamite to set off a huge explosion. The most volatile revelation in the NBC story was based on a Justice Department intelligence report claiming that a Vesco associate "allegedly paid approximately $100,000 per month to Bahamian officials, among them the prime minister."[12]

In addition to Pindling, Brian Ross reported the involvement of Kendal Nottage, a cabinet minister and member of the Bahamian Parliament. But real hard evidence was missing. The broadcast cited only an aborted FBI sting designed to compromise Nottage by offering him a bribe on a yacht outside Bahamian waters and then arresting him.[13] The FBI plan failed when the then U.S. ambassador (to The Bahamas) Lev E. Dobriansky objected on the grounds that it would undermine U.S.-Bahamian relations and threaten ongoing talks concerning a U.S. submarine-testing base in The Bahamas.[14]

Suddenly, The Bahamas was the subject of major media attention, and Prime Minister Lynden Oscar Pindling did not like it one bit. A week later, on September 12, 1983, an angry Bahamian Prime Minister submitted to an interview by Jane Pauley on NBC's morning magazine, "Today," and fiercely denied any wrongdoing. Pindling lashed out at reporter Brian Ross early in the interview, calling him a "faker." As a somewhat flustered Jane Pauley fought to regain control of the interview,[15] Pindling proved a formidable adversary. He charged Ross with engineering a midnight ambush during which a tired Pindling refused to be interviewed. Not content with that broadside, Pindling followed it up by citing President Reagan and Vice President Bush's chief of staff, Admiral Daniel Murphy, in his defense. In an interview with Admiral Murphy, who then ran the South Florida Drug Task Force, Brian Ross had attempted to label the Bahamian Government "corrupt." But Murphy had wryly observed: ". . . you'll find that it is very difficult to get adequate corroborating evidence to make a strong case."[16]

When Ross finally confronted Pindling, the Bahamian

Prime Minister turned the tables on the reporter and demanded the names of the U.S. government officials who were Ross's alleged informants. The interview became heated and although it may seem that Pindling was somewhat incoherent, in reality, he cleverly manipulated the interview to his benefit:

Ross: Mr. Prime Minister, the federal authorities say they have information from one drug dealer after another.

Pindling: I'm not interested. Bring—bring the—bring the drug dealer.

Ross: Hm, hm.

Pindling: You see, bring the drug dealer. I know how to deal with convicted people.

Ross: Have you . . .

Pindling: Bring the drug dealer. What's his name?

Ross: My question. Have you not authorized . . .

Pindling: What is the name of the drug dealer?

Ross: There are a number of different ones.

Pindling: I don't mind the different ones. Give me one. Just one.

Ross: Who is that?

Pindling: Of a drug dealer. Give me one who you say tell the FBI this, who tell you?

Ross: About corruption in The Bahamas?

Pindling: No. What you were talking about just now. You know what I am talking about, Mr. Ross. Are you going to play crazy on me now?

Ross: There are a number of . . .

Pindling: Then name one my brother. Just one. You can't name one?

Ross: Do you know Michael Yamanis?

PINDLING: I never heard of Michael Yamanis.

Ross: Well, that's one. I'm here too . . .

PINDLING: Do you know Ca— do you know Casey Cartwright?

Ross: Pardon me?

PINDLING: Do you know Casey Cartwright?

Ross: I know Ken Cartwright.

PINDLING: Ken Car— Ken Cartwright.

Ross: Let me ask you a question . . .

PINDLING: Mr. Ross, are you going to name for me please right here now, in front of the same audience that you fraudulently and scandalously carried my name—the name of the informer you relied for the truth of your statements and on who NBC relies?

PAULEY: If he does, he's going to do it sometime after this station break.[17]

He didn't. And once off the air Pindling remained on the offensive against NBC. Represented by noted attorney F. Lee Bailey, the Bahamian Prime Minister sued Brian Ross and NBC in The Bahamas and Canada. Filed in Toronto in April 1984, the suit charged the reporter and the network with libel and slander, and demanded $2 million in compensation.

The Canadian courts were chosen for this unprecedented action because Canada's libel laws do not require the tough criteria established by U.S. libel laws. Rooted in the English common law, Canadian law places the burden of proof on the defendant, who must bear out the veracity of the disparaging statements and demonstrate that they were not, in fact, maliciously intended.

For the next five years, the legal wheels turned as both sides filed claims and counterclaims. In October 1989 a secret agreement was reached and Pindling dropped the suit.[18]

The NBC report had a dramatic effect on Pindling and he took an unusual step to lessen its impact and sent a letter to the U.S. Attorney General William French Smith. "I, Lynden Oscar Pindling, Prime Minister of The Bahamas, became the victim of circumstances beyond my control . . . on . . . NBC's nightly news," he wrote. "Ever since then a series of 'inspired' leaks have fueled the torrid fires of the press, mainly U.S.-based with incredible stories . . . despite official requests . . . in spiking the stories. I have endured the anguish . . . of repeated assassination attempts on my character and reputation by the press, by convicted felons and even by U.S. attorneys who have used perjured evidence knowing it to be false . . . primarily for purposes of launching themselves in U.S. politics."[19]

As The Bahamas is a member of the British Commonwealth, the Prime Minister went on the offensive and called for a Royal Commission of Inquiry to examine the charges against him. Royal commissions perform roughly the same function as an independent counsel does in the U.S. federal government. Such commissions have the advantage of being able to draw on the legal and law enforcement talent of the entire commonwealth, thus supposedly adding to the potential for objectivity and thoroughness. However, in the case of The Bahamas, the Royal Commission was unable to conduct a fair inquiry. The fact that its members were outsiders and foreigners in The Bahamas served Pindling well. Pindling was able to maintain full access and control of the documents. He also brought to bear great influence over the members of his government and other witnesses called to testify before the commission. Pindling's manipulation of the commission was no secret to American, Canadian, and British law enforcement agents, many of whom believed the investigation was a farce that he artfully controlled, directly or indirectly.

The Royal Commission was established by Bahamian Governor-General, Sir Gerald Cash, representing the Crown. Commission members included Sir James A. Smith, retired Bahamian Supreme Court Justice; Edwin Willes, retired assistant commissioner of the Royal Canadian Mounted Police (RCMP); and the Right Reverend Drexel W. Gomez, Bishop of Barbados.

Chief counsel to the commission was Robert J. Ellicott, an outspoken former Attorney General of Australia. Aiding Ellicott through the intricate maze of charges and counter-charges were three senior police officers: Superintendent David Stockley, head of the Central Drug Squad from Scotland Yard; Inspector Andrew Wells of the Special Investigative Branch from Australia's Federal Police Force; and Inspector Frank Richter from the Criminal Section of the RCMP.[20]

The Royal Commission received its mandate from Queen Elizabeth and was given a year to produce its report. The Crown and the Governor-General of The Bahamas made it explicitly clear that it was the direct result of the NBC news report. The commission invited NBC's Brian Ross and his producer, Ira Silverman, to testify, but they declined.[21] The hearings took place in The Bahamas and in Miami, Florida.

For 146 days, commission members listened to witnesses—360 of them—in public and secret sessions, and examined more than 1,000 documents. Those who testified comprised a wide range of government officials, policemen, drug traffickers, businessmen, anyone, in short, who seemed knowledgeable about illegal drugs and related industries. The documents included transcripts of telephone conversations, bills of sale, letters, affidavits, and bank and financial statements from people involved or suspected to be involved in the trade. The conclusions of the Royal Commission inquiry were published in a 307-page fine-print report. It painted an appalling picture of what The Bahamas had become under the one-party rule of Prime Minister Pindling.

Released in December 1984, the report described how, by the late 1960s, drug smugglers had already discovered The Bahamas as a transshipment point to the United States. First came marijuana dealers and later the more profitable and deadly cocaine traffickers. The report detailed how Bahamian officials, supported by a small army of well-connected lawyers, had helped Colombian and U.S. drug dealers and how they had been handsomely compensated.

The Royal Commission also found that drug consumption skyrocketed in The Bahamas. It was spurred by "spillage," the Bahamian term for small-scale thefts of drugs by the locals. Drug addiction resulted in the loss of nearly an entire generation of youth in this once closely knit and conservative family-oriented society. Drugs brought crime and violence in their wake. Once the smugglers realized that their drugs were being stolen by Bahamians, they armed themselves and entrusted their caches to armed guards. This inevitably led to increased violence.[22] With cocaine consumption, especially the highly addictive free-basing variety popular in the islands, came a tidal wave of violent crime—rape, murder, and armed robbery—unprecedented in the archipelago's history. Some islands, such as Bimini, were lost to the drug traffickers, whose small armies moved in and took control.[23]

It was a shocking indictment. But there was more. Names were named and their criminal behavior aired. Included was cabinet official George Smith, at the time Minister of Agriculture, Fisheries, and Local Government. Smith subsequently resigned from the Cabinet, but retained his seat in Parliament.[24]

Smith's constituency included Norman's Cay, the headquarters for Carlos Lehder and his drug-trafficking activities. Lehder offered Smith a BMW, which Smith accepted. That, at least, was the conclusion of the Royal Commission. After weighing the evidence, the commission carefully suggested that "the funds for the purchase of the BMW in Miami on 4 June 1979 were provided to the Minister by the Lehder organization."[25]

The Royal Commission addressed yet another of Smith's problems. According to a convicted drug smuggler, Edward Ward—also based at Norman's Cay—Smith was offered $100,000 to provide Ward and his wife "protection" while they worked in The Bahamas. Arranged by Everette Bannister, one of the most formidable wheeler-dealers in The Bahamas, a meeting took place on a houseboat at Paradise Island. The commission noted that Bannister used his political influence to solve legal and other problems for the drug smugglers and received handsome payments for his services. Bannister, who had been born in Marsh Harbour, The Bahamas, some sixty years ago, had spent many years working as a doorman in Manhattan. In 1951, he obtained U.S. citizenship, an event he denies. Bannister returned to The Bahamas in 1966 just before his good friend Lynden Pindling was elected Prime Minister. Bannister funneled more money in "gifts and loans" to Pindling's accounts than anyone else, even though his only reported income at the time of the commission probe was a consulting fee of $50,000 from Resorts International. He reportedly received $1,000 pocket money whenever he acted as a "fixer" on behalf of Pindling or The Bahamas.[26] An independent Bahamian parliamentary committee investigated Bannister for influence peddling and noted that "Mr. Bannister is obviously a very persuasive person who has been able to obtain loans from various entities under circumstances and for amounts that are simply amazing and inconsistent with known usual business practices . . ."[27]

Everette Bannister was also instrumental in relieving Robert Vesco, the American fugitive, of part of his stolen fortune. Bannister obtained $14 million in "loans" that were never repaid. Of the $14 million, $10.5 million went to Everette Bannister's Bahamas World Airways (BWA) and Bahamas Catering. The rest financed yet other companies in which Pindling had undisclosed interests. As the *Miami Herald* reported, "When it came to BWA, the Vesco bank was 'a continuous tap that somebody forgot to turn off' according to [bank] liquidator David Jones."[28] At the houseboat meeting between cabinet minister Smith and drug smuggler Ward, Bannister did most of the talking. In the course of their conversation, according to Ward, Smith made it clear that the $100,000 would go to the Prime Minister. Smith denied the incident. He claimed he never met Ward and never accepted money for himself or on behalf of Lynden Pindling. The Royal Commission did not believe Smith's denials and sided with Ward. Its conclusion rested on Smith's inability to provide a convincing explanation for the $96,000 that appeared in his bank account in May 1979. The commission's report recommended that the Bahamian Attorney General "review the evidence relating to Minister [Smith] to determine what further action may be appropriate in the circumstances."[29]

What was the Prime Minister's role in all of this? Edward Ward was not the only one who reported payoffs to Lynden Pindling. The testimony of Timothy Minnig, also known as Robert Fuller or T.T., in June and July of 1984 probably did the most to damage the Prime Minister's reputation. It had already played a leading role in the NBC story.

Minnig was an American drug trafficker in need of protection. He was told by Robert Vesco that for a fee he could obtain such protection in The Bahamas for himself and his associates, one of whom was Robert L. Frappier. The cost according to Minnig: "one million dollars, part of which would go to the prime minister."[30] Minnig claimed he saw Vesco hand Pindling an envelope stuffed with $100,000 as a down payment. But to Minnig's annoyance, he did not actually get to talk to Pindling. Instead, he only observed the transaction from a distance. Minnig stated that:

the prime minister was saying goodbye to people who looked like they were finishing a formal type meal; it was

23

mid-afternoon: Vesco said "wait here for me" and he walked over; Mr. Pindling separated from the group of people: there were five . . . ten feet apart; the Prime Minister spoke; Vesco handed him the envelope, the prime minister turned: they went up a little walkway into the house . . . the prime minister and Vesco came out of the house; neither of them had the envelope.[31]

Later over drinks Minnig asked Vesco what happened and was told: "Well, everything will in due course work itself out . . . you have been taken care of."[32] Pindling denied knowing anybody by the name of Timothy Minnig, Robert Fuller, or T.T.

Commission members rejected Minnig's story because they did not believe he had that much cash in his possession at the time. But others in The Bahamas were not so sure. One Canadian investigative journalist, William Marsden, of the *Montreal Gazette*, checked Minnig's story. He found that Minnig had somewhat unusual relations with the Nassau branch of the Bank of Nova Scotia and its manager, Eric Sawyer. Minnig had repeatedly deposited and withdrawn large sums of cash with no formal registration of the transactions.[33] Marsden also discovered that shortly before Sawyer testified at the commission inquiry, Prime Minister Pindling met with the Nova Scotia bank manager. There were two other witnesses present. According to Marsden, Sawyer changed his story after talking with Pindling. In spite of his earlier testimony to the commission that Minnig had withdrawn large sums of money on short notice, on the stand, Sawyer could not recall anything about it.[34] Not surprisingly, the commission found the incident disturbing.

In the end, Minnig's account contained no proof of bribery even if the envelope was filled with cash. All he saw was an envelope, which, according to Vesco, contained $100,000. Much depended, therefore, on Vesco's reliability; and Vesco was not a trustworthy witness. Besides, he did not testify about any of these and it is unlikely that he will. However, Minnig's associate, Robert Frappier, told the *Miami Herald*, "I felt that the government of The Bahamas was a payable situation. If you paid enough money, you were protected in The Bahamas."[35]

While the Royal Commission could find no conclusive proof linking Pindling to drug money-laundering, there was ample evidence from other sources. Some of this evidence was made available to me on the written condition that I *never* reveal the source, a reliable person with inside knowledge of Vesco's and Pindling's business dealings. The source spoke about Pindling's direct knowledge, participation, and approval of kickbacks and bribes in The Bahamas. From the start, he emphasized that he knew Pindling. "The Prime Minister is *very* smart. . . ." he said. "Vesco was dealing with Prime Minister Pindling and one of his ministers [who] handles everything." This source also explained how it all happened. When Vesco was under investigation in the United States in 1972 for his role in the Investors Overseas Services (IOS) scandal, he had scouted many islands in the Caribbean: "Vesco was welcomed everywhere, everybody wanted to have him. . . . Everybody thought—and Vesco did everything to confirm the impression—that he had $224 million in stolen money but he actually 'ripped off' no more than $60 million, keeping only $10–12 for himself. Thirty million dollars were invested in The Bahamas and the rest of the money is unaccounted for," my source told me. This was the reason "Vesco had to walk around like he owned the world when in reality he had a cash flow problem. After 1974 Vesco didn't have any more money. He couldn't even raise $200,000 in cash when it was requested of him. . . . Vesco visited many islands, everybody wanted [him] but Vesco chose The Bahamas because of its higher living standard. . . . Banking in Panama is okay but living there stinks. . . . Vesco also went to Haiti and after three days, Jesus Christ . . . he left. . . . When Vesco opted The Bahamas, the arrangement with Pindling was that Vesco would invest in The Bahamas to . . . enhance the capitalist system and the independence of The Bahamas . . . and everybody will make a lot of money."

Vesco used his money very carefully. The $30 million invested in The Bahamas were "loans for friends in high offices." Vesco made these loans usually under "pressure" from the Bahamian Government. For example, when a well-connected Bahamian requested a loan from Vesco for a new venture, one of Pindling's ministers made sure that Vesco provided the "loan." "I hope the loans are going well with this guy," the minister told Vesco, and this was enough to convince Vesco that he didn't have much choice. When Vesco was under the gun in the United States, Barclay's Bank in The Bahamas refused to clear Vesco's checks. Vesco went immediately to the minister, who, in turn, threatened the director of Barclay's with the loss of their clearinghouse privileges. The threat went so far as to suggest that Vesco's bank, the Commonwealth Bank, would take over this role if Barclay's didn't cooperate. Barclay's caved in.[36]

The most recent indictment against Vesco handed up by

26

a federal grand jury in Florida in September 1989 accused him of collaborating with Pablo Escobar-Gaviria, José Gonzalo Rodriguez Gacha, Jorge Ochoa Vasquez, and Fabio Ochoa Vasquez, the Medellín drug cartel kingpins, in trafficking drugs from Colombia through Nicaragua, Andros Island in The Bahamas, and Cuba to the United States. Vesco reportedly is living in Cuba and it is doubtful that he is in charge of his fate.

After reviewing all the allegations made by Ward, Minnig, and others, the Royal Commission concluded that Pindling's alleged guilt had not been conclusively proven. There was not enough evidence, they claimed, to prove that Pindling was receiving protection money and bribes. Yet, records showed that the Prime Minister and his wife had received nearly $17 million in gifts and loans from foreigners over a period of twelve years; "the money came from investors and businessmen who owned or sought government-sanctioned enterprises in The Bahamas."[37] Even Pindling's wife owned an office building built with "loans" from Vesco.[38] This was not all. The Royal Commission reported:

Between January 1, 1977 and December 31, 1983, the prime minister and Lady Pindling made deposits into their bank accounts of $3.5 million over and above his official income as prime minister. . . . According to Inspector Richter [from the RCMP] the sources and the amounts of the various items which made up the sum of $3.5 million were from [loans from banks, loans from friends, identified deposits and cash deposits]. This liability far exceeded the prime minister's official monthly salary. . . . these loans were unsecured; there was no documentation and no provision for the payment of interest thereon. . . . In answer to the question: "Do you ever expect to be repaid?": Edward St. George [a major partner in the Grand Bahamas Development Company in Freeport, and one of Pindling's friends who "loaned" him money] said . . . "we certainly do not expect to be repaid, and we would not be suing him. We certainly would not be taking any action. We would write it off." He further stated "as a result of further information of the prime minister's financial difficulties, Jack Hayward and I have agreed unconditionally to waive the repayment of these loans." Thus the prime minister has been relieved of the obligation to repay to Mr. Hayward and Mr. St. George a total of $750,000.[39]

Yet another friend of Pindling and a cabinet minister, Kendal Nottage, was a member of the law firm that facilitated the transactions. However, Pindling did not escape criticism entirely. The Royal Commission examined his finances, which were—to put it mildly—tangled almost beyond comprehension even to a battery of certified public accountants. The commission easily confirmed that the Prime Minister was spending far more than he was earning. Interest payments on bank loans alone ranged from $7,000 to $8,000 a month plus a $4,500 payment on a mortgage held on a house described as something between a "villa" and a "palace."[40] These liabilities greatly exceeded the Prime Minister's relatively modest annual salary of $100,000. Nevertheless, Sir Lynden, who was knighted in 1983, and Lady Pindling managed to deposit $3.5 million between 1977 and 1983 in various bank accounts.[41]

Despite great efforts made by the Royal Commission and

its chief detective inspector, Frank Richter, the origin of some of these deposits could not be identified. The Bahamas has no income tax and, therefore, financial records are not required. The Prime Minister, furthermore, kept skimpy financial records. Most of the "loans" to Pindling were invariably unsupported by any documentation and there was no provision for interest payments—a detail that should have called into question the real nature of these "loans."

On other occasions, the commission discovered that the Prime Minister had received large amounts of money and that neither he nor his benefactors were very clear as to what the transactions were all about. For example, Everette Bannister gave Pindling $550,000 for the Prime Minister's alleged undisclosed shares in a catering company. The Prime Minister thought the deal had actually involved $650,000. Both men were vague about details.

This tangled financial relationship with Everette Bannister turned out to be far more damning to Pindling than it first appeared. Bannister left a distinctly unfavorable impression on the Royal Commission. Its report, especially its chapter on "Influence Peddling," described him as an uncooperative, arrogant, and rude witness. "Apart from that," the commissioners wrote, "his demeanor did not permit us to place confidence in his evidence."[42]

Every time Bannister was questioned about known drug dealers, including deposed Nicaraguan dictator Anastasio Somoza, he denied having any connection with them. On June 5, 1984, John J. Roll, a former Bahamian immigration officer who was arrested and served time in the United States on drug conspiracy charges, testified that in the summer of 1979 Bannister gave him $5,000 taken from a bagful of money given to Bannister by Somoza. Pindling and his then Foreign Affairs Minister, Paul Adderley, assigned Bannister to "handle" Somoza. Seeking asylum in The Bahamas, the deposed dictator apparently did not have what it took to buy protection there and had to leave. A year later, on September 17, 1980, Somoza was assassinated in Paraguay. Bannister, whom Pindling described as "a good friend," bragged about helping the Prime Minister on many occasions. The wife of American drug dealer Edward Ward testified before the Royal Commission that Bannister told her: "Our Prime Minister and other people are just figureheads and it's actually people like us who run the government. We have all the say so. We are the ones who do all the work."[43]

The commission chose to believe Mrs. Ward, whose memory for details seemed nearly impeccable. Specifically, the commissioners found: "We have concluded that Mr. Bannister did meet with Mr. and Mrs. Ward and promised to use his political influence to solve their legal problems in The Bahamas."[44]

Although the commission could not substantiate a direct link between the Wards, Bannister, and the Prime Minister, Bannister's deposits of large sums of undocumented money into Pindling's bank accounts left the question of propriety wide open. Despite strong circumstantial evidence, the commission took the narrow view: there was no evidence that Pindling's money was drug-related; not even the money whose origin has yet to be identified.[45]

But the Prime Minister did not escape unscathed. While two out of three commission members agreed with the report's indulgent conclusions, Bishop Gomez was not fully satisfied and filed a minority opinion concerning Pindling's finances. His findings were far less charitable.

In his opinion, Bishop Gomez addressed other discrepancies. The Barbadian clergyman pointed out that Bannister had given Pindling an enormous sum of money at a time when Bannister's reported income was only a yearly consulting retainer of $50,000 from Resorts International. The bishop noted that some of the alleged shares involved in the undisclosed financial agreements between Bannister and Pindling were worthless.[46]

Bishop Gomez could not find any direct evidence linking drug money to Pindling. But that, the clergyman argued, was the wrong question. He wrote:

> I would think that those who deal in drugs are unlikely to make or receive payments on account of their activities in a way which could easily lead to identification of the source of the payments. So that the title given to payment does not necessarily indicate its true character.[47]

Bishop Gomez found that substantial loans had been made, two of which were soon converted into outright gifts. These transactions were carried out with minimum or no documentation and the bishop argued that some of the individuals involved in these transactions had the shadiest of reputations. Consequently, the clergyman raised serious doubts about the entire business:

> . . . in my opinion, the circumstances raise great suspicion and I find it impossible to say that the payments were all

non-drug related. Some could have been but, however that may be, it certainly cannot be contested that the Prime Minister did not exercise sufficient care to preclude the possibility of drug-related funds reaching his bank account or being applied for his benefit. In the absence of the inquiry he could have unwittingly received drug related funds. [Bishop Gomez's final judgment:]To this extent, at least, he left himself, in my opinion, open to criticism for lack of prudence by a person holding the high office of Prime Minister.[48]

The good bishop proved to be more worldly-wise than his fellow commissioners who had spent their working lifetimes dealing with criminals. The bishop's minority opinion placed a dark cloud over the integrity of Prime Minister Pindling, his close associates, and The Bahamas.

Another opinion critical of Prime Minister Pindling can be found in the investigative report published in London's *Sunday Times Magazine* on September 29, 1985. The article stated that the Prime Minister was motivated by his constant desperate need for money. The money was received from "close associates and friends accused by the Commission of Inquiry of direct links with drug traffickers." The article went on to say, "Chief among those is Everette Bannister, who gave Pindling $640,000 in various 'gifts' and 'overdue debts.' Pindling apparently took [the money] without asking too many questions. One of the reasons, according to the Royal Commission, might have been 'his great folly'—Lakeview—the Prime Minister's palatial residence in which he allegedly 'invested' $10 million."[49]

Rather surprisingly, the Royal Commission paid little attention to drug trafficking and drug money-laundering and their influence on The Bahamas.

In 1980, Kendal Nottage, an affluent and high-flying attorney, was a member of the Bahamian cabinet as Minister of Youth, Sports, and Cultural Affairs, and a close political ally and friend of Lynden Pindling. They were so close in fact that, when Pindling was knighted in 1983 by Queen Elizabeth, Nottage and his wife were part of Pindling's entourage. Three years earlier Nottage had been accused of laundering $1 million on behalf of indicted American drug smuggler and mobster Salvatore Michael Caruana. Caruana, who disappeared in 1984, was a lieutenant in the New England mob long headed by Raymond Patriarca. Before turning to drug trafficking, Caruana served time for bank robbery in the United States. Caruana was a member of the Sicilian Cuntrera-Caruana clan, whose tentacles extend throughout the world. He and other members of his family in Venezuela and Canada had been using The Bahamas as a "clearinghouse" for heroin from the Near and Far East and cocaine from South America, and, of course, as a laundry for the proceeds.

When queried by the Royal Commission about his relationship with Caruana, Nottage claimed he had never met him and, therefore, could not have laundered money on his behalf. Arnold Katz, the witness who claimed to have seen Nottage at the Fort Lauderdale airport carrying what was purported to be Caruana's drug money, is himself a confessed smuggler. Katz did not actually see the money and had only Caruana's word that the Bahamian cabinet member was the bagman. Later, Katz was introduced by Caruana to the "minister" and recalled in his testimony that " 'the minister's' first name [was] 'Kendal.' " Worse, Katz also proved to have a poor memory. He failed to identify Nottage from a photo shown to him by commission investigators.[50]

"Handsome, smooth-faced, impeccably dressed," was Katz's accurate description of Kendal Nottage, but he guessed him to be in his mid-twenties. Nottage at the time was forty years old.[51]

But Nottage's denials and Katz's faulty memory did not refute the money-laundering accusations. For one, Nottage could not explain why his unlisted phone numbers were found in Caruana's address book. Nor could he explain bank records that showed hundreds of thousands of dollars deposited by four Bahamian companies established by Kendal Nottage's wife, Rubie, also a lawyer, and then transferred to U.S. corporations that were later identified as Caruana's.

In 1980 Katz flew with Caruana from North Carolina to Fort Lauderdale aboard Caruana's private plane. According to testimony before the Royal Commission, during the flight Caruana told Katz that he was meeting in Fort Lauderdale with a Bahamian minister. The plan was to give the minister $1 million to be laundered on behalf of Caruana in The Bahamas. A Nassau bank account registered to Tiberon Investments, Ltd., recorded a $999,960 deposit the very next day. "Tiberon has been identified by investigators as a Caruana-controlled company formed by Rubie Nottage, who was also its president," reported the *Miami*

Herald. Two days after it was deposited, the money was withdrawn from the Tiberon account. Robert Ellicott, a member of the commission, referred to this incident as "a very significant illustration of laundering."[52]

The *Miami Herald* investigative team broke its story about drug trafficking and corruption in The Bahamas four months before the Royal Commission filed its report. The commission was sufficiently concerned with the Nottages to devote an entire chapter to them. The report expressed a rather "dim view of the Nottages," their dealings with American criminals, and their involvement in money laundering.

The Royal Commission stated in part: "The bank account and related documents of Tiberon Investments of which Mrs. Nottage was the sole signatory, disclose a pattern of deposits and withdrawals from January 1980 onwards which indicate a money laundering operation."[53] As for the Nottages, the commission concluded that if they did not know what was going on, they should have:

> . . . a prudent man, such as we would assume Mr. Nottage to be, would make inquiries of the character of the person with whom he was dealing behind the corporate veil and thus avoid the risk of entering into a joint venture with an apparent criminal and the consequent effect upon the reputation of a person of Mr. Nottage's standing as a Cabinet Minister.[54]

But money, not reputation, motivated the Nottages. Greed triumphed; money, lots of it, was everywhere to be made and temptation simply proved irresistible.

In March 1989, about four years after the commission completed its report, a federal grand jury in Boston indicted Kendal Nottage and his wife, Rubie, for conspiring with Salvatore Michael Caruana to launder $5 million in drug profits. The Nottages proclaimed their innocence from the safe distance of The Bahamas. Neither has come to the United States to stand trial and dispute the charges. About the same time, Everette Bannister was indicted by a federal grand jury in Florida on charges of conspiring with members of the Medellín drug cartel to bring cocaine illegally into the United States by way of The Bahamas.[55]

The Nottages and Everette Bannister are only a small cog in a much larger money-laundering machine in The Bahamas. Corruption was not the exclusive domain of government officials. Money-laundering flourished in The Bahamas in part because it was supported by a cottage industry of lawyers and fix-it men and women who willingly served their clients without asking questions about the money's origin. And even if they knew the provenance of the money, they were not deterred from providing the vital services for which cash-loaded drug traffickers paid them handsomely.

The Bahamas, like other offshore tax havens such as the Cayman Islands, the Netherlands Antilles, and Panama, has attracted significant foreign capital. "Free port" haven regulations were not designed to lure criminals or encourage corruption but to improve local economies. Since their inception, however, these regulations have been exploited by criminals and money launderers as well as by legitimate businessmen.

Tax havens are often used by the wealthy as private

and discreet vehicles for further enrichment. Capital tax shelter nations have strong bank secrecy laws that protect their investors. Unlike drug trafficking, money-laundering *per se* did not constitute a crime in the United States until 1986. In The Bahamas drug trafficking seemed to be only illegal *de jure*; *de facto* was another matter. First-time drug-trafficking offenders who could pay their way out were often freed by Bahamian magistrates.

The Royal Commission discovered that between 1977 and 1983, eighty-four indicted drug offenders had been released on bail set at around $10,000. At least fifty of those indicted failed to appear for trial. Bail money often represented little more than small change to drug traffickers.

Chapter Nineteen in the commission's report, "Bail, Penalties and Confiscation," was devoted to the Bahamian courts and drug trafficking. The commission concluded that: "The percentage [of those who fled trial] may well be even higher because there are recent cases, where substantial cash bail has been [deposited], which are still awaiting trial."[56]

Had the commission looked harder it would have found even more discouraging facts. Until 1984 only one person had been arrested on drug-trafficking charges in drug-drenched Bimini, and he served time only because he was a minor street dealer who could not afford the fine. Although everyone living on the island was aware of the prevailing commerce, no American or Colombian served any time in Bimini for drug trafficking.[57]

Offering protection for local bank accounts, The Bahamas have strict banking secrecy regulations contained in

Section 10 of the Bank and Trust Companies Regulation Act of 1965.[58] These laws provide the privacy that tax evaders depend on. No one, not even agents from foreign governments, including the U.S. Internal Revenue Service, is allowed to examine bank records in pursuit of delinquent tax evaders, unless granted special permission by a Bahamian court. In The Bahamas, as in other tax-haven countries, local banking officials, from manager to teller, are criminally liable if they reveal any detail about their clients and their transactions. The penalties are severe.[59]

U.S. Justice Department officials told the Royal Commission that Bahamian banks rarely cooperated with U.S. investigators and were seldom ordered to do so by local courts. Thus, it was difficult to obtain the information necessary for U.S. grand jury indictments.

In the sixties, Meyer Lansky delivered beer cartons filled with U.S. dollars—the proceeds from his gambling operations in The Bahamas—to Miami banks. By the mid-1980s, drug smugglers and criminals were walking into Bahamian banks with suitcases and black plastic trash bags stuffed with cash. In twenty years, only the containers changed, not the contents. No questions were asked by the banks and, on average, a nominal 2 percent "counting" fee was charged—although the bankers often haggled with the customers. A major complaint voiced by drug traffickers in The Bahamas was that the old-fashioned local banks were slow to install automatic money counters. To ensure their silence, tellers would usually be given "tips" for their hard manual work, thus further corrupting an already corrupt system.

From evidence provided by veteran drug smugglers like

Timothy Minnig, it was apparent that the larger the deposit—invariably from drug trafficking—the more personal the attention given by the bank manager. Huge sums of money were personally accepted by managers, and the already minimal accounting procedures became even more informal and highly irregular compared to normal banking practices. Minnig and his full-service banker, Eric Sawyer, became such close friends that they often went on snorkeling holidays together. Establishing and maintaining a personal relationship with their bankers was essential to traffickers operating in The Bahamas. Canadian investigative journalist William Marsden discovered: "One group of smugglers was so close to their manager that they followed him to another branch on another Bahamian island after he was transferred by the Bank of Nova Scotia."[60] When the money was safely deposited into a Bahamian bank, drug traffickers would then wire-transfer the money to another bank, usually foreign. North Americans preferred U.S. or Canadian banks; Colombians chose banks in Panama.

Cautious traffickers often took advantage of another Bahamian service. With the help of a local lawyer, and for a proper fee, a foreigner laden with money was able to hide his identity behind a newly created but fictitious corporation. This arrangement provided the trafficker with an additional layer of protection. The trafficker's name never appeared in the registration papers; only "nominees," such as the Nottages, along with a generic corporate name would be listed. The company's activities were couched in obscure and vague terms that satisfied the lenient and permissive legal requirements. According to Bahamian bank regulations, beneficiary owners should be listed on corporate papers but in the easygoing Bahamas that requirement, like much else, was simply overlooked.[61]

Once the money was safely deposited in a "corporate" account, it was usually transferred outside the country. Particularly popular with Latin Americans was a double shell arrangement, in which the Bahamian cover was overlaid with Panamanian corporate shells. Panamanian lawyers were equally adept at creating fictitious companies. The money would be wired from one corporate account to another without revealing the identity of the real owner.

How this all worked is well illustrated by Bruce Griffin's career. A middle-aged, heavy-set American marijuana and cocaine smuggler operating in the late 1970s and early 1980s, Griffin, nicknamed Peewee, was no flower child turned trafficker. He was a serious businessman whose goal was to amass a fortune. Until Griffin's indictment in the United States in 1983, along with 100 of his associates, the Florida drug dealer owned racing cars, boats, and a Texas ranch where he bred Appaloosa horses, which he sold for a million dollars apiece.

Between 1975 and 1981, Griffin poured $100 million in drug money into Bahamian bank accounts. But Griffin was no fool. The cash was deposited anonymously into accounts of some forty different Bahamian-registered companies. According to William Marsden: "The money was . . . wired to Scotiabank's Cayman Islands branch and into the account of a company called Cobalt, Ltd. From there, the money was wired back to the U.S. into Scotiabank's New York City branch. Griffin then dispersed it among numerous corporations he owned in the U.S."[62] The lawyer who helped Griffin with this elaborate deception was none other than Nigel Bowe. George William Baron, another American drug trafficker, and a key government witness against Carlos Lehder in 1988, testified that Nigel Bowe was the middleman who introduced him to Pindling in 1980. The meeting took place at a casino on Nassau's Paradise Island. According to Baron, he gave the briefcase stuffed with $400,000 to Pindling. When Bowe got up to leave, Pindling "reached into the briefcase and took out two or three of the packets of money . . . and gave them to Mr. Bowe."[63]

Nigel Bowe was arrested in The Bahamas in 1985. Following a meeting between the Bahamian Attorney General and a U.S. representative, some thirty individuals involved in drug trafficking in The Bahamas were targeted for arrest. The local police carried out the raid and Nigel Bowe was among the thirty swept up. He was charged with RICO[64] violations and the United States filed an extradition request with the Bahamian Government, but Bowe was released on bond. He still roams freely in The Bahamas.

How large a part of the Bahamian economy was and may still be based on drug trafficking and money-laundering is open to conjecture, but the phenomenon can be better understood by examining Bimini. There are two Biminis, the north and south islands. The bulk of the population, 2,000 in all, lives on North Bimini; South Bimini has the all-important airstrip. Since the islands lie only fifty miles from Miami, the Biminis have long been favored by drug traffickers. At least 500 locals were employed in the drug-trafficking business, making the islanders relatively well off although they lacked other visible means of support. Even the small tourist and fishing trade, which once attracted

41

Ernest Hemingway, lost its dominant role in recent years.[65]

In 1984 tiny Bimini was awash in dollars. The *Miami Herald* investigative team learned that:

> According to the Royal Bank of Canada, transfers of U.S. dollars from its Bimini branch to Nassau rose from a modest $544,360 in 1977 to a remarkable $12.3 million last year [1983]. "We are talking about U.S. dollars, actual cash," said William Allen, governor of The Bahamas Central Bank. He said the historic Bimini windfall can only be the result of one factor: drug trafficking.[66]

What the *Miami Herald* left out of its report was the fact that in 1983 the Bimini bank had transferred an additional $12 million directly to the United States.[67]

> According to the Governor . . . the bank had not been able to identify them as coming from any ordinary business transaction. The only conclusion arrived at by the bank is that the large increase in U.S. dollar deposits is directly related to the flow of drugs . . . a small part of U.S. dollars [is] in circulation in Bimini and the bulk of it finds its way back to the United States of America.[68]

Bimini was a slightly exaggerated version of the rest of The Bahamas. According to The Bahamas Central Bank figures, nonresident dollar holdings in 1983 in Bahamian banks amounted to $5.3 billion. The following year, the year of the Royal Commission's inquiry, they totaled $4.3 billion, and by the first half of 1985, the sum had climbed to $4.9 billion. How much of it was drug money cannot be determined because Bahamian banking and government officials didn't know—or weren't saying—and they apparently were making little effort to find out.[69] The fluctuation of the dollar holdings has been the result of drug money moving from The Bahamas to parts unknown.

For a better appreciation of The Bahamas' banking system, several features must be understood. First, it is dominated by Canadians. Four of the six most important banks in The Bahamas are Canadian-owned: The Bank of Nova Scotia, the Bank of Montreal, the Royal Bank of Canada, and the Canadian-Imperial Bank of Commerce. The other two are British and American. Canadian banks have long been dominant in the tax-sheltering business in the English-speaking Caribbean. They control, among other things, much of the banking and insurance industries, as well as bauxite mining rights. With thirty-six branches on the islands, the four big banks control some 80 percent of the Bahamian banking business. They also dominate real estate and trust companies that are known to have sheltered drug profits.[70]

The Canadian involvement in the Caribbean began when a Bank of Nova Scotia branch office was established in Jamaica in 1889. Another branch shortly followed in The Bahamas. Since then, the Canadian share in the banking community has remained relatively constant.[71]

By the early 1980s, however, both American and Canadian officials had become frustrated with the Canadian banks' lax attitude toward drug money-laundering. The banks' home offices exercised little or no control over their Bahamas branches. The Bank of Nova Scotia, for example, claimed it couldn't monitor the local branches because they operated under Bahamian and not Canadian law. It repeatedly resisted subpoenas of its Bahamian records by a U.S. federal grand jury investigating the activities of American drug trafficker Frank Brady, aka Robert Wade. The bank protested, claiming that local bank secrecy laws forbade them from revealing any information. The stonewalling continued for four years and did not end until U.S. prosecutors won a landmark court decision that forced the Bank of Nova Scotia to pay $1.8 million in fines.[72]

The Bank of Nova Scotia's eventual compliance contradicted its earlier legal argument. So did subsequent actions by other Canadian banks. For example, in 1985 the Royal Bank of Canada, the largest in The Bahamas, established a special committee to study the problem of money-laundering and to find ways to prevent it from occurring in its offshore branches. Two years later, the new procedures were implemented. Other Canadian banks followed suit but these new procedures are known only to the banks.[73]

The Canadian Imperial Bank (CIB) has been an exception, at least nominally. In 1985, its officials told the *Montreal Gazette* that the bank's Bahamian branches no longer accepted cash deposits of $5,000 or more. The CIB and other Canadian banks also claimed to monitor more closely wire transfers from The Bahamas.[74]

Money-laundering in The Bahamas has not ceased. Canadian banks remain dominant in The Bahamas and there is no noticeable decline in their dollar deposits from countries in the Western Hemisphere. The money is usually transferred out of the islands. Business continues as usual, despite claims that controls have been tightened.

In August 1985 the U.S. Senate Subcommittee on Crime had detected several loopholes in the new controls:

It is impossible to know which banks adhere to these policies and for which customers. The reporting of large transactions does not apply to customers who have an existing relationship with the bank. Nor does it apply to those customers recommended by reputable parties, a term that broadly encompasses law firms, accounting firms and other professionals.[75]

But there were some changes. Bimini was shut down as a money-laundering haven, thus returning the population to its predrug poverty.[76] Some private airstrips have been closed and maritime patrols increased with the addition of a frigate contributed by the British Royal Navy. This activity has had some effect on the actual volume of drug trafficking throughout the islands, but not on money-laundering. Frigates are not the weapon of choice in scuttling money-laundering.[77]

The U.S. Senate Subcommittee on Crime looked into the effect of the new measures and concluded that they have done nothing to discourage continued laundering through the islands' banks. The subcommittee did not think matters had improved much. Personal contacts between drug traffickers and the Bahamian establishment paid off.

What worked for Bahamian banks also worked for Bahamian trust companies that served as major money-laundering outlets. The Royal Commission, while inclined to accept the banks' claims of tightened controls, was particularly harsh with trust companies, many of which were controlled by Canadian capital.

The commission's report illuminated two examples of trust company abuse. The first case involved Columbus Trust Company, Ltd., which set up shop in 1969. Kendal Nottage was a director and one of its shareholders. The

Royal Commission learned that Nottage had acquired 5,000 shares "for the benefit of the Prime Minister." In the early seventies Robert Vesco appeared on the scene, using Butler's Bank, his local bank, as an intermediary for purchasing shares of Columbus Trust Company. By the early eighties, Vesco had become the majority shareholder.[78]

Shortly after its establishment Columbus Trust began to attract funds from known drug traffickers. The practice had become so blatant that the trust companies' regulatory agency, The Bahamas Central Bank, could no longer ignore it and initiated an inquiry, as did the Royal Commission. But, according to the commission's report, the Central Bank probe was considerably hampered: "[M]any of [the] records had been destroyed. It was [the manager's] practice to destroy annually or biennially the records relating to each client after their accounts had been audited."[79] One of Columbus Trust's prominent clients was Dennis Markle, an American drug dealer who had managed to attract the attention of *The Wall Street Journal* following his testimony before a grand jury in Pittsburgh in August 1979.[80]

According to his testimony, Markle flew to Nassau with $49,000 in cash and deposited it at Columbus Trust. The account he used was listed as "Wilder Resources Ltd.," a Bahamian shell company with no assets. The title was furnished to Markle for $1,500 by the trust company. Conveniently, Markle's name was absent from the registration documents. Instead, Columbus Trust's officers and shareholders acted as nominees.

The commission concluded: "It illustrates how Columbus Trust was used either knowingly or unknowingly to erect a corporate structure to facilitate the laundering of funds."[81] The report went on to say: "In the true sense there may be a legal responsibility that is not taken very seriously in The Bahamas and that Columbus Trust was not the only firm adopting that attitude." The commission added that it "dealt with Columbus Trust in some detail to illustrate how institutions of that type in The Bahamas could be exploited by drug smugglers and other criminals."[82]

Dennis Markle was hardly the only dishonest customer at Columbus Trust or even the biggest one. Columbus Trust was small potatoes, however, compared to Guardian Trust Company, Ltd., in Nassau, which acted as the principal money launderer for Carlos Lehder.

Enormous sums of money were deposited at Guardian Trust by Lehder and his associates. Yet Ian Davidson, the trust company's manager, claimed he never suspected anything was wrong until the infamous September 1979 raid on Norman's Cay. Only then, according to Davidson, were "measures" taken to halt Carlos Lehder's drug money-laundering activities. Despite those claims, however, Lehder's money continued to flow to Guardian Trust for seven months until April 1980. Under investigation, Davidson was unable to produce records indicating the "measures" he claimed had been implemented.

The Royal Commission would have none of it:

> We do not accept, given the amount of cash he handled for Lehder and the notoriety of Norman's Cay, that he [Davidson] did not at least have a strong suspicion concerning the activities there prior to the raid of September 1979. In our view his contention that he immediately decided to termi-

47

nate his dealings with Lehder after the raid is not believable. We have concluded that a more plausible explanation is that the relationship ended upon the instructions of Lehder himself.[83]

Despite this discouraging pattern, the commission took heart from more vigorous policing of trust companies by The Bahamas Central Bank. In 1984 it reported that Bahamian officials were "revoking trust licenses when the companies have been perceived as having failed to make sufficient inquiries regarding their clients and the sources of the latter's funds."[84]

But even with these measures and the hopeful conclusion of the Royal Commission's report, many remain skeptical.

Have matters really improved since the mid-eighties when The Bahamas and its Prime Minister received so much unflattering attention from North American law enforcement officials and the media?

The Royal Commission has long since folded its tents and the Florida federal grand jury probes of Sir Lynden Pindling were left in limbo. Hopes for Pindling's indictment peaked in 1988 as a result of testimony given in the trial of Carlos Lehder in Jacksonville, Florida. That evidence, said sources in the U.S. Attorney's office in Tampa,[85] would have convicted Pindling. One prosecutor even promised an indictment by 1989. But more than four years later there is no indictment in sight.[86] And according to high-ranking officials in U.S. law enforcement agencies who were close to these investigations, the Department of State blocked the grand jury from hearing the evidence which clearly demonstrated Pindling's role in drug money-laundering. Former U.S. attorneys and other law enforcement officials provided documentation for proving these allegations. The review of those documents proves beyond a shadow of a doubt that the Department of State stalled the investigation until the statute of limitations had run out.[87]

Meanwhile, despite all the negative publicity, the Bahamian premier won easy reelection in June 1987, and he will probably do so again in 1992.[88] Pindling was not the only one to be reelected. Kendal Nottage and George Smith retained their seats in Parliament. In addition, Nottage was appointed chairman of The Bahamas Broadcasting Corporation in August 1987.

Since his reelection Pindling appears to have slowed down the campaign to clear his name. However, he paid for newspaper advertisements to denounce former U.S. Attorney Robert Merkle and other U.S. officials. The tart-tongued Merkle replied: "In a nutshell, Sir Lynden is full of hot air." Although the suit with NBC had been settled, Pindling threatened to reinstate it when NBC reneged on its agreement not to discuss the affair any further. Yet in a public statement issued by NBC, the network claimed victory. Pindling didn't follow through.[89]

In September 1988, Pindling requested that then-Attorney General Richard Thornburgh appoint a special prosecutor to probe Merkle's investigation of his activities. The Justice Department promptly declined. Pindling, in turn, issued an official denial of all allegations about him which surfaced during the trial of Carlos Lehder.[90] In May 1988, Carlos Lehder was tried, convicted, and sentenced to life imprisonment without parole plus 135 years, in Jacksonville, Florida. He was found guilty of masterminding the transhipment of 3.3 tons of cocaine from Colombia to the United States through Norman's Cay, the Bahamian island. He is serving time in the federal system's most secure prison—Marion, Illinois.

Meanwhile, Pindling and his supporters sound the continuing refrain that there is an official American conspiracy to get him.

Paradoxically, the Prime Minister is running his own idiosyncratic campaign against drug trafficking. Over the last few years, he submitted several proposals in international forums to combat drug trafficking. At the same time he continued to accuse the United States of creating the problem, by failing to control its citizens' appetite for drugs and generally not doing enough to wage war on drugs. For example, he has urged the United States to recall all large-denomination currency and issue newly designed large bills. This, he argues, will leave drug traffickers with money not worth the paper it is printed on.[91]

Along with Jamaica's Prime Minister Michael Manley, Pindling has advocated the formation of a UN-sponsored multinational antidrug armed force with a writ to dispatch troops around the world to assist governments fighting the drug trade. The force would interdict drugs, help eradicate illegal crops, collect intelligence on drug traffickers, and launch commando-style raids against them.[92]

Official U.S. response to these proposals has been lukewarm at best. Even those who do not suspect the Prime

Minister's motives outright argue that the high cost of the UN antidrug force might be better spent on more effective bilateral programs.

As for his plan to recall U.S. currency, experts claim that it would be too expensive and ineffective. The time allowed legitimate dollar holders to trade in their notes would permit drug traffickers to do the same.

U.S./Bahamian relations hit bottom in 1984. Since then, U.S. pressure on Pindling has evaporated. By the end of 1991, the official U.S. stance was to sing his praises.[93] Considering that The Bahamas continues to have serious drug-trafficking and money-laundering problems and that this commerce is aided and abetted by a corrupt government led by a Prime Minister who at best is willfully blind, the U.S. attitude is incomprehensible. Even the Royal Commission reiterated that it had "established that corruption in various forms invariably accompanies the drug trafficking trade. In our opinion the peddling of influence, on behalf of persons involved in drugs, constitutes one of the most insidious forms of corruption." However, legal opinion on the evidence of Sir Lynden's activities was divided.[94]

Uncovered by the Royal Commission, corruption in The Bahamas—and Pindling's alleged role—could no longer be overlooked. Nor could an aggressive and determined U.S. ambassador who took her post in Nassau in early 1986. Ambassador Carol Boyd Hallett, a Reagan appointee from California, was determined to eradicate drug trafficking and drug money-laundering in The Bahamas. Bahamian officials found her "pushy," but they could not ignore her or the forces that stood behind her. The Bahamian Government grudgingly began to cooperate with U.S. law enforcement agencies. The Bahamas went as far as becoming the first nation to sign the UN Convention Against Illicit Traffic in Narcotic Drugs and Psychotropic Substances in 1988 (although it had not laid the complex legal foundations to comply with it). This leadership role in the new UN Drug Convention served Pindling well and helped shake off U.S. public criticism. The United States has stopped issuing public statements concerning Pindling and his government's involvement in the drug trade. Pindling himself helped by distancing himself even further from direct contact with drug traffickers or open links with money launderers.

Since the late eighties State Department reports consistently cite the Bahamian Government as "cooperative" in fighting the drug trade, while privately expressing concern about the degree of corruption rampant in the islands.[95] Bahamian collaboration consists mainly in allowing U.S. government airplanes to fly over Bahamian airspace, and in permitting a U.S. Customs radar balloon station to operate over Grand Bahama Island. An expanded Bahamian police force also works more closely with its U.S. drug-fighting counterparts.[96] In addition, U.S. law enforcement officials have expressed approval of new Bahamian drug legislation, the Dangerous Drugs Act of 1989 and its 1990 amendments. Enforcement and the weight of penalty, however, appear to be less than commendable. The law now stipulates that anyone possessing over two pounds(!) of cocaine must be held without bail. Those convicted face ten years to life imprisonment. Drug-related arrests, mostly of foreigners, are up and the total amount of confiscated drugs has increased as well.[97]

This cooperation has made The Bahamas eligible for U.S. assistance, and given it access to funds to control drugs. Should this cooperation cease, the aid will be automatically cut in half. Although cooperation as a precondition for aid has been required since 1986 by the U.S. Congress under a federal certification law, the White House, and the State Department in particular, are reluctant to decertify any government as long as some cooperation exists.[98]

Many in Congress have pushed for decertification of The Bahamas and other nations until and unless they make greater efforts to control drug trafficking. But congressional attempts to overturn the President's certification have met with obstinate resistance. For example, then Speaker of the House, Jim Wright, a Democrat from Texas, was successful in preventing decertification requests from ever reaching a vote in the House of Representatives.[99] The last attempt in the Senate was defeated by a comfortable 57–40 margin, in 1989.

One unintended consequence of Bahamian cooperation has been the development of alternative drug-running routes. In recent years Colombian drug traffickers have shifted their air routes from The Bahamas to other countries in the region, including isolated airports in Mexico's Yucatán or Baja peninsulas as well as the northern states of Chihuahua, Nuevo Leon, Sonora, and the northwestern state of Sinaloa. The cargo is transferred to cars and trucks and smuggled into the United States across the border.[100] Puerto Rico, Panama, Brazil, and Guatemala, to name a few, are heavily used as drug transshipment points to the United States and to growing European markets.

As for money-laundering, Washington is still seeking Nassau's cooperation. The United States has been negotiating a Mutual Legal Assistance Treaty (MLAT) to help authorities obtain necessary information from Bahamian banks. Talks began only after The Bahamas charged in 1983 that the United States had shown little interest in the Bahamian Attorney General's proposal to begin negotiations—an accusation that the Royal Commission willingly endorsed.[101] Discussions on the treaty began in 1985 and a treaty text was negotiated by the summer of 1987. Ironically, the MLAT has since been held up in the U.S. Senate, home of The Bahamas' most vociferous critics. Once the MLAT is approved by the Senate, U.S. officials hope to negotiate a new extradition treaty with The Bahamas.[102] At present most U.S. extradition requests remain stalled in Bahamian courts.

Even the most optimistic U.S. officials acknowledge that huge quantities of drugs still pass through The Bahamas. Moreover, they admit that real progress on money-laundering is difficult, if not impossible to measure. In the words of one recent State Department report:

> Banking regulations have made money laundering more difficult in The Bahamas. Absence of control over laundering money through purchases of goods and services makes it difficult to measure accurately the extent of money laundering in the country. However, U.S. officials believe that large amounts of drug money continue to enter the Bahamian economy.[103]

The Bahamas and Prime Minister Lynden Pindling were once again exposed to the limelight during the trial of deposed Panamanian General Manuel Noriega, which began in Florida in Miami in September 1991 and ended with Noriega's conviction in April 1992. Pindling and his associates were named as recipients of large sums of money from drug traffickers throughout the world. Pindling, as usual, denied the allegations.

The device Lansky set in place in the early sixties has evolved into an awesome machine that continues to produce the drug-trafficking and money-laundering nightmare that haunts us all.

The Treasure of La Mina

> It may not be good business to be moving money around in the street, but it's not illegal . . . if they caught me I'd say I'm sorry, I'd pay the tax, walk away and that's good, that's my cost of protecting that money and there's a lot of good ways to do it.
>
> —EDUARDO MARTINEZ ROMERO to DEA undercover agents, Aruba, March 1988

CAST OF CHARACTERS

Eduardo Martinez Romero—money launderer for the Medellín cartel, one of the few who was extradited to the United States by the Colombian government

Vahe and Nazareth Andonian—Los Angeles jewelers of Armenian descent, owned Nazareth Jewelers, the VNA Gold Exchange, among others, famous drug money launderers

Raoul Vivas—the owner of Cambio Italia

Robert Bonner—Director of the Drug Enforcement Administration and former U.S. Attorney in L.A.

Jack Kilhefner—senior vice president of the Wells Fargo bank in San Francisco

Wanis Koyomejian—Armenian from Aleppo, the oldest of La Mina operatives, who owned the Ropex Corporation

Raffi Kouyoumjian—son of Wanis Koyomejian, worked with his father at Ropex, used different spelling of last name

the Goldstein family—father Jack and his three sons, Donald, Allen, and Richard, owner of Loren Industries and Ronel, a Florida-based corporation importing and selling gold

Nellie Magdaloyo—alias used by FBI special agent acting as undercover cleaning woman

Bruce R. Stephens—FBI special agent

Ghaith Pharaon—Saudi Arabian businessman fronting for BCCI in the United States

Vagram Tankazyan—better known as Mario, Armenian drug money launderer in L.A.

Krikor Chahinian—(aka Koko) Armenian drug money launderer in L.A.

Richard Ferris—former president of Ronel Industries

Carlos Desoretz—employee of Ronel Industries, subordinate to Ferris

Sergio Hochman—from Argentina, worked for Raoul Vivas in the United States and South America

Vagram Marion Dangasian, better known as Tio—an Armenian jeweler and drug money launderer with Latin American connections operating out of L.A.

Jimmy Brown—alias for DEA undercover agent in Atlanta

Alex Carrera—alias for DEA undercover agent in Atlanta who worked with Jimmy Brown

Clara Garcia de Paredes—Banco de Occidente's commercial manager in Panama

Stephen A. Saccoccia and wife, Donna—gold jewelers and drug money launderers from Cranston, Rhode Island. This ring included Arboleda-Gonzalez, Mollicone, Sharir, and Slomovitz and was part of Polar Cap.

Jose Duvan Arboleda-Gonzalez—Colombia citizen who owned money-laundering businesses in Rhode Island, New York, Miami, and California

Joseph Mollicone, Jr.—former director of Heritage Loan and Investment Bank in Providence, Rhode Island, who had a major role in the Rhode Island operation and disappeared with $13 million

Aharon Sharir—New York jeweler who laundered drug money through Banco de Occidente's branch in Panama

Barry Slomovitz—jeweler, part of the Saccoccia ring, also known as Steve "Yerukim"

ONE OF THE HARSHEST prison terms ever imposed in the United States—505 years without parole—came down in August 1991 against Vahe and Nazareth Andonian, Los Angeles jewelers of Armenian descent, and financial wizard Raoul Vivas, their Argentinean counterpart. Along with other conspirators, they were convicted in the U.S. District Court in Los Angeles for drug trafficking and drug money-laundering, felonies that do not carry a life sentence but that will be expiated consecutively rather than concurrently. The Andonians and their accomplices laundered the proceeds of cocaine sales for the Colombian Medellín cartel and heroin sales for Turkish drug traffickers. It was amid the Los Angeles jewelry district that their work began in 1985.

The Spanish conquistadores came to the New World in search of gold and fresh converts. Gold was infinitely more profitable—initially at least—and they found it in great abundance throughout their vast empire, except in Alta California. Although a handful of men would later climb into the San Bernardino mountains in search of a few golden traces in the washes of an arroyo, this largely barren territory showed little promise. Centuries later, Alta California, now Spanish in name only, beckoned successive waves of English-speaking immigrants. Blessed with clement weather and a steady supply of water, the once small and unremarkable Pueblo de Nuestra Señora Reina de la Ciela et de Los Angeles became the sprawling megalopolis known to the natives simply as L.A.

But, as events would demonstrate, gold had not been forgotten. Not entirely.

Colombia's drug cartels dubbed one of their laundering organizations "La Mina," Spanish for *the mine*. As Eduardo Martinez Romero, their chief money man described it, "La Mina is a gold multinational that really exists . . . as an entity throughout the world."[1] In existence fifteen years before the authorities first learned about it, La Mina, whose tentacles stretched throughout the world, also extended into the Los Angeles jewelry district.

A haphazard melding of cities and towns within a city, Los Angeles has swelled in recent decades as new waves of immigrants continue to squeeze into its 400 square miles, notably Vietnamese, Cambodians and Koreans from Asia, and Mexicans, Salvadorans, and Nicaraguans from Latin America.

And L.A. continues to be a magnet. Some 40,000 people move to the Los Angeles basin every year. In addition to drought, gang wars, crime, traffic, and pollution, all of which have made life in the region less than ideal, drug use, once the glamorized pastime of a few, has rapidly become the hellish habit of thousands of Angelinos.

Since the early 1980s, Los Angeles has not only been a major drug-consuming market, it has also become a top national distribution center. Pushed in part by the rigorous efforts of the federal drug Task Force of South Florida—then administered by Vice President George Bush—Colombian drug traffickers shifted their attention from Miami to Los Angeles. The change in locale was gradual. By the late 1980s telltale signs began turning up in the Los Angeles Federal Reserve Bank receipts. By 1989 L.A. banks were producing a $3.8 billion cash surplus—a 2,200 percent increase in four years.[2]

What happened was simple. Southern California banks were suddenly awash in *cash* deposits; more currency was in the till than was needed to carry out normal daily cash transactions. Since banks do not want large amounts of noninterest-producing money, they usually hand over the excess to the Federal Reserve in return for credit against their accounts.

In late 1980 that surplus was steadily building up in L.A. while nationwide the Federal Reserve was reporting a deficit of $16.5 billion. The measure of L.A.'s meteoric rise is easily demonstrated by comparing Federal Reserve surplus figures. In 1981, in Miami, the city's banks were drowning in cash—some $4.5 *billion* in excess—while L.A. reported a mere $343 million. By 1991, Miami had $5.7 billion and Los Angeles soared to $5 *billion.* In 1990, unseating San Francisco, L.A. became the financial capital of the West Coast. On the East Coast, Miami and Jacksonville continued to report large surpluses of cash entering their financial institutions.[3]

California authorities soon suspected that the sharp rise in cash was the result of heightened drug-marketing and money-laundering activities, of which L.A. had become a center. Selling illegal drugs is strictly a cash and carry business. One of the confidential informants for the government disclosed that the drug money-laundering business was conducted like any other business by placing "bids" for the right to launder money on behalf of the Colombian cartel. The bid consisted of agreement to launder money at a certain rate of commission with guarantees to launder the funds by a certain date. The bidding is lively and is awarded to whoever can handle the money quickly and at the lowest rate. Armored cars such as Loomis and Brinks are used constantly to deliver cash as well as some gold as are Federal Express and other courier services. The Cali and Medellín Colombian cartels don't take credit cards. Personal checks are just as useless. But they sell on credit and they use certified checks.

Soon, this new and huge, cash-only business distorted the monetary flow in a very noticeable fashion. Robert Bonner, Director of the Drug Enforcement Administration and former U.S. Attorney in L.A. noted: "There is certainly a correlation between the figures [and] . . . Los Angeles . . . the principal distribution center for cocaine . . . is becoming the principal financial center for the drug trade in the United States."

The reason: drugs were relatively easy to move into the city—compared to the now tougher Miami market—because the 2,000-mile U.S.-Mexican border was proving as porous for drugs and money as it had been for illegal aliens.

L.A.'s newfound prominence was no small feat considering the historical dominance of Miami and New York. Narcotics trafficking had over decades developed an enormous institutional infrastructure through which drugs, among them cocaine and heroin, were distributed throughout the United States.

For the most part, Southern California banks did not look upon the cash surplus as a problem, but as a gift from heaven. By the mid- and late 1980s banks were experiencing the first flush of easy success that their Florida counterparts had enjoyed until Miami's reputation as a drug capital began to affect business. The domestic institutions used by members of the Medellín drug cartel included Chemical Bank, Continental Bank International, Morgan Guarantee Trust, Security Pacific International Bank, and Republic National Bank, New York. Branches of foreign banks in the United States were patronized by the Colombians as well. These included DAIWA Bank of Osaka, Japan; Banco de Santander of Madrid, Spain, and Miami; Union Bank of Switzerland; Swiss Banking Corporation in New York, Toronto, and California; and Lloyds Bank International of The Bahamas, to name a few. Altogether U.S. law enforcement agencies identified thousands of bank accounts all over the world from Italy and Switzerland to Luxembourg, the United Kingdom, Spain, Germany, France, and Liechtenstein as well as Hong Kong, Japan, Korea, and Taiwan, containing drug money.

But not everyone in California accepted this sudden prosperity blindly. In 1988 a bank official at a downtown L.A. bank became suspicious about one account. The account belonged to a gold trading company, which within three months, had deposited $25 million in cash, mostly in small bills. The account belonged to brothers Nazareth and Vahe Andonian.

Nazareth is slightly built with dark thinning hair and a fair complexion. His brother, Vahe, is dark, somewhat taller and heavier. Both emigrated to the United States from Aleppo, Syria, in 1976. Vahe was twenty-four when he left Lebanon to seek work in the United States. He found a job as a mechanic in Bergen, New Jersey. Shortly after Syria's occupation of Lebanon, Nazareth, who was twenty-one and an experienced diamond setter, joined his brother in the United States. Both were happy to escape Lebanon and war-shattered Beirut.

It was Nazareth who insisted that the brothers leave the East Coast for L.A. There they joined other recent Armenian immigrants from Syria, Lebanon, and Iran. They all may have been strangers in a strange land, but Armenian immigrants had long found the California climate to their liking. For generations of Armenians, as writer William Saroyan had chronicled in his many stories, the great Central Valley of California offered land and an opportunity to work it in peace after centuries of Turkish and Soviet tyranny.

Numbering in the thousands, new Armenians—mostly young and very ambitious—converged on the cities, notably Los Angeles. Many were familiar with the gem and gold trade, an occupation which provides the most secure and portable assets possible in the violently uncertain world of the Levant.[4] The Andonians moved to L.A. and Vahe found a job as a mechanic in Glendale. His younger brother, Nazareth, peddled gold chains on the streets. By 1979, the determined Nazareth had accumulated enough capital to begin manufacturing gold jewelry. Vahe and Nazareth became partners by the early 1980s and within a year were selling bulk gold, wholesale and retail.[5] They settled in L.A.'s Hill Street jewelry district, a decaying downtown enclave that occupied a few square blocks. Scattered among thirty buildings and often spilling into the sidewalks, L.A.'s Hill Street gold and jewelry trade employs about 50,000 people.

Shops and offices are well equipped for this mostly cash business, boasting money-counting machines, blastproof safes, armed guards, armored delivery trucks, and other high-security measures dictated by a growing wave of crime.

The Andonians and their fellow Armenians overlooked the blight. They had known far worse. Relying on tight, extended family ties, the new arrivals began setting up various enterprises all involving gold and jewelry.

Determination and hard work paid off. By the mid-1980s the Andonians, the Koyomejians, the Anouchians, the Moroyans, and the Momdijians, to name a few, were doing quite well. Pushing sixty, Wanis Koyomejian, an Armenian from Aleppo and the oldest of La Mina operatives, owned the Ropex Corporation, an enterprise that rivaled the Andonians' rapid success. Meanwhile the Andonians operated at least half a dozen jewelry businesses in the Hill Street area, including their flagship Andonian Brothers Manufacturing Company, Nazareth Jewelers, and the VNA Gold Exchange with branch offices located on Fulton Street and Sixth Avenue in Manhattan, New York. Through marriage, the Andonian brothers held interests in other firms, including Joyce Jewelers and A&P Jewelers, both in Los Angeles.[6]

The Andonians purchased handsome homes in West Los Angeles and the San Fernando Valley's La Crecenta and Sylmar districts. They could well have afforded Brentwood and Beverly Hills.

If the conquistadores could not find gold in Southern California, the Armenians did, trading briskly in the precious metals, particularly at the height of world crises. They feverishly exploited the nervousness caused by steep hikes in the price of oil and sudden free-fall drops in the stock market. Paper lacked the substance offered by gold and jewelry.

The new Armenians, it seemed, were adding a fresh chapter to the great American success story. All it took, as everyone knew, was sheer hard work and a little bit of luck. Or was it luck?[7]

Jack Kilhefner had an uneasy feeling. He harbored no prejudices against immigrants, much less Armenians. Yet something was wrong. As senior vice president of the Wells Fargo bank in San Francisco, Kilhefner was responsible for tracking suspiciously large cash deposits flowing into California banks, particularly in small bills.

This assignment had come in the wake of congressional legislation charging financial institutions with the responsibility of verifying the origins of large cash deposits. Like it or not, bank officers—by law—had to play detective.

One Los Angeles account worried Kilhefner. The account belonged to the Andonian brothers. It took six weeks, however, before Kilhefner became suspicious enough to order the investigation of the Andonian brothers' account at the downtown Wells Fargo branch. When the Andonian account grew to $25 million in three months' time, Kilhefner recommended that his boss call the Internal Revenue Service.

The suspicious bank vice president knew that gold and jewelry traders deal mostly in cash, and that large sums can be generated in wholesale transactions. Such an amount, however, all of it in relatively small bills, was almost unheard of, even in the jewelry trade. The extent to which cash plays a major role in the jewelry business, moreover, is arguable. According to one Hill Street diamond merchant, "legitimate wholesale transactions are conducted through bank checks rather than cash. . . ."[8]

At the height of the Wells Fargo investigation, a curious incident took place on a Loomis Armored Transport Company armored car. Armenian jewelers regularly used Loomis to ferry gold and jewelry between their Hill Street shops and the Los Angeles International Airport. One night in January 1988, a Loomis employee was checking a shipment that had just been unloaded from a United Parcel Service jet. He noticed a torn edge on a box belonging to the Ropex Corporation that listed its contents as gold scrap. The box was much too light to contain gold. Upon closer examination, he discovered that it contained neatly bundled stacks of American greenbacks.

When the Loomis employee checked with Ropex he was offered a puzzling explanation: there had probably been a clerical error on the manifest. The currency was being dispatched from New York to Los Angeles to take advantage of higher short-term interest rates.

Having often handled similar shipments and being familiar with the transfer of cash and commodities, the Loomis employee questioned this answer. Why not, for instance, use electronic funds transfer? Why take time and risk to move the money manually when an electronic keystroke would do the same instantaneously?

The Ropex story made no sense to Loomis, which ordinarily transports items with few if any questions asked. The carrier completed the delivery, but the suspicious employee informed the Los Angeles field office of the Federal Bureau of Investigation.[9]

Reported separately by Wells Fargo and Loomis, the incidents sparked an investigation by local, state, and federal officials. The case led to 127 indictments spanning California, Florida, New York, Georgia, Texas, Panama, Colombia, and Switzerland, breaking up what is considered the largest money-laundering operation so far uncovered in the United States. In excess of $1.2 billion in profits from drug sales were washed clean of any association with drugs over a period of three years.

Cooperation among federal agencies was not swift. But more and more evidence of this huge and integrated laundering operation poured into the Internal Revenue Service (IRS), the Federal Bureau of Investigation (FBI), the Drug Enforcement Agency (DEA), and the U.S. Customs Service. By spring 1988, an investigation was underway, coordinated by a forty-member Washington-based committee led by senior officials from the Departments of Justice and Treasury and overseen by Attorney General Richard Thornburgh. The operation was dubbed Polar Cap, an oblique reference to the fact that the feds were casting their eagle eyes from the Eastern to the Western parts of the United States—poles apart. Further deflecting attention from its target, the codeword Polar Cap would never be associated with an investigation in sunny California—a wise precaution considering the number of agencies and people involved.

Begun in 1985 and still underway, Operation Polar Cap

is the culmination of several separate investigations, including "Operation C-Chase"; "Operation Cash Web Expressway"; "Operation Pisces"; and "Operation Catcom." The investigations focused on members of the Medellín cartel, such as Pablo Escobar-Gaviria, Jorge Ochoa Vasquez, Jose Gonzalo Rodriguez Gacha, Geraldo Moncada, also known as Don Chepe, and many of their associates. All of them were accused of smuggling narcotics into the United States, maintaining control over the sale of these drugs, laundering the proceeds, and moving the money out of this country.

Polar Cap also penetrated deep into the Medellín cartel and resulted in the arrest of Eduardo Martinez, the principal money launderer for Don Chepe. Don Chepe was indicted under his pseudonym in the BCCI Tampa case, also known as Operation C-Chase, which was the beginning of the end for BCCI.[10] He was also linked to the latest wave of the Polar Cap probe in Atlanta. This time the indictment tied Don Chepe with the Patriarca organized crime family operating out of Providence, Rhode Island, and Canada. The same family has been implicated in drug-trafficking and money-laundering cases involving the Colombia cartel and The Bahamas on one side and the Syrian Government and Middle Eastern terrorist organizations on the other.

When U.S. investigators examined evidence uncovered in Operation C-Chase, they noticed that documents from the Bank of Luxembourg belonging to Cambio Italia, also known as Letra, and transferred through Republic National Bank and Banco de Occidente, Panama, matched the account numbers of the La Mina organization's Atlanta and L.A. money-laundering operations. On July 26, 1988, an alleged trafficker named Francisco Serrano, later indicted in the case, went to Los Angeles with a Polar Cap undercover agent and pointed out the building that housed La Mina offices headed by Raoul Vivas. It was 500 South Hill Street.

The genius behind this huge money-laundering operation was Eduardo Martinez Romero, who surfaced in 1987 in connection with an undercover investigation in Atlanta, Georgia. He worked on behalf of the Colombian Medellín drug kingpins. He was extradited to Atlanta from Colombia in 1989, pleaded guilty, and plea-bargained his sentence to six and a half years.

In the Polar Cap investigation the U.S. Government traced $1.2 billion in drug money, of which $412 million went from the numerous bank accounts of the Ronel Refining Company. Ronel was a Florida-based corporation engaged in the importation, refining, and sale of gold. It was a subsidiary of Loren Industries, Inc., a publicly owned company controlled largely by the Goldstein family; father Jack and his three sons, Donald, Allen, and Richard. The Ronel connection figured heavily in the unmasking of the Andonians and other L.A. and New York jewelry fronts.[11] Ronel moved money from their bank accounts in the United States to Banco de Occidente in Panama and Cali, Colombia, to Cambio Italia and Letra, in Montevideo, Uruguay, and other foreign banks in the United States. The government was able to recover $50 million in the United States. In all, 1,035 bank accounts and 179 banks were involved.

Cash went to Los Angeles from drug sales in Miami, Houston, and New York. Money was transferred from L.A. to New York, wired to Panama, Bolivia, and Uruguay and ultimately to Europe. Money transferred to Banco de Occidente and Banco Cafetero in Panama went through a chain of middlemen servicing the Medellín cartel, among them Eduardo Martinez Romero. Eduardo Martinez, one of the few big money launderers the Colombian government extradited to the United States, is serving time in a maximum-security prison. He was the closest the U.S. Government was able to get to the Medellín cartel's tightly controlled financial circle. His immediate superior—perhaps his equal—"Doctor" Geraldo Moncada, also known as Don Chepe, was a major target of Operation C-Chase.

Intergovernment agency cooperation helped make Polar Cap a success. While the DEA watched the Colombian and Mexican connection, the IRS and the FBI were hot on the trail of the money as it moved throughout the United States. No one agency could claim absolute right of turf. Moreover, Polar Cap proved so complex that every warm body and resource was needed to figure it all out.

Penetrating the closemouthed and secretive Los Angeles Hill Street district was difficult enough. Communicating in the vernacular was exceedingly more difficult but the normally monolingual U.S. Government was somehow able to recruit Armenian, Turkish, and Spanish-speaking undercover agents. Undercover work was often further complicated by the very security measures the gold and gem district had devised for its own protection.

According to Evan Lowell Maxwell of the *Los Angeles Times*:

> Security is tight on Hill Street. The sidewalk is the enemy, so gold brokers, gem dealers, jewelry designers, casters, pol-

ishers and retailers try to cluster together in the same building. Armed guards and closed-circuit television cameras blankly monitor the hallways. There are hold-up alarms in every office. When an alarm is triggered, elevators rise to the top floor and lock, becoming traps for the unwary stickup man.[12]

And presumably for any unwary law officer as well.

In addition to multilingual operatives, agents also posed as janitorial help, messengers, and repairmen who planted TV monitors in the back rooms and hallways of suspected businesses, including Ropex.

On one occasion the camouflage was simply too good. Disguised as a prostitute, a DEA agent was chased out of the building she was staking out by a suspicious security guard, himself an off-duty L.A. policeman.

A special task force was also set up to track the money as it made its circuitous way in L.A. to the vaults of the Colombian cartels. It took time but the result was a cornucopia of intelligence on the inner workings of money-laundering. Polar Cap's successes have since spawned numerous other investigations by the U.S. Government.

Nellie Magdaloyo enjoyed her job and was good at it. Every night she supervised the office cleaning crew on the ninth floor of the International Jewelry Center, a boxy sixteen-story glass and marble Hill Street office building facing Pershing Square, one of the few patches of green space left in the smog-soaked L.A. downtown area.

Never late or absent, Magdaloyo was meticulous and

cheerful. At the end of her shift, stealthily and with great aplomb, she systematically stole the trash that other workers had gathered and placed it in the service elevator. Odd, but not illegal. Nellie had a warrant in case anyone asked. Nellie Magdaloyo was a special agent for the FBI.

From April to July 1988, the FBI carefully picked through the bits and pieces discarded by Wanis Koyomejian's Ropex company, looking for evidence of money-laundering. And the agents found plenty, including tags from two bank currency bags. The tags indicated the bags contained a total of $480,000, all in twenty-dollar bills. Better yet, after reviewing the scrupulously kept records of the Loomis company, FBI agents discovered that this very same amount had been delivered by Loomis to the Federal Reserve Bank eighteen days earlier.

A week later, evidence of similar transfers was found on scraps of paper, including a handwritten note dated April 12, 1988, containing the words "out," "A.I.B." and "670,000." A.I.B. stood for the American International Bank, where Ropex had an account, and the figure represented the total amount of cash to be delivered to it via the Federal Reserve Bank. Loomis records bore evidence that the same amount was delivered to the Federal Reserve that very day.[13]

There would be many other matching dates of cash deliveries, all performed by Loomis, and the FBI was soon able to give the lie to Ropex's claim that a box containing cash instead of gold scrap had simply been mislabeled.

Cash, lots of it, was frequently transferred from Ropex to its bank accounts and short-term interest rates had nothing to do with it.

Nellie Magdaloyo's trash collection revealed other intriguing details about Wanis Koyomejian and Ropex. Koyomejian controlled five separate companies, including the Ropex Corporation (aka RAFCO), with offices in L.A., Houston, and New York; Orosimo Corp. in New York; S&K Sales, L.A.; ATAYAN & Sons Jewelers, also in L.A.; and SAV-A-Lot Liquors in Sunnyvale and San Jose, California.

On April 27, the day's trash yielded a series of invoices typed on company stationery. According to the affidavit of FBI special agent Bruce R. Stephens: "These invoices list names, countries, the amount of gold allegedly purchased and notations that payment was in cash."[14] The names listed on that date were those of Canadian and Mexican citizens. A typical invoice read "Manuel Melendez, Mexico, April 25, 1988, gold purchase, $140,000, paid in cash." Another read: "Evan Laiman, Canada, April 25, 1988, gold purchase, $188,620, paid in cash." Similar invoices containing other Canadian and Mexican names would also be retrieved by the FBI's trash patrol. Curiously, the alleged Ropex customers always bought gold and paid cash in sums greater than $100,000.[15]

The FBI subsequently ran the Canadian names through the Royal Canadian Mounted Police (RCMP) and learned that:

Of the ten names checked by the RCMP, no records were found to confirm the existence of such persons. Of the ten addresses checked, all ten street names were found to exist. Seven of the addresses, however, were found to be fictitious, [sic] and no connection was found between the remaining

75

three addresses and the purported gold purchasers who supposedly provided them.[16]

As for Mexico, Special Agent Stephens learned from U.S.
Customs "that checks of purported gold purchasers from
Mexico [had] produced similar findings." In other words,
the well-heeled Mexican gold buyers were as phony as the
Canadian ones.[17]

Ropex trash yielded more information. On May 17, the
FBI found a piece of paper with the heading "N.Y." and a
cash denomination in tens and twenties of $1.5 million.
Under that figure was a note saying "extra $150," which
was scrupulously appended to the total. But this time
"$150" was not a contraction for $150,000 but meant precisely $150, adding up to a total cash sum of $1,500,150.
Again, Loomis records indicate that on May 16, it delivered
parcels containing the same amount to Ropex from
Orosimo, located in New York City.[18]

Orosimo proved to be a year-old Fifth Avenue wholesale
jewelry business. Simon Kouyoumjian was listed as president. Born in 1965, and at that time a mere lad of twenty-
three, he was—despite the slight difference in the spelling
of his surname—the son of Wanis Koyomejian, the owner
of Ropex in L.A. The "office" closed in May 1988 but
while it was in business Orosimo had an interesting role in
the La Mina operation. According to FBI Special Agent
Stephens: "This location is also believed to have been a
collection point for narcotics proceeds ultimately shipped
via common carrier to ROPEX-LA."[19] Wanis Koyomejian
ran the business with his sons. Born in 1967, Raffi
Kouyoumjian was apparently Wanis's second in command.

According to an FBI affidavit, Raffi worked in "the daily counting, delivery, distribution and sorting" of money brought into ROPEX-LA for laundering. Houston, Texas, in addition to New York, figured heavily in the business of the Ropex company. On May 18, a piece of paper retrieved by FBI agents listed "H-1,499,000." This information matched Loomis's records for an amount sent from Houston to Ropex in L.A. A $1.5 million entry for New York was similarly recorded. That same piece of paper listed banks and individuals with numbers next to them. The FBI concluded that these were in fact the true recipients of the cash forwarded from New York and Houston. Among the financial institutions on this scrap of paper was the L.A. branch of the Independence Bank, Encino, California, the bank later discovered to have been purchased illegally by Ghaith Pharaon, the Saudi Arabian businessman who fronted for BCCI.[20]

Careful analysis of the trash had yielded some major clues and raised huge suspicions about Ropex and other jewelry firms. But false invoices could not, by themselves, prove Ropex was laundering money—at least, not beyond the shadow of a doubt. More solid evidence would soon turn up. The DEA had mounted a surveillance of the Andonian brothers' operations located just blocks away from Ropex, at 220 West Fifth Street. The Andonians controlled five different companies all listed in the same building. Unlike Koyomejian's, the Andonian trash was not as rich and rewarding to the DEA—and the FBI. But here, too, a few shipments of cash disguised as gold or gold scrap could be matched with Loomis's and Brinks's records.

The reason for the smaller harvest of evidence can be

traced to the more cautious Nazareth Andonian, who installed a paper shredder in October 1988. Andonian employees also attempted to deface return addresses on the cardboard boxes used for shipping currency to the office. However, the DEA managed to remove paint from one of the boxes and exposed the sender's address—Z&G Jewelry in New York.[21]

Z&G Gold Exchange was located on West Forty-eighth Street in Manhattan, but it was not recorded with the state or city of New York. Dun and Bradstreet had never heard of Z&G either. Subsequent investigation found that No. 1107 at 64 West Forty-eighth consisted of a small room with a telephone, a desk, and a chair. No gold or jewelry were found.[22]

Despite the meager information gleaned from the Andonian trash, some important evidence was uncovered, and it was enough to lead to La Mina's demise. On August 12, 1988, the DEA trash collectors found a handwritten note that cryptically read: "1,000,000 L.A. 34,000 L.A. INV under RONEL's." Two other invoices gathered on that day said: "Sold to RONEL REF., 2801 Greene Street, Hollywood, Florida." According to the DEA's affidavit, "the stated value of the two invoices totaled $1,034,000 and indicated the amount was paid for in cash."[23]

Rifling through trash was only one technique used to collect information. Closed-circuit television was another. Armed with a court order, the FBI installed cameras in the Andonian and Koyomejian offices and let the tapes roll. This police version of "Candid Camera" documented daily deliveries by Brinks and Loomis couriers of large boxes and duffle bags stuffed with money. In one five-day period—November 28 to December 2—Loomis delivered forty-four boxes of cash and picked up twenty-seven duffle bags stuffed with currency. Videotapes also confirmed that the Andonians had sold a small amount of gold jewelry as well.[24]

On December 20, at the Andonians', the camera taped Vagram Tankazyan, better known as Mario, and Krikor Chahinian (aka Koko) sorting $120 million with the aid of a high-speed money-counting machine.

According to the DEA affidavit:

KOKO sorted bundles of currency while MARIO (out of camera range) was recorded via concealed microphone and audio tape, operating a high speed money counter (machine) in the room and confirming the addition of the currency. Upon completion of the counting of the currency, MARIO placed a telephone call to THEO (believed to be in N.Y.) . . . and engaged in a spanish [sic] conversation. These telephone numbers were not being intercepted and thus only one side of the conversation was recorded. It is apparent from MARIO's statements that a discrepancy existed in what THEO had claimed the total to be when the currency was delivered to ABI-LA [Andonian Brothers Manufacturing Company, Inc.] and the actual count arrived at by KOKO and MARIO.

At Ropex the hidden video camera recorded couriers making the rounds to area banks, coming and going. In his affidavit, FBI agent Stephens noted one incident involving the L.A. Police Department.

[FBI Special Agent] FRANKIE T. ISHIZAKI has informed [me] that on May 13, 1988, CHANES KHAWALOUJIAN was observed by close-circuit TV departing ROPEX-LA at about 11:50 AM with a large jewelry display case. LAPD surveillance units lost KHAWALOUJIAN in the vicinity of 6th Street and Grand Avenue. KHAWALOUJIAN returned to ROPEX at approximately 12:16 PM with the case. CHANES was observed again departing ROPEX with another display case at approximately 12:20 PM and was surveilled by LAPD units to CITY NATIONAL BANK, 620 South Olive Street. He returned to ROPEX at approximately 1:00 PM.[25]

Three days later, Special Agent Ishizaki arranged for a DEA surveillance team to shadow Chanes Khawaloujian to the Independence Bank, a few blocks from Ropex. A subsequent query at the bank revealed that $350,000 was deposited to the bank and then credited to Wanis Koyomejian's account. On January 19, 1989, Nazareth Andonian was taped inside his office standing over a table, counting stacks of U.S. dollars and placing them into heat-sealed envelopes.[26]

Telephone and fax taps and planted electronic microphones also yielded a harvest of intelligence for Polar Cap. The La Mina money launderers used mostly coded language in their conversations and preferred untappable cellular and pay phones, beepers, and fax machines. La Mina began to use faxes between individual businesses during the summer of 1988. The U.S. Government caught up with the fax transfers a year later. Despite their precautions, however, they used their regular office phones on occasion, especially when their colleagues called. On January 20, 1988, Nazareth Andonian and Harout Beshlian discussed on the phone the difficulty of maintaining a cover. Beshlian was an executive officer of Geminor, Inc., another L.A. Hill Street wholesale jeweler.

Nazareth Andonian told his colleague:

> "One, how did I buy it? How did I ship it? Where did I ship? There is nothing showing these. Have I not bought it? If they say that, O.K. you have bought this . . . where did you go and buy it? I have not bought anything. We are directly making it explicit that the matter is like this, Harout."[27]

Andonian further explained that it was vital that the drug money move while the gold stayed in one place without ever really changing ownership. This was the master principle of his operation. Having revealed the equivalent of state secrets on the phone, Beshlian suggested the next conversation take place in person. A wise precaution, though a bit too late.[28]

Even more revealing were Nazareth Andonian's numerous phone conversations with, and fax transmissions to, his Ronel company contact, Richard Ferris. These communications were all intercepted and recorded by the DEA. At first, according to the intercepts, both men expressed pleasure at their booming business, ostensibly Andonian's purchase of gold from Ronel in Florida.

Soon enough, however, difficulties began to arise and both parties, especially Ferris, grew worried.

One of the main problems came from their legitimate gold broker. Cargil Metals had been selling small amounts of gold to the Andonians, but it soon expressed lively interest in the destination of the precious metal. Smooth-talking Nazareth Andonian assured a Cargil salesman on December 7, 1988, that some of the gold was being shipped by Brinks to jewelry manufacturers in Italy. The younger Andonian further explained that he was using Ronel's account at London's Phillip Brothers because the Andonians were not registered with the British gold broker. This arrangement, he added, was quite legitimate as the Andonians sometimes "traded" gold with Ronel. Cargil seemed reassured for the moment, but on the following day, December 8, Ferris called Andonian. He was anxious to know whether Cargil had called Andonian and what Andonian had told the broker. Unfortunately, Andonian and Ferris were not reading from the same script. "I obviously gave him the same answers as you did," Ferris told Andonian.[29] In fact, his answers were totally different. Ferris told Cargil that the Ronel account was being used for hedging gold investments in London. He had said nothing about Italian manufacturers, a fabrication that only Nazareth Andonian used. Ferris added that Cargil already knew that Ronel was selling the same gold back to the Andonian brothers rather than to other customers—yet another discrepancy.[30]

During the rest of their troubled conversation, Ferris and Andonian tried to reconcile their stories. Unable to do so, they decided to drag in other gold brokers, a scheme designed to make transactions seem smaller, thus more believable and legitimate. Still upset by Cargil's phone call, Ferris later suggested doing business with a respectable gold exchange firm such as Shearson Lehman in New York. The Ronel manager briefly considered the ask-no-questions Hong Kong gold market, but decided that the thirteen-hour time difference would cause too many problems.[31] On December 12, a worried Ferris told Andonian by phone that he could not risk Ronel's relationship with Cargil. He suggested that Andonian limit his use of Cargil to "only a couple of days a week."[32] He also instructed Andonian to confirm all transactions supposedly untapable by fax.

Although the wary Andonians tried to avoid electronic surveillance, the Koyomejians didn't seem to care. Ropex was anything but vigilant in conducting business over the phone and Wanis Koyomejian was downright foolhardy. Adopting his father's cocky stance, Raffi bragged on the phone to a woman friend—despite her warnings—that he owned a quarter of Ropex and with profits rolling in, he would clear at least a million dollars.[33]

For a professional money launderer he had yet to learn much about security. Unlike the Andonians, Wanis was regularly captured on government cameras counting a steady green avalanche of money, the proceeds from the sales of cocaine. If a picture is worth a thousand words, Koyomejian's words were well worth their weight in gold as well.

In a stir of paternal benevolence Wanis was recorded giving his son Raffi sound advice: "Work only in cash." Getting rich, he added, was only part of the game. Real gratification, the elder Koyomejian bragged, came from "faking" the government—in this case by failing to report $25,000 Wanis had just earned laundering Colombian cocaine profits. Wanis was in the habit of using office phones to talk to his employees even though they were only a few feet away. All these conversations were intercepted by government taps. Koyomejian must have thought that speaking in Armenian and Arabic or in guarded and coded English would discourage eavesdroppers. It did not. FBI and

DEA agents assigned to the case spoke Armenian and Arabic. Some also spoke Turkish, a language widely used by the Andonian brothers.[34]

But Koyomejian also incriminated himself in English. On November 4, 1988, he had a lengthy conversation in his office with Randy Matiyow, manager of Prosegur, Inc., also located at 550 South Hill Street. Prosegur rented safes to brokers who bought and sold gold but did not find it necessary to physically transport the bullion from place to place. Wanis informed Matiyow that law enforcement officers had picked up someone with a half a million dollars in cash and that an Armenian jeweler had already been questioned by the FBI. The jeweler had asked Koyomejian for some cover in the form of an invoice for the cash—a request Wanis had denied.

The topic changed and the two men talked about the fees charged for large currency transactions. Koyomejian explained the dos and don'ts of money-laundering. "If you put cash in your account and issue a check, then you are laundering money directly," he told Matiyow. But if you were to do it as a "service" and then charge for the service, then "no one can knock on your door, no one can come to you."[35]

It was, to say the least, a strange reading of Title 18 of the U.S. Code, which deals with money-laundering, but the confident Koyomejian must have been convinced he was immune from prosecution. He went on to tell Randy Matiyow about Ronel and the special services that firm performed for him. He then added gratuitously that if Ronel's employees went to jail it would be at least for ten years while he, Wanis, would only get six months, "maybe."[36]

Still, Wanis was not entirely without guile. Like the Andonians, he worried about the circular nature of the gold trading arrangements, which in time, he feared, would arouse official suspicions. Eventually, like the Andonians, Koyomejian would have a series of discussions with Richard Ferris of Ronel.

On October 21, 1988, at his Ropex offices, Wanis Koyomejian met with Richard Ferris and his partner, Carlos Desoretz, to discuss the shortage of gold. Koyomejian suggested they establish a pool of 300 kilos (66 pounds) of gold to be exchanged only within "the group," a scheme that would permit the selling of the same gold back and forth within the laundering network. This way they would avoid sudden and possibly costly shortages of the metal.

Ferris, for his part, said he and his associates had recently been scared by arrests and seizures in Miami, the result of Operation C-Chase. "The owners," Ferris told Koyomejian, "are frightened men." Ferris seemed to endorse the gold pool idea but warned that some of the metal had to be sold to "outside" people, lest passing it back and forth among themselves would eventually raise suspicion.[37]

But the problems facing the La Mina money launderers had not been resolved. On January 17, 1989, Ferris warned Koyomejian that the gold "sales" were beginning to look funny. In spite of his advice to the Andonians, the ring had been able to involve very few legitimate gold brokers as cover. On February 23, 1989, worried sick and no longer able to handle the stress, Ferris voluntarily turned himself in to the DEA.

Following his arrest, Ferris also sang to the FBI, U.S.

Customs, and the IRS. In August, he pleaded guilty to money-laundering charges under Title 18. What Ferris had to say was at least in part self-serving, but during lengthy periods of questioning the Ronel president provided the government with fresh details on La Mina's inner workings—information which greatly bolstered data officials had previously obtained through surveillance.

Richard Ferris knew how things worked. He had been at Ronel for thirteen years, four years as its president. The company had begun business as an honest refiner and assayer of precious metals including gold, platinum, and palladium. According to Ferris's statement that meant that ". . . Ronel would melt down and refine scrap jewelry, sweepings of dust from jewelry manufacturing processes, and computer circuit boards."[38] Ronel was a subsidiary of Loren Industries, Inc., owned by the Goldstein family. The Goldsteins also controlled half a dozen other gold and jewelry businesses and a Florida realty firm.[39]

By the spring of 1986, however, business at Ronel was bad. Gold prices had peaked long ago in the waning Carter years and had dropped during the Reagan administration. Gold had been a panic purchase at a time of U.S. inflation and seemingly endless international crises, such as steep oil price increases. But now investors were more interested in the stock market, which by the mid-1980s was well into another bullish period.

It was no wonder that Ferris then took an immediate interest in an offer from a South American firm to sell Ronel "mine gold." Unrefined gold, direct from the mine, is freely available from parts of the old Spanish empire. Ronel would refine the metal and sell it to its customers. Ferris's principal employee, Carlos Desoretz, vouched for this South American firm and was the sole person to communicate with Ronel's new partner. Meanwhile, all monies paid by Ronel for the Latin American gold would go into a New York account called "Orofe."[40]

This mum's-the-word approach did not reap immediate dividends. For the first few months of operation in 1986, the South Americans sent only a few kilograms of gold at a time and only a couple of times a week. But then the trickle suddenly turned into a torrent of gold, first from a few kilos to twenty-five and then forty kilos per week.[41]

Accustomed to supplying modest amounts of gold to Loren Industries' other subsidiaries and to a number of local jewelers, Ronel found itself holding a large and unprofitable inventory of the metal from somewhere in South America. Even worse, the gold needed to be refined, a process that only added to Ronel's business costs.[42]

Ferris, however, would soon find a way out of his dilemma. Ronel's president was also one of forty directors of the International Precious Metals Institute (IPMI). At the institute's annual convention, Ferris met Randy Leshay, of the A-Mark Trading Company of Los Angeles. A-Mark was a very large gold broker, far bigger than Ronel, and Leshay expressed an interest in buying Ronel's leftover inventory. The two men quickly reached an oral agreement—common enough in the gold business—and Ronel's Ferris was suddenly relieved of the excess metal from South America.[43]

By the summer of 1986, Loren Industries chief financial officer Moe Lakhani began to have doubts. What he found was a curious circular exchange of bullion between Orofe, Ronel, and A-Mark. Soon other L.A.-based firms had become involved, including the Andonian brothers, and Wanis Koyomejian felt relieved. The money Orofe generated from the gold purchased from South America would be transferred by wire from the Chase Manhattan Bank in New York to Banco de Occidente in Panama, then on to Occidente's branch in Montevideo, Uruguay.[44]

It became even more interesting when Ferris poked further into this arrangement. According to Ferris's statement:

> [Ferris] . . . created a unique mark on several of the plastic bags which contained the gold shot [measure] bullion and recorded the serial numbers of several of the gold bullion bars and discovered that some of the same bags/bars of gold were repeatedly being traded within the circle of Orofe, Ronel and A-Mark. Since these companies were the only ones involved in this circular flow of gold from Florida to California and back it was suggested that a gold depository account be set up in this case with Prosegur Security Agency headquartered in Los Angeles. Prosegur would simply save the expense of physically transporting the gold while keeping account of who was owner of the metal at any one time.[45]

After discovering this arrangement, Ferris continued to buy gold. But he noticed other changes. Ferris and Desoretz were told the Orofe account would be discontinued and replaced with one called Letra, S.A. Still later it would become Omensal. No explanation was given for these sudden switches and no questions were asked. But Ferris knew perfectly well that sudden changes in name and address were usually the hallmark of illegal money-laundering operations—standard practices to throw off government investigators.

The Loren owners, the Goldsteins, were completely satisfied. Arrangements with Orofe/Letra/Omensal proved profitable, especially after the gold depository arrangement was put in place with Prosegur of Los Angeles.[46]

But in April 1987, according to Ferris, another incident broke Ronel's serenity. A-Mark discovered that some of the South American gold shot was thinly gold-plated silver. A-Mark had purchased the "gold" from Ronel although the Florida company had never been in possession of the metal, thanks to the depository arrangement with Prosegur of L.A. After that, Ferris claimed, Ronel tested all gold shot coming from South America, although gold bar bullion continued to be traded through the old arrangement.[47]

None of this helped allay Ferris's suspicions, or so he claimed to federal officials, and by the summer of 1987 he sought legal advice to determine Ronel's liability should the South American gold turn out to be a money-laundering scheme. He was reassured that there would be none. Nevertheless, he lowered Ronel's risk by ending its physical possession of the metal. Ronel would merely act as a conduit of convenience. Only wire transfers of money from A-Mark and other deals would be sent to the Letra accounts and, again, on to Montevideo, Uruguay.[48]

The simplicity and apparent safety of the scheme appeased the Ronel organization for a while, but yet another oddity emerged from a further examination of the circular transactions. While Ronel, A-Mark, the Andonians, and the other American firms made money, Ferris discovered that Letra, S.A., never made a profit on any of the transactions. In fact, the South Americans were losing money. Lots of it.[49]

In September 1987, Ferris now openly told the lawyer for Loren Industries of his virtual certainty that money-laundering was behind the Letra account. Once again he was brushed off. But, as he claimed in his affidavit, Ferris would not stop there. A-Mark officials were also becoming suspicious. They prompted Ferris to approach members of the Goldstein family on several occasions between September and November 1987, and to inform them of their concerns.

The Goldsteins refused to discontinue the Letra account. They shunned calls from A-Mark officials presumably to avoid hearing the suspicions. By this time, thanks to the South American connection, Ronel had become so profitable that it was able to absorb losses from some of the less successful companies owned by Loren Industries. In November 1987, Loren's officers boosted Ferris's salary and worked out a bonus plan, an incentive that, to Ferris's great dissatisfaction, proved illusory. According to Ferris, the bonus was phony since the Goldsteins shifted operational and overhead expenses of their other firms to Ronel, thus radically reducing its "profitability."[50]

A month later, now certain of the illegal nature of the Letra enterprise and unhappy over his compensation from Ronel, Ferris worked out a kickback scheme with Letra using Carlos Desoretz as the go-between. According to Desoretz, Ferris earned some $300,000 in kickbacks. Desoretz made twice that amount. Ronel made profits in excess of a million dollars.[51]

To keep this useful conduit open, the South Americans had to keep Ferris happy. By early 1988, he had become a co-conspirator, and he now frequently discussed the mechanics of money-laundering with the Andonians.[52]

But Desoretz was beginning to scare, especially after the BCCI money-laundering scandal broke in Tampa, Florida (Operation C-Chase). BCCI was one of the financial institutions used by Ronel and Letra, S.A.[53]

To cover their tracks, both Ferris and Desoretz attempted to persuade the Goldsteins that the Ronel gold transactions were frauds. But the Goldsteins did not take the warnings seriously. Ferris said in his affidavit:

> Richard Goldstein said he didn't want to hire a private investigator, as previously recommended by Loren Attorney Bruce Rich [of Spengler, Carlos, Gubar & Frischling law firm] and also commended that as soon as Ronel could "get by" without the Letra account, Ronel would stop doing business with them. Richard Goldstein also decided that he would stop selling Ronel pool gold to Letra, yet authorized the sale of physical gold to Letra.[54]

This was the stance maintained by Loren/Ronel owners until Ferris and Desoretz were arrested for money-laundering. None of the Goldsteins were arrested.

On February 21, 1989, Sergio Hochman was arrested in Los Angeles. Hochman had been in trouble before. Trouble, in fact, seemed to stalk the young Uruguayan wherever he went.

By the 1960s, Uruguay had long ceased to develop and its young people had grown restless. Many immigrated to more promising societies; others joined extremist movements such as the Tupamaros, which promised revolution and delivered terror. In 1980 Hochman was neither an adventurous émigré nor a romantic revolutionary but an underpaid jewelry shop clerk in downtown Montevideo. In 1982 Hochman became acquainted with Wilton Gutman and, after a suitable period of courtship, married Gutman's sister, Liliana.

Originally from Argentina, the Gutmans had lived in the United States before moving to Uruguay. Gutman had casually explained that he had been forced to leave the States on an immigration technicality. Only later, after Hochman had married Liliana, did the jeweler learn that his new brother-in-law had served a year in jail and been deported on drug charges.[55]

Wilton Gutman also got into trouble in Uruguay for passing bad checks. He hastily retreated to Buenos Aires in 1982. Hochman complained to Gutman that his future in the jewelry business looked bleak. Gutman offered to help him by way of a nebulous business deal that turned out to involve the laundering of Colombian drug money. Hochman would later claim that he was unaware of such activity even though the numerous trips he made on behalf of his brother-in-law took him to Colombia, the United States, and Panama, and always involved the transport of large sums of cash neatly packed in suitcases.[56]

Sergio Hochman continued to serve Gutman in Argentina until an argument erupted, not over money, but over a Colombian woman who Hochman thought was taking up too much of his business partner's precious time.

In December 1985 Hochman returned to Montevideo to try his hand at the legitimate precious metals trade. It took him less than two months to realize that he was not going to make it. In February 1986 Hochman met three men in Montevideo, a Cuban émigré named Pedro Martinez, a Chilean named Jorge Masihy, and the Argentine Raoul Vivas. Hochman had met Vivas briefly a few months earlier in Miami. Then as now Vivas clearly seemed in charge. Unlike Hochman's old partner Wilton Gutman, Vivas was direct, forceful, and self-assured.

Vivas proposed a straightforward business deal that Hochman liked—and badly needed. He invited Hochman to Montevideo to work for his newly acquired business. Vivas explained that he owned a gold refinery in Montevideo. Hochman did not find this unusual since many Argentines preferred putting their money into reasonably tranquil, democratic, uninquisitive Uruguay rather than tumultuous and dictatorship-prone Argentina.[57]

Uruguay had an abundance of currency exchange offices. The country's banking laws freely allowed dollars to flow in and out—unlike Argentina, its close neighbor, which had long imposed strict currency controls. Vivas, the Argentinean, moved to the Uruguayan capital of Montevideo to realize his financial ambition. Vivas purchased a failing money-exchange business in Montevideo called Cambio Italia. Established in 1982, the firm had lost so much money that by 1986 the owner happily sold out. With all the competition, Cambio Italia had made little if any money. That was to change, Vivas hoped, when he bought it with his three partners, Pedro Martinez, Jorge Masihy, and Mauricio Mejia.

Vivas looked for a profit from Cambio Italia because he

planned to use it as a front to launder money for his Colombian clients. Vivas kept its corporate name, Letra, S.A., and installed Sergio Hochman and Ruben Priscolin as corporate officers. Cambio Italia was, in fact, only a cover for its holding company, Letra, S.A., which had branches in the United States. Hochman served as a vice president while Vivas remained in the shadows, his name never to appear in any of the companies' documents. Despite the title, Hochman's real job was to count the money and keep his mouth shut. All along he suspected he was also being used as a front man and perhaps a fall guy, but having gotten nowhere in his own business, he agreed to take the risky new job.[58]

After several months Hochman followed Vivas to Los Angeles, where Vivas had purchased a house and invested in a jewelry business called Paolo, Inc., in the Hill Street district. Vivas renamed the business Standard Commodities Trading, Inc., but used the acronym (RAOF). By July 1986 Vivas, Hochman, and their associates were collecting cash for the Medellín cartel. In the cocaine-happy, prosperous Southern California of the mid-1980s, business boomed. From the gang turf of the sweltering, depressed flatlands of South Los Angeles to the cool and affluent canyons of West Los Angeles drug money rolled in, mostly in $20 bills. Ten to fifteen pickups were made each week and the hauls ranged from a paltry $20,000 to a respectable $300,000. The weekly minimum was around $200,000. For Hochman, now aswirl in easy money, the wretched Montevideo jewelry store job seemed a universe or two away.

At first, Vivas, Hochman, and the others picked up the cash at prearranged locations from beeper-equipped Colombian couriers. The money was counted at RAOF, placed in containers, and transported to Astro Jewelers, S&H Imports, and, in the fall of 1986, to Wanis Koyomejian's Ropex. Soon, high-speed money counters borrowed from a neighboring jewelry firm owned by a squat, popeyed Armenian named John were installed to keep up with the volume. In this secretive business, last names were rarely shared and Sergio Hochman didn't ask.[59]

RAOF used the money to buy and sell gold. Vivas put his profits in U.S. banks and U.S. branches of foreign banks and wire-transferred them out of the United States. In early 1986 Raoul Vivas and a confederate met in Hollywood, Florida, with Richard Ferris, the president of Ronel, and his employee Desoretz. Vivas was interested in selling his unrefined gold to Ronel. Ferris accepted the offer not knowing that Desoretz had brought Vivas to Ronel for a kickback of fifty cents per ounce of gold sold to his employer. Vivas shipped the gold from Los Angeles to Ronel and received payments to accounts in the name of Orofe and Letra held at Chase Manhattan Bank of New York. The proceeds were then wire-transferred to Vivas's accounts in Uruguay.

In less than a year, at the end of 1986, the profitable enterprise had turned into a bonanza, a round-the-clock business that never slept, except in Uruguay's summer months—mid-November to mid-January—when the country reveled in a three-month siesta and Cambio Italia, afraid to raise suspicion, also went on vacation.[60]

Deluged with money, Vivas soon needed larger quarters and he moved to 550 South Hill Street in L.A.[61] South Hill was a good place to meet other jewelers, all dependable and greedy Armenians who acted as middlemen in the laundering process. By late summer 1986, Vivas had worked out his best arrangement yet with a firm called Ropex, fortuitously located in the same building as Vivas's operation. The drug cash would be boxed and moved from the Argentine's office to the Armenian's in exchange for gold bars or gold shot, which were hand-carried to Vivas's office. This was, quite literally, an in-house operation. Working in such close quarters, however, soon proved less than practical as neither Vivas nor his employees entirely trusted the blustering blowhard Wanis Koyomejian. As a result, Vivas and company reduced the amount of currency they were willing to launder for Ropex and instead redirected a good deal of it to the more discreet Andonian brothers.[62]

Late in 1986, when Ronel was unable to sell all the gold it refined, Ferris made contact with A-Mark, the gold brokering company in Los Angeles. The gold shipped from Los Angeles to Miami took a round-trip back in Los Angeles to A-Mark. This convoluted paper trail, inefficient and inconvenient as it seemed, was essential to disguise the money's real source. It also served to deflect suspicion. In February 1987 Ronel opened a depository account with Prosegur in Los Angeles. This arrangement allowed Vivas's gold suppliers to deposit the metal with Ronel in Florida without incurring shipping delays or costs, since Ronel sold much of the gold into A-Mark's Prosegur depository account. The business expanded and the tentacles spread.

Around the same time Vivas sent Hochman to New York to open a new cash collection network. Hochman operated out of a penthouse suite on Sixth Avenue under the name S&H Imports. He gathered payments from drug sales in the greater New York–New Jersey–Connecticut area. The packets of money carried a La Mina code number indicating the member of the Medellín cartel who "owned" them. After counting the money in the office, Hochman delivered the cash to Orosimo, another storefront in New York's jewelry district operated by Simon Kouyoumjian. From there the money was transported by Loomis and Brinks to Ropex in Los Angeles, then on to Ronel in Florida or to Ronel's account at Prosegur. When he received the cash, Hochman would make a confirmation call to Cambio Italia in Uruguay and Raoul Vivas in Los Angeles. Vivas soon established another money collection conduit in Houston, Texas, and assigned yet another associate to manage it. Fearing detection, Vivas shut down that operation within a year. In the summer of 1987 A-Mark began to suspect that some of the gold from Prosegur had been adulterated. Upon closer examination A-Mark found silver pellets thinly plated with gold and from then on refused to accept deliveries from Prosegur. Ronel remained the main dealer. Toward the end of 1987 Vivas visited Hochman in New York and instructed him to do business with the Andonian Brothers Manufacturing Company, Inc., and Nazareth Jewelers.

Vivas also decided to let the Andonians quench his voracious thirst for gold. Beginning in early 1988, after notifying Vivas, Sergio Hochman sent the New York collections to the Andonians via Loomis or Brinks.[63]

The key man in this group was Vagram Marion Dangasian, better known as Tio. Dangasian's best contact in Latin America was his son-in-law, Avetis Tokaltian—Avo for short—who owned a prosperous jewelry store, Rose Marie Joyeria, in the center of Buenos Aires.

Tokaltian and his partner, Eduardo Comerci, also from

Argentina, were soon introduced to Tio Dangasian's nephew, Mario Tankazyan, a young émigré from Soviet Armenia, who, with his brother Arutyun, operated a small but successful jewelry business in Los Angeles. By 1984, Uncle Tio was referring his South American friends and relations to Mario and his brother, Arutyun. Soon the Latin trade made up the bulk of their jewelry repair business. Later, Tio introduced his nephew to his son-in-law Avo Tokaltian and Eduardo Comerci. The three would form a partnership and name the business Rose Marie, Inc., of Los Angeles.[64]

With multiple sources of gold, Raoul Vivas and his partners could next perform an act of reverse alchemy. The pure gold was mixed with silver giving it the appearance of impure gold of foreign origin. The adulterated gold was then transported by armored truck to New York City, where a Vivas associate sold the metal to either the Republic National Bank, the Central Bank of New York or Manfra, Tordella, and Brooks, a precious metals broker.

The banks, in this case, were innocent middlemen. But Vivas had found another financial institution that was far from innocent. One of Vivas's partners at the Cambio Italia personally knew a bank president who proved willing to cooperate. His bank, the Guarantee International Bank (GIB) located in Stamford, Connecticut, cheerfully created an account for Letra, S.A. GIB had a reputation for being a "fast" bank. It moved money by wire very quickly without ever asking a question. For that service, Guarantee charged a whopping 5 percent to 6½ percent.[65]

In all cases, Vivas's gold was credited to the account of Letra, S.A. Upon fax instructions from Cambio Italia in

Montevideo, the money was then wire-transferred from the New York banks to several different foreign bank accounts, all in Panama.[66]

The critical element in Vivas's scheme was a simple but brilliant sleight of hand. The Argentine had to convince the New York banks that the gold he sent, while coming from California, originated in Uruguay. To do that, Vivas was able to create false import documentation papers, ironically with the unwitting help of the U.S. Customs Service.

Sergio Hochman in his statement spelled out the scheme in filigreed detail:

> [We] were able to arrange documentation that made the gold appear as if it was coming from Uruguay by having Cambio Italia, Montevideo, send to the United States via Skorpios Transport or Juncadella gold plated lead bars weighing a certain amount. United States Customs would then document a certain weight of gold being shipped from Uruguay into the United States. They would then present the documentation to the banks and the gold plated lead bars would be replaced with the gold which had been purchased and melted down in Los Angeles.[67]

Vivas's legerdemain was a work of art. It was a simple but elegant fraud, almost foolproof—and immensely profitable because Vivas charged his Colombian clients a 5 percent fee for the total amount of money laundered. After Vivas's overhead and business expenses were deducted—including Hochman's meager salary—Raoul Vivas kept 1 percent. That meant the Argentine made—at a bare minimum—even in the early, start-up days in Los Angeles

$2,000 a week. As time went on, it would be much, much more.[68]

Still, the Argentine never became complacent. In mid-September 1986, Vivas decided to stop melting the Armenian gold in his offices and had it instead transported to Ronel Refining for reworking in Florida. His contact—fellow Argentine Carlos Desoretz, whom he met on several occasions—once in January 1988 in Punta del Este, Uruguay's famous beach resort—to discuss the laundry operation.

With his Los Angeles business booming, Vivas decided to expand into New York and Houston. The Andonians had already laundered for Vivas $8 million in 1986 and $80 million in 1987; 1988 proved to be a banner year: $290 million.[69]

In 1987, when Sergio Hochman, now trusted to do what he was told, was put in charge of the New York branch, he operated from a swank penthouse suite on the Avenue of the Americas, better known to New Yorkers as Sixth Avenue. The Uruguayan was soon collecting money in Manhattan, the proceeds from cocaine sales in the New York area.

As Vivas's New York partner, Jorge Gallina, in Vivas's opinion, spent too much time out of town and away from the workbench, Hochman was also to oversee bank transfer operations to Montevideo.[70]

Gallina, however, was not the only one Vivas found wanting. His partners, Martinez and Masihy, he felt, were no longer doing their share of work, which was to act as liaison with the Medellín drug traffickers. In addition, Vivas thought Martinez, the Cuban, had earned a reputation as a chatterbox, a fatal weakness in this kind of business. As a result, the Argentine severed his relationship with the two men and began to work directly with the Colombian bosses.[71]

More trouble was on the way.

Celio Merkin, another fellow Argentine and Vivas's partner in his Houston money-laundering operation, decided he could do better on his own and moved to New York to set up a rival laundry. More bad luck attended the Houston venture. Finding a suitable replacement for Merkin proved difficult for Vivas. Two new men had been hired in less than six months but neither proved acceptable. Worse, on advice of an employee who suspected police surveillance—legitimately so—Vivas shut down his Houston operation in the fall of 1988.[72]

Even the loyal Sergio Hochman was not without blemish. To be sure, he was in no position to betray his boss, but ill-fortune would continue to shadow him in New York.

In May 1988, Hochman was supervising the collection and shipment of a large consignment of money to California from his Sixth Avenue penthouse office when he heard a knock at the front door. A closed-circuit TV monitor revealed what appeared to be New York City police detectives standing in the hallway. In fact, they were FBI agents. Hochman managed to escape through an opening to the roof, abandoning over $2 million in cash. On the same day he jetted back to home and refuge in Montevideo.[73]

Vivas summarily fired Hochman for desertion. Hoping to resume his money-laundering career, Hochman returned to Los Angeles. His luck ran out on February 21, 1989, when he was arrested moments before he was to board a New York-bound airliner.[74]

Sergio Hochman's unlucky star soon began to follow

Raoul Vivas as well. Hochman's arrest was bad news. Vivas knew his former employee would turn state's evidence, which Hochman did. But things got worse. On the day of Sergio Hochman's arrest, the Andonians and Mario Tankazyan had met in Vivas's office to discuss the loss of over $4.8 million to U.S. Customs at New York's John F. Kennedy Airport a month earlier. They had already engaged in long distance phone calls to sort out the matter, but had reached no conclusions.

As was often the case, the seizure was a matter of random luck. Loomis had picked up about thirty falsely manifested boxes of currency destined for delivery to the Andonian brothers in L.A. A Loomis employee had inadvertently torn a hole in one of the boxes and a U.S. Customs dog on a routine patrol at the airport's warehouse had detected the presence of cocaine residue in the boxes.

Vivas was caught unaware; he was vacationing at the time in Punta del Este on Uruguay's Gold Coast. On the advice of the Medellín cartel, he had no choice but to absorb the loss. Nor would Nazareth Andonian's panicky calls to New York and Montevideo help. They were all being tapped.[75]

At a subsequent meeting in Los Angeles, the money launderers sadly concluded that the confiscation of nearly $5 million would be chalked up to experience. They vowed to be more vigilant in the future. The future was well behind them, however. Vigilance would be useless. Over a period of five months, the FBI and DEA had accumulated 3,000 reels of audio and videotape evidence of the Andonian and Koyomejian money-laundering activities. Nor could prudence ever have prevented accidents caused by innocent third parties such as Loomis.[76]

To make matters worse, Vivas earlier learned from one of his Los Angeles banks that the federal government was investigating La Mina. A Los Angeles grand jury had subpoenaed the records of one of his accounts. Like Hochman, Vivas had panicked and caught the first flight out of Los Angeles to Montevideo.

On February 22, 1989, following Hochman's arrest in Los Angeles, Vivas was arrested by Uruguayan police on a warrant issued by U.S. authorities. Uruguay swiftly approved Vivas's extradition in December 1989 and he returned to the United States to face a series of trials. Vivas and his co-defendants, the Andonian brothers, were held on thirty counts of money-laundering and conspiracy. In a separate indictment naming the Koyomejians as co-conspirators, Vivas was also held on seventeen counts. Vivas's career with La Mina was over.

In contrast with the Andonians and Koyomejians of Los Angeles, the firm of Brown and Carrera had not yet made the big league in 1987. They had gone into business in 1986 after a brief dalliance with drug smuggling. Laundering money would prove safer and more lucrative. Their budding business relationship with the Medellín cartel began—as it invariably does—through a trusted intermediary, a U.S.-based drug trafficker who recommended Brown and Carrera to his Medellín bosses.

Jimmy Brown appeared to be a fast-talking Irish-American blessed with a shrewd business mind and an ability to work smoothly with just about anybody. His apparent ties with the New York Sicilian Mafia proved it. He also impressed everyone with his masterful grasp of accounting and with his willingness to put this complex science at the service of crime.

No one seemed to notice the fact that for an Irishman, his last name was wrong. The Irish version of the Anglo-Saxon name Brown is spelled with an "e" as in Mr. Browne of Dublin. Born in Cuba and raised in Miami, Alex Carrera, Brown's partner, was suave and spoke English and Spanish with equal ease, a talent which would help their new Atlanta-based business considerably. Both exuded confidence, both had street smarts—useful virtues for money launderers. Shrewdly, Brown and Carrera had chosen Atlanta, rather than Miami, as their headquarters. While not sharing in the glamour or the intense scrutiny of the overworked Miami area, Atlanta was a sophisticated financial center brimming with a wide variety of banks. Unlike their Floridian counterparts, however, Georgia banks had little experience with money-laundering and could be counted on to be far less cautious.

At that time, cartel chieftains were anxious to get their profits safely out of the United States. Laundering networks were still in their infancy, and the Brown-Carrera partnership looked ideal. They both maintained a low profile and their reputation as spunky, skillful operators was benevolently vaunted by their friend, an American drug trafficker who in 1985 was indicted in Atlanta for cocaine smuggling, and volunteered to work under cover for the U.S. Government. The drug trafficker had a Colombian business partner who had previously acted as an attorney for the Ochoas in purchasing real estate in the Medellín area. The Colombian's advocacy proved all-important. Not unlike the legitimate business world, it is who you know, who you trust, and who vouches for you that count in the narcotics trade.

Brown and Carrera were in, almost, pending a final exam orchestrated by their Colombian bosses. In late 1986, a courier met Jimmy Brown in the bar of an Atlanta hotel and surrendered $94,000. Brown was outraged. He told the courier that he did not work in bars much less take money stuffed in shoeboxes like some lowlife street peddler. He added that he never, never touched cash personally. That was the work of underlings. Besides, Brown said with an air of disgust, that amount was hardly worth the trouble. The Colombians were impressed. Brown was no stereotypical *gringo* money grubber after all.

Instead of thousands, millions in dirty U.S. money were soon rolling into the offices of Brown, Carrera, and Company on their way to be laundered through such ultra-respectable institutions as Citizens and Southern Bank as well as New York's tony Chase Manhattan and Republic banks. The circuit would be completed with wire transfers going to Panama's Banco de Occidente.

In August 1987, Brown and Carrera's Colombian sponsor and the drug trafficker were invited to Medellín where they met with Eduardo Martinez. Posing as a cattle rancher and financier, Martinez did not have the credentials of an Escobar or a Gacha, but he was vital to the cartel's worldwide money-laundering operation. Martinez was of a new breed of entrepreneurs. At thirty-six, he was well educated, with an advanced degree in finance, and his Rolodex was packed with the names of bankers worldwide. Charming and affable, he knew how to put people at ease. He oozed respectability. He did not smell of cocaine or death.

Fascinated with the Atlanta operation, Martinez wanted to learn more from his contact about Brown and Carrera. The man obliged, singing the praises of the Atlanta duo. Martinez embellished his own story, claiming to be a top launderer connected with the most powerful members of the Colombian cartel. The Atlanta operation looked sound enough and he wanted to diversify. But he had no desire to go to Atlanta. That was too risky. Still, Martinez was anxious to meet Brown and Carrera before expanding his business with the Americans.

Thanks to Martinez, about $17 million eventually went through the Atlanta money-laundering operation. In a few months, however, Martinez grew impatient. Atlanta seemed safe enough but in contrast to the La Mina operation in Los Angeles, Brown and Carrera were slow, something that displeased both Martinez and his superiors.

Brown and Carrera's strategy was to keep the Colombians at bay. It hastened the much anticipated face-to-face meeting with Martinez.

Instead of joining his partner, Brown directed Carrera to go alone. It was chancy. Martinez might not like having to meet with a subordinate; but it fit the professional image Jimmy Brown was trying to project. He would tantalize Martinez with Carrera while remaining in Atlanta to mind the store. Besides, Carrera spoke perfect Spanish while Martinez spoke very little English. Martinez had the meeting in the boardroom of Panama's Banco de Occidente—instead of the hotel suites to which Carrera was accustomed. The encounter went remarkably well.

Both Brown and Carrera knew that the Panamanian bank was being used as a key transit point in the money-laundering chain, but they were astonished at the extent of Occidente's collusion. Attending the meeting were two of the bank's officers, William Guarin-Pulencio and Clara Garcia de Paredes, who were, in fact, on the cartel's payroll. The Occidente officers treated Martinez with great courtesy and Martinez called Clara Garcia "Clarita," a term of endearment. To Carrera, the officers acted as if Martinez owned the bank. In any event, Martinez had no qualms about using the bank as his business address in Panama.

Still, Carrera felt uneasy. This time around he carried no weapon and was not wired for sound. He was alone. He had no backup. These elaborate precautions would have been difficult to arrange in General Manuel Antonio Noriega's Panama.

Weapon? Wired for sound? Backup?

Precisely. Carrera was no crook, no drug money launderer. He was and is a special agent for the Drug Enforcement Agency. His real name: Cesar Diaz—Cuban-born, Miami-raised, and blessed with a talent for fast talking himself out of tight spots. That's not all. The drug trafficker who had recommended Brown and Carrera to Martinez was a confidential informant for the DEA. His or her identity remains a secret. Diaz's partner Jimmy Brown's real name is John Featherly, a red-blooded Irish-American who also was a DEA agent.

And fast talking is what Diaz did best in Panama, later recalling that he made things up on the spot hoping no one would detect his desperate improvisation.

Although calm and polite, Martinez insisted on knowing why $5 million of *his* money was somehow tied up in North American banking red tape. Martinez didn't want excuses; he wanted his money. Now. Carrera-Diaz bobbed and weaved as best he could, smiling, trying not to appear nervous, and diverting the increasingly exasperated Colombian's attention. The reason for the hang-up: the DEA was painstakingly photographing every ten- and twenty-dollar bill to keep track of the money's flow through the world's financial network.

Carrera-Diaz kept smiling and blamed the delays on senior management, namely his "boss" John Featherly, alias Jimmy Brown. But Martinez was buying none of it, insisting that phone calls be placed to the States, to Brown, to the banks, to anyone who could explain the delay. Fortuitously, Banco de Occidente had a direct line to the United States. Now concerned, Carrera-Diaz suddenly remembered that it was Martin Luther King's birthday and that the banks would be closed. He was off the hook—temporarily.

The reward for Diaz's considerable risk was Martinez' boastful description of his service to the Medellín cartel. First, the Colombian explained, one of the cartel members would inform him that a certain amount of drug money was available for laundering in the United States. Next, Martinez would arrange for couriers in the States to deliver the cash to trusted launderers who could get the money into the American banking system and then on to wherever in the world he wanted it to go. Using his own working capital, Martinez would then pay off 93 percent of the total to his clients in Medellín, the remaining 7 percent constituting his profit as soon as he collected the money from the States. If, for some reason, the money was lost, the risk was Martinez's. Moreover, every day the funds remained in the U.S. banking system, he also lost on his commission.[77]

The Panama talks yielded other rewards for the DEA. Now that Carrera-Diaz had met Clara Garcia, the Banco de Occidente's commercial manager would tell the DEA agent of her bank's corresponding account at the Continental Bank International, an affiliate of the Continental Illinois National Bank located on Madison Avenue in New York.

After chatting with Clara, Carrera-Diaz and a special agent of the IRS interviewed the Continental bank officer whom Garcia had recommended as being particularly helpful. Posing as associates of the Colombian cartel, the two undercover agents taped the officer's copious revelations. The bank officer taught the undercover agents how to set up an account for wire transfers without arousing the suspicion of her bank's legal department. Despite this highly compromising behavior, the bank officer (who is not identified in the government's affidavits) was never indicted. Nor was the Continental Bank cited for improper behavior or even named in a federal civil suit filed in New York in which nine banks and three Uruguayan corporations were listed as assisting in the laundering of $433 million. None of the banks was found guilty of illegal activity, but under the suit the money was the property of the U.S. Government and the banks were instructed to make full restitution.[78] Evidence had been given to the Treasury Department to follow through and investigate the activities of Continental Illinois and its officer's complicity in laundering drug money. Yet nothing happened, perhaps because the U.S. Government had paid an unusually high price to rescue the failing bank. It was apparently important to keep Continental Illinois solvent.

Back to Panama, feeling lucky to be still alive, Cesar Diaz cheerfully agreed to meet again in two months, this time

accompanied by "Jimmy Brown." It was agreed that th
meeting would take place in Aruba, another in a string o
sun-drenched islands where money was safe from gover
ment scrutiny. Diaz and Featherly had suggested meetin
Martinez in the United States where they could nab him
but the cautious Colombian insisted on Aruba. The meet
ing took place in a hotel suite Featherly had suitably wired
This time a backup agent was there to run the audio an
video equipment and to provide protection just in case
Diaz acted as interpreter.

Much to the DEA's delight Eduardo Martinez freely er
gaged in name-dropping. The men he worked with in C
lombia, he said with unmasked pride, were the kingpins o
narcotics: Pablo Escobar-Gaviria, Jorge Ochoa Vasquez
Geraldo Moncada. Close to them as to his own family
Martinez was their trusted broker, seeking out the bes
possible deals in U.S.-based money-laundering outlets.

Although relaxed and affable, Martinez voiced a numbe
of complaints. Two months earlier, for example, a millior
dollars that the Atlanta duo had laundered was confiscate
by L.A. police. The Colombian drug lords were angry
Geraldo Moncada in particular, wanted to sever the Atlant
operation. Tempers cooled and business with Atlanta con
tinued. Martinez also needled the Atlanta pair for being s
slow in laundering money. His friends in Los Angeles too
only forty-eight hours to get the money to Panama; Dia:
and Featherly took seven to ten days. Yet both organiza
tions charged the same amount.

Featherly assured Martinez he too was interested ir
speed, but that safety was equally, if not more important
Hinting at high-level contacts in the Atlanta banking com

munity, Featherly promised to do better. All it would take to move the money faster would be "more oil"—more money. Martinez seemed to buy the explanation.[79]

Featherly bragged that through his Las Vegas connections he could use gambling winnings to disguise laundered cash. He also described a complicated scheme designed to fool U.S. Customs by switching merchandise for cash. The DEA man rubbed it in: "They don't look, they don't care."[80]

Quite casually, Martinez divulged the name of his California operation. He called it "La Mina"—the mine. This was the first time federal agents had heard of it. They also learned how jewelry stores were fronting for La Mina and how gold had been brought in at inflated prices to help disguise the drug cash as an innocent bullion transaction. Martinez even bragged that La Mina had been in business for years and that no one at the IRS had ever gotten wind of it. He described the Los Angeles operation as

> . . . gold. They export gold. They have mines in Uruguay. They export gold to the U.S. and they pay taxes and everything. And from the U.S. they make wire transfers to pay for the gold imports that were made from Uruguay which in the case of Uruguay exported the gold. They receive it in the U.S. as an import and pay for the importation of gold with dollars. They get it in Uruguay. And through them I know how the system works.

Martinez added that:

> . . . the idea is to work with Banco de Occidente. Why? Because the Banco de Occidente is going to make it easy for

us to open the account as Banco de Occidente's in the bank with which you will work in Atlanta.

Martinez further added:

it is better to use Banco de Occidente because it has branches in Panama, Aruba and the Cayman Islands . . . an offer can be made to the bank manager, the friend, that we make a commitment to leave the funds for one day in the Banco de Occidente account. That is, in his bank. In other words we are giving it one free day. . . .

Martinez even instructed the undercover agents on proper dress code.

. . . we have to keep the people who make the rounds alert . . . they have already been told to dress properly, not to wear Bermuda shorts, to try to refrain from wearing gold watches, jewels . . . nothing flashy. The idea is to look like business men, well dressed. . . .

Martinez went on to describe La Mina's objectives as the exploitation of legitimate gold mines for the purpose of laundering illegitimate monies. This involved linking up with and taking control of gold mines in Peru, Venezuela, Chile, Uruguay, etc., of gaining access to U.S. gold refineries and jewelry stores and of amalgamating money generated through legitimate gold sales with drug money to conceal its origins.

Some of the money was reinvested by the cartel to fund the operation. Laundered drug money paid for airplanes and boats in the United States and bought coca paste in Bolivia and Peru. Later, accounts in Banco de Occidente and BCCI were identified by the U.S. Government and the Canadian RCMP as having been used to purchase aircraft used to ferry drugs. The RCMP also identified a number of cartel operatives and airplane manufacturers and fixed-base operators (FBO) such as Aviel in Colombia, Eagle Air, in Memphis, and Downtown Air, in Oklahoma City.

The Colombians would usually arrange for cash transfers in parks, in the dead of night, during which they handed over bags filled with money to aircraft employees. Several aircraft manufacturers were convicted of tax evasion for failing to declare their earnings. The cartel also purchased drug-processing machinery. U.S. agents identified several law firms in the United States and elsewhere during the investigation that used the addresses of their legitimate business to register fictitious corporations. These corporations were then used as purchasing agents for aircraft. The lawyers involved were handsomely recompensed.

An interesting twist of events was the discovery of the Schroeder International Bank's involvement with La Mina. This is the same bank that the CIA used to facilitate the transfer of U.S. dollars to Mohamed Shakarchi in Zurich, Switzerland, money destined for the Afghan rebels. Shakarchi was allegedly involved with the Swiss end of the La Mina organization. Shakarchi said he had legitimate business with Wanis Koyomejian, the owner of Ropex, on behalf of an Italian client. Following lengthy investigations in the United States and Switzerland, Shakarchi was found innocent but Armenian brothers Jean and Barkev Magharian, who operated a big money-laundering business in

Zurich, were not so fortunate. Their contact with the La Mina organization was Dikran Altun. Altun supplied the Magharians with cash from the United States. They, in turn, wire-transferred the money from Switzerland to Panama and Uruguay. Their drug money-laundering services were originally established on behalf of a Turkish heroin-trafficking organization long before Altun delivered the Medellín cartel's drug money. Altun turned government informant when U.S. authorities seized three suitcases in his possession containing $2 million while he was traveling from Los Angeles to Switzerland in November 1986. Altun continued to work with the Magharians until their arrest in 1988. He revealed that from March through December 1988, he and the Magharians laundered $60 million through Crédit Suisse and Union Bank of Switzerland. Altun identified at least ten more couriers who worked with him on the Swiss/Southern California line. Altun did not have to stand trial and is currently back in Turkey.

When the Magharians were arrested in July 1988, they claimed that they laundered the money for Altun for fear he might be killed if they stopped. This argument did not fare well with the Swiss court, which convicted and sentenced them to four and a half years in prison.

The DEA Aruba sting was carefully lubricated with good meals and alcohol—lots of it. Grateful they did not have to take notes, elated at their interlocutor's volubility, Diaz and Featherly sat back instead and let Martinez do the talking.[81] During this meeting Martinez talked about his dealings with BCCI in Panama, Miami, and Luxembourg, and fondly remembered the bank's kindness toward him and his organization, particularly when it recommended that they avoid Panama during the chaotic events of 1987. Instead Martinez suggested they use Uruguay as a banking center. "So, from Panama I think we could do the operation," he told Diaz and Featherly, who marveled at the convenience of modern banking.

Even . . . the U.S. itself. Find out which are the U.S. banks that operate in Uruguay. Okay? Open accounts in the U.S. in the bank that operates with Uruguay, and request forms so that the bank can fill out the correspondence, send it to Uruguay, and have accounts in Uruguay. . . . You can do it without going to Uruguay. For instance, I open at the BCC because the bank was a friend. I filled out the account opening forms of the Miami BCC in Panama . . . and the manager sent the documents via the bank mail to Miami. They authorized my account, they gave me my number, and I started operating from Colombia. You understand? Without having to go to Uruguay. You guys can do the same thing. In the correspondent bank in the U.S. to Uruguay, you open an account in the U.S. in Atlanta, for instance, on behalf of the company with which you are going to work and you can ask for a favor from a friendly banker. "We need to open an account in Uruguay without going to Uruguay. Give me the paper work and I'll sign it, you know me."

An investigation of the Polar Cap–La Mina connection determined that the correspondent accounts of the defendants maintained very low daily opening and closing balances. During the rest of the day, however, many millions of dollars went through the accounts. The banks should have suspected foul play. They appear to have been willfully blind.

Diaz and Featherly's last task would be to arrest Martinez and to bring him back to the United States. Aruba was not the place, so they scheduled another meeting. After the arrests of the Andonians, Koyomejian, Hochman et al., this time in Panama, presumably with General Antonio Noriega cooperating in the bust.

Martinez showed up but no arrest was made. Panama's Defense Forces and DEA agents had the Banco de Occidente staked out, but Martinez evaded the trap. The DEA continues to suspect that Noriega tipped off Martinez. After all, Noriega cooperated with the DEA only when there was something in it for him. The cartels were now angry with Noriega and he did not want to risk the fury of Medellín's hit men.[82]

The Atlanta laundry service remained in place. After La Mina was put out of business in Los Angeles with the arrest of the Andonians and their confederates in February 1989, Martinez called Diaz and Featherly in Atlanta and instructed them to be ready to take over. The money once funneled through Los Angeles's jewelry fronts would now go to Atlanta. Martinez kept his word.[83]

Diaz and Featherly would have to wait for the Colombian Government to finish the job they had started in the summer of 1989. Following the murder of the Liberal party presidential candidate, President Virgilio Barco declared war on narco-traffickers. Army units moved into Medellín and, for a while, drug lords were on the run. Their vast properties were temporarily confiscated and thousands were rounded up on a variety of charges.

Most of the cartel's leaders, however, proved remarkably elusive. Some fled to other countries. Others vanished in Colombia's dense jungle.

Having been indicted by an Atlanta grand jury in March 1989, Martinez was subject to extradition, the first major cartel figure to be brought to U.S. justice since Carlos Lehder was turned in two years earlier. Within a few days of his arrest in Colombia, Martinez was flown to Georgia for arraignment and trial.[84]

On August 14, 1989, the Panama branch of Banco de Occidente pled guilty to the indictments for laundering drug money for the Medellín cartel, but only in the Atlanta case. It was fined a mere $5 million. The other Banco de Occidente branches, including the Cali, Colombia, home office, were not touched. Originally, the banks' parent, Banco de Occidente of Colombia, had been indicted but charges were dropped after President Barco of Colombia assured senior officials in Washington that the bank was not under the thumb of his nation's drug lords.

Eduardo Martinez at first protested his innocence and denied any knowledge of drug money-laundering. The evidence against him, however, was overwhelming. In August 1990, Martinez admitted to helping launder $1.2 million and, in April 1991, plea-bargained himself into a six and one half year jail sentence—he could have gotten thirty—plus five years of federal supervision after his release. Martinez must have been mortified when the *New York Times* identified him as a mere "bookkeeper."[85] Despite the affront, he remains Polar Cap's biggest catch.

Raoul Vivas and Nazareth and Vahe Andonian did not fare so well. They fought and lost. In late December 1990, they were each convicted of twenty-five felony counts of money-laundering and conspiracy, with each count drawing 20 years' imprisonment.[86] In August 1991 they were individually sentenced to serve 505 years without parole.

Not all of the Los Angeles indictments turned into convictions. Joyce Momdijian (Joyce's Jewelers) and Sepur Moroyan, both young cousins of the Andonians, and their employees, were acquitted.[87]

On November 25, 1991, the U.S. Government was able to score yet another victory with multiple indictments in Atlanta, New York, Miami, Providence, Rhode Island, and Los Angeles. In addition to Customs, IRS and FBI investigators played a more active role in uncovering drug money-laundering activities with jewelry and gold trading companies fronting for the Medellín and Sicilian-American organized crime families. Fifty indictments were handed down for laundering at least $500 million dollars in a three-year period but only thirty-five arrests were made when the case broke. The leader of this ring, Stephen A. Saccoccia and his wife Donna from Cranston, Rhode Island, were picked up in Geneva, Switzerland. The Swiss are considering extradition of this couple to the United States. Another member of this ring, Jose Duvan Arboleda-Gonzalez, fled to Colombia. Arboleda is a Colombian citizen who owned money-laundering businesses in Rhode Island, New York, Miami, and California and forwarded the profits to both the Cali and Medellín drug cartels. The most recent changes to the Colombian constitution do not allow for extradition of Colombian citizens to the United States. Fugitive banker,

Joseph Mollicone, Jr., the former director of Heritage Loan and Investment Bank in Providence, Rhode Island, which played a major role in this money-laundering operation, disappeared in 1990 with $13 million from cash deposits. He surrendered seventeen months later and was arrested in Cranston, Rhode Island. This incident triggered the collapse of the Heritage Bank and a state banking crisis. The Heritage Loan and Investment Bank reportedly accepted duffle bags full of bills in small denominations without reporting these transactions as required by law. The laundering ring used other banks to deposit cash and transfer money including Citizens Bank, Old Stone Bank, and Rhode Island Hospital Trust. But all of these institutions except the Heritage Bank aided the government investigation.

While pursuing Polar Cap, U.S. authorities had obtained information about more operations using jewelry and gold trading companies to remit money to the Cali and Medellín cartels. Although the first Polar Cap investigations named only the Medellín cartel as the benefactor, further probes revealed that the Cali and Medellín cartels were working in cahoots more than U.S. law enforcement anticipated. The fact that Geraldo Moncada (Don Chepe) was mentioned in all Polar Cap indictments, including the latest, and in the BCCI case indicates that the collaboration between the Medellín and Cali cartel has been going on for a very long time without the knowledge of U.S. authorities. In the November 1991 indictments some of the original Polar Cap defendants played an important role, including Sergio Hochman, the Andonian brothers, Raoul Vivas, and Wanis Koyomejian. The 1991 indictments stemming from the

initial Polar Cap investigations rounded up other partici
pants from Sicilian-American organized crime families i
New England and Canada. This is the second case tha
uncovered cooperation and close ties between "Mafiosi
and Colombian cartel members.

Cambio Italia, the money exchange business in Monte
video, Uruguay, owned by Raoul Vivas, and Banco de Oc
cidente in Monserrat and Panama functioned a
clearinghouses through which all laundered drug mone
passed. These funds were laundered through many bank
in many cities and in many countries under accounts calle
Letra, S.A., and Omensal, S.A., among others.

One of the spinoffs of the 1989 Polar Cap investigatio
was the arrest and conviction of Aharon Sharir, a jewele
from New York's Forty-seventh Street jewelry district wh
also laundered drug money through Banco de Occidente'
branch in Panama. In November 1991 another case with
similar modus operandi was identified in the Polar Ca
investigations. Jewelry stores, gold refineries, and coin dea
ers served as storefronts for this highly illegitimate busi
ness. The Andonian Brothers, Ropex, and others mixe
illegal with legal business; however, the storefronts tha
were uncovered in the November 1991 indictments did no
bother to conduct any legitimate business at all. They wer
strictly drug money-laundering operations.

The 1991 indictments tied yet another big money-laun
dering operation to the vast pool of the Polar Cap probe. I
the Sharir case, the U.S. Government managed to seiz
over $11 million after tracing the drug-tainted money t
Banco de Occidente accounts in its corresponding bank i
Hawaii. Sharir was sentenced and is now serving time i
prison in the United States.[88] Sharir was arrested in 1989

d his collaboration with the government helped bring
wn his former confederates Stephen Saccoccia and Barry
omovitz. When Slomovitz was arrested the police found
vo unregistered loaded Uzi submachine guns in his posses-
on. Everybody knew what Saccoccia was doing. It was no
cret in the diamond district in New York, for his nick-
ame was Steve *Yerukim* (literally green in Hebrew and
mmonly used to describe U.S. dollars). Neither Sharir nor
ccoccia filed IRS forms 8300, which are required any
ne a business receives more than $10,000 in cash. This
lped the government to nail them for IRS violations.
hen the Sharir operation in New York collapsed at the
d of 1989, Saccoccia's money-laundering business got
to trouble. Sharir laundered the money on behalf of Sac-
ccia and the Colombians by breaking it into small depos-
s under $10,000 and by buying cashier's checks. Suddenly
hen Sharir was busted Saccoccia was flooded with huge
antities of cash that he was unable to handle. In the
mmer of 1990, Saccoccia and his partners deposited large
nounts of cash into his company's account in various
nks in Rhode Island. He tried to cover his tracks through
series of gold purchases and sales to justify the huge
nounts of money but this did not fool either the bank's
ecutives or government investigators. When Citizen's
ank in Rhode Island ordered Saccoccia to close down his
count in April 1991, he moved his money-laundering
erations to the Bank of America in Los Angeles. But it
as too late. The government was already on his trail.
  Polar Cap remains the largest and most complicated anti-
ug money-laundering operation ever undertaken by the
.S. Government—or any government for that matter.
nd its poles are still apart.

The Whip at the End of
the Polar Cap

There is no dirty money, there are only dirty people.

—HANS KOPP, June 10, 1991

Cast of Characters

Elizabeth Kopp—former Minister of Justice and President-elect

Hans Kopp—Elizabeth's husband, Swiss businessman and former vice president of Shakarchi Trading Company

Mohamed Shakarchi—Lebanese owner of Shakarchi Trading Company

Dick Marty—district attorney in Ticino, the southern Italian-speaking canton of Switzerland, who broke the Kopp case

Kathrina Schoop—Hans Kopp's assistant, formerly Elizabeth Kopp's assistant

Renate Schwob—Elizabeth Kopp's former assistant at the Ministry of Justice

Rudolf Gerber—the Swiss chief prosecutor

Jacques-André Kaeslin—Swiss federal public prosecutor

Jean and Barkev Magharian—Syrian brothers, money launderers of Armenian descent

Rudei Ernst—American businessman, partner of Hans Kopp

Mehmet Ali Agca—the Turk who attempted to assassinate Pope John Paul II on May 13, 1981

Turkish organized crime figures:
Yasar Musullulu
Haci Mirza—a Turkish Kurd
Paul Waridel
Celenk Bekir

Nicola Giulietti—Italian drug trafficker and partner of Haci Mirza

124

Wanis Koyomejian—owner of Ropex, a gold refining and jewelry company in Los Angeles and major defendant in Polar Cap investigation who did business with Shakarchi

Andonian brothers, Vahe and Nazareth—Armenian drug money launderers and major defendants in the Polar Cap investigation in Los Angeles

Dikran Altun—Turkish drug trafficker and money launderer in L.A. working on behalf of Carlos Pineda, a member of the Medellín cartel. Altun was a friend of the Magharians

Carlos Pineda—Colombian drug dealer, in Los Angeles

Ivanoff Tochkov and Stoyan Paunov—Bulgarian secret police operatives in charge of Kintex and Globus trading companies

Lyndon LaRouche—head of U.S. extreme right wing organization

Hashemi Rafsanjani—Iran's president

Edmund Safra—owner of National Republic Bank

Dr. Alfred Hartmann—former chairman of Banque de Commerce et de Placements (BCP), a partly owned subsidiary of BCCI in Switzerland. He was also the director of Lavoro Bank in Zurich, a fully owned BNL subsidiary.

Mehmet Emin Karamehmet—president of Çukurova group that bought BCP from Hartmann

HOLDING FINE-CUT wineglasses, we passed from the elegant living room into a small but comfortable dining room where the round table was impeccably set and decorated with fresh-cut flowers. Platters of colorful crudités and salad were prominently displayed. But in spite of the elegance, the atmosphere was heavy and the mood somber. When we sat down to begin the meal, the conversation turned to the events that had put our hostess on front pages around the world. Her eyes filled with tears as she began to talk. At first, she fought to regain control of herself, but her tears spilled over and she abruptly left the room. The memory of the Kopp affair had proved too painful for the sophisticated woman who had served as Switzerland's first female Justice Minister and was in line to become its president. I was invited to dine with Hans and Elizabeth Kopp in their lavish home in Zumikon, an affluent suburb of Zurich, Switzerland. Kathrina Schoop, a buxom, blond young woman, Hans Kopp's assistant, was present too.

The bitter memories for Elizabeth Kopp go back to January 12, 1989, when Mrs. Kopp was forced to resign her post because she had warned her husband, Hans, a vice president of Shakarchi Trading, that his company was being investigated on allegations of laundering drug money. After a lengthy probe in February 1990, a five-judge Swiss federal tribunal cleared her of wrongdoing. Ironically, her resignation triggered the passage of the anti-drug money-laundering laws that she had initiated while in office. The "Kopp affair," also known as the "Lebanon Connection," is actually the Swiss terminus of a major investigation conducted in the United States, Panama, and Uruguay. Code-named Polar Cap, the investigation, detailed in the previous chapter, involved many players, including the notorious Colombian Medellín cartel, but the Swiss link was composed of Shakarchi Trading Company, a Zurich-based currency and precious metals trader, Hans and Elizabeth Kopp, and the Magharian brothers.

I decided to go to Switzerland to interview the major players: Elizabeth and Hans Kopp, Mohamed Shakarchi, brothers Jean and Barkev Magharian, government officials, magistrates, lawyers, reporters who covered the case, and others. Before leaving for Switzerland, I was full of praise for the swift passage of laws and regulations to keep dirty money out of Swiss banks. I returned convinced that these regulations are window dressing.

Nothing that I had read or heard about the so-called Kopp affair prepared me for what I found in Switzerland. It's one thing to go touring in this pristine, antiseptic, and orderly country, quite another to scratch beneath the surface. What most visitors do not realize is that Switzerland is a police state. *Habeas corpus* does not exist in Switzerland and the police can hold you incommunicado for as long as they see fit. A foreigner will get inextricably lost in the bureaucratic shuffle. Remember, this is Switzerland—not a KGB-haunted U.S.S.R. Yet, the Kopp affair revealed that the police had compiled over 900,000 secret files on the activities of "suspect" Swiss citizens and that the information had been obtained through illegal surveillance. The Swiss media dubbed the scandal "Big Brother in the Land of Heidi." When you go to Switzerland as a tourist, enjoy crystal-clear lakes, high snow-peaked mountains, and green sparkling valleys alive with flowers; just don't ask any question about money-laundering.

Minutes after checking into my room at the Baur-au-Lac Hotel in Zurich, I called Hans Kopp to confirm a meeting scheduled for the next day. There were strange clickings on the phone and Mr. Kopp became very nervous and asked repeatedly, "What's wrong with the phone?" The mysterious static must have upset him and he abruptly ended the conversation.

The next morning I met with a couple of Swiss reporters who provided me with background material on the Kopps and on other individuals involved in the case, including government officials. The reporters suggested that there might be CIA involvement in the Kopp affair and that Elizabeth Kopp did not resign her office because of wrongdoing but was forced out because she lacked political support from her own party. The reporters further suggested that the real target was the Swiss banking system and shared with me documents claiming that the Kopp affair "illuminates the situation of the Swiss financial center—meaning the pressures to which the financial center is exposed. Foreign countries are apparently able to achieve their interests in an aggressive and offensive manner . . .

[this case] shows the extraordinary influence that American authorities hold over Swiss bureaucracy." The reporters also alleged that the U.S. banking community was envious of the success and prosperity of Swiss banks, so "assisted by the U.S. government, the American banks framed Elizabeth Kopp to force the passage of anti-drug money-laundering laws." In doing so, the reporters rationalized, "American banks hope to reduce the power of the Swiss banks." The truculence with which they alleged CIA and DEA involvement in Swiss domestic affairs left no doubt about their anti-American feelings. To prove their point, the reporters cited a DEA sting during which U.S. agents uncovered and confiscated a drug laboratory in Switzerland. The incident led to a parliamentary report which criticized Swiss cooperation with the DEA as "too extensive." The reporters also said that "the DEA started the rumors that Switzerland is one huge money-laundering machine." These rumors, they claimed, helped U.S. objectives—to diminish Switzerland as a world financial center and, perhaps, they added, "to monitor the activities of Swiss banks and gain access to secret bank accounts." What the reporters conveniently overlooked is that Switzerland's reputation as a major money-laundering center long precedes the founding of the DEA.

That afternoon I went to see Hans Kopp. His office occupies a spacious townhouse on a narrow residential street just down the hill from the Grand Dolder Hotel, the most expensive hotel in Zurich. I was led into a sparsely furnished conference room, decorated with Chinese art and modern paintings, with windows that overlooked the Zurich Lake. A few minutes passed and an attractive young blond woman walked in, said hello, smiled, and sat down. Hans Kopp arrived shortly after. He introduced the woman, Kathrina Schoop, as his assistant and said she spoke no English. I found this odd since the meeting was conducted in English. In retrospect, her comments in German, a language I understand, left no doubt in my mind that she had no problem understanding English. Kathrina Schoop was there, Hans Kopp insisted, to advise him and "to look out" for him. Hans Kopp did not strike me as particularly vulnerable—middle-aged, medium height, Teutonic in bearing, balding, armed with a direct aggressive gaze and cautious manner. But playing the victim may have been a useful stratagem for no sooner had we begun to talk than he informed me that his wife was Jewish, a plausible reason, he explained, why he and his wife had been so unfairly treated. As I expressed interest in his revelation, he revised his story somewhat, admitting that it was one of his wife's ancestors—four generations removed—who was Jewish. I politely informed him that "Jewishness" is maternally "transmitted." Even Hitler claimed that Jews had to be at least one quarter Jewish to be considered Jews, I pointed out. Hans Kopp overlooked the clarification and said, "But I'm proud to be married to her."

Hans Kopp continued to portray himself and his wife as "the victims of a CIA and DEA conspiracy." I found that difficult to believe and told him so. I asked him if he could support his allegation. After all, following lengthy discussion and interviews with U.S. officials, it was clear to me that everyone in the U.S. Government liked Elizabeth Kopp, praised her, and appreciated her for having the courage to promulgate anti-drug money-laundering laws. If anything, it seemed that the United States would have done all it could to keep Elizabeth Kopp at her ministerial post. Under the circumstances, Kopp's accusations sounded irrational. He said, "I don't have any tangible evidence but Elizabeth and I are convinced that the CIA and the DEA are behind the case." He went on to explain the Kopp affair from his vantage point. He said, "I had never been officially accused of any wrongdoing in connection with the Shakarchi Trading Company. The only connection linking me to charges of drug money-laundering was my position as vice president of the Shakarchi Trading Company since 1984, a year after the company was founded." He continued, "It was the company that was under investigation, not I."

It is clear that Hans Kopp was tried by the media, but then Hans Kopp had had problems with the media before. Curiously, he claims that the press has fabricated everything they published about him, even though he has "championed freedom of the press" in the past. This seems improbable, since libel laws in Switzerland are very strict and the subdued and repressed Swiss media are unlikely to fabricate stories. But then again, Hans Kopp is a controversial man given to some peculiar habits. He has been frequently targeted by the press for a number of questionable business dealings, in connection with his military career and with regard to his sexual proclivities. The most recent investigation involving Hans Kopp, an American partner, Rudei Ernst, and the Trans-K-B Investment Company ended in September 1991 when the court in Zurich found Kopp guilty of fraud. He was given a suspended sentence of one year in prison, a term he will have to serve *only* if he commits a similar felony within the next three years. This is little more than a slap on the wrist for Hans Kopp. His American partner, Rudei Ernst, was sentenced in absentia to two years imprisonment without suspension. An earlier scandal involving Hans Kopp broke in 1987, when it was discovered that Trans-K-B–owned Kapital Beratung, A.G., yet another investment company, declared bankruptcy on February 4, 1983. Kapital Beratung was liquidated on September 14, 1982, after receiving $1.824 billion from Iraq, as advance payment for ten corvettes and frigates built by Cantieri Navali Riuniti shipyards in Genoa, Italy. The Italians received only $441 million, and the rest is unaccounted for.[1]

Hans Kopp has been under investigation by Swiss authorities for tax evasion and fraud charges in the past. One of Zurich's prosecutors commented in his office on June 6, 1991, that "Kopp has always been the go-between for tax evaders, currency and gold smugglers and the banks, creating fictitious companies in order to accommodate all the parties." He is said to be sought after because of his extensive political connections and his standing in the community. When Shakarchi, on advice of his lawyer, approached Kopp to sit on his board, Kopp was already on the Board of Directors of at least thirty other companies. One of his more unusual schemes involved the hybridization by genetic engineering methods of a new agricultural product, the "Tomoffel," a cross between a tomato and a potato (kartoffel). Kopp and an American partner raised over SF12 million for research and development. The scheme failed. Investors sued but were able to recover only SF4.5 million.

What shocked the prim and proper Swiss were media reports that Kopp had been eased out of his military command—he was in charge of the internal psychological propaganda unit—for "improper behavior." It is most unusual for a high-ranking Swiss military officer to be removed from his post. In a letter to his subordinates explaining his departure, Kopp invoked health reasons. There is more. In 1972, Hans Kopp, who is a lawyer, was disbarred for six months by a special judicial commission (in keeping with a 1938 Swiss law that regulates conduct within the legal profession). Short of total disbarment, this is the most severe penalty that can be imposed on a lawyer for misconduct in Switzerland. Juicy accounts in the Swiss media attributed the disbarment to Hans Kopp's unusual methods of maintaining office discipline.[2] If someone on the staff made an error, Kopp would whip his naked buttocks with a bamboo switch. None of the participants will discuss the matter publicly. This practice went on for some time until a new employee spilled the beans.

Hans Kopp claimed these stories are untrue and said "the press has been manipulated against me by the former mayor of Lucerne. This goes back to an old family feud when my father [Kopp's] was the mayor of Lucerne." Skepticism must have been painted all over my face because Kopp reiterated, "I was manipulated by the CIA and the DEA to force my wife's resignation." Swiss reporters noted that Mr. Kopp, in his arms dealings, might have had connections directly or indirectly with Turkish organized crime figures such as Yasar Musullulu, Haci Mirza, Paul Waridel, and Celenk Bekir. These are the very same figures who were involved in major heroin and gold smuggling investigations spanning from Turkey through Bulgaria to Switzerland, as well as the financing of Mehmet Ali Agca, the Turk who attempted to assassinate Pope John Paul II on May 13, 1981. Mohamed Shakarchi's name surfaced in that investigation too, but he was never directly implicated.

Before our encounters, I was told that Kopp would control the meeting by staring and speaking in a low monotone, almost as if he were trying to hypnotize his visitor. And that is just what he did. Perhaps he was play-acting or he was obeying his training as head of the Swiss Army's internal psychological propaganda unit.

He often declared, "I have nothing to hide." He said, "I first learned of the investigation from Mohamed Shakarchi himself," the owner of Shakarchi Trading Company, who phoned him *six weeks before* his wife had called him in panic, and offered him an opportunity to resign from the board. In addition to the phone call, Mohamed Shakarchi sent him an article from a Turkish newspaper reporting the investigation. Kopp did not resign from the board. Instead, according to Mohamed Shakarchi, "Kopp sent me an invoice for SF700 for the translation of the article into German." When I asked Kopp, "Why didn't you tell your wife you knew about the investigation?" he rehashed his old apologia—that six weeks later his wife was informed by one of her assistants about rumors concerning the Shakarchi Trading Company, in which he served as a vice president, that it was under investigation for drug money-laundering. There were other vice presidents at the Shakarchi Trading Company, but the others were not mentioned, only Hans Kopp and Mohamed Shakarchi. "I was only a titular vice president and had nothing to do with daily operations," he protested, so why all the fuss? U.S. authorities, on the other hand, assured me that the Swiss had participated in the investigation well before it surfaced in the press. Where was Elizabeth Kopp all this time? Is it possible that the Minister of Justice did not know about this highly charged inquest?

According to testimony before a Swiss parliamentary investigative committee, and in conversation with me later at her home, Elizabeth Kopp maintained that upon learning that the Shakarchi Trading Company was under scrutiny, she panicked, called her husband, and urged him to resign from the board forthwith. Hans Kopp concurs and, in fact, he did resign at once, "in order to protect my wife from any political embarrassment." In hindsight, had he not quit, the probe might have turned out differently.

"What were you afraid of?" I asked Elizabeth Kopp. "Why did you panic?" She said that by that time her husband was under investigation—"not for the first time"—and she feared for her career. "It was too much," she said.

Many questions were left unanswered. Why all the fuss? After all, Elizabeth Kopp was exonerated by the Swiss court probing her fateful phone call. The judges ruled that notifying her husband was not illegal. Hans Kopp himself was never investigated as vice president of Shakarchi Trading Company for drug money-laundering activities and even Mohamed Shakarchi was hardly investigated by the Swiss. The whole incident seems like "much ado about nothing." If the U.S. Government was anxious to have the new drug money-laundering laws passed in Switzerland, why go after Elizabeth Kopp? A plausible conclusion is that certain forces at work in Switzerland desperately wanted to prevent these laws from passing and decided to punish Mrs. Kopp for initiating them. The Swiss banks had the most to gain. The more I learned about the case, the more convinced I became that the banks were behind the Kopp case. But they were not the only ones.

Leaving Kopp's office, I hurried back to my hotel to meet with Renate Schwob, Elizabeth Kopp's former assistant at the Ministry of Justice. Schwob is a tall, slim, intelligent woman who doesn't smile often. Like most Swiss, she was exceedingly polite. She sang the praises of her new employer, the bank Crédit Suisse, and about its efforts to prevent drug money-laundering. She was careful not to go into details. We chatted about her work at the bank, about the new Swiss banking regulations, but she offered very little about her relationship with Mrs. Kopp at the Ministry. She was eager to know how my interview with Hans Kopp had gone and whether I was impressed with him. I told her about the non-English-speaking assistant present at the meeting. She said, "I thought Kathrina Schoop was fluent in English." She should know. After all Schoop and Schwob both worked at the Ministry. Renate Schwob paused and then said, "I'm no longer in touch with the Kopps." Odd. After all it was Mrs. Kopp who gave me Ms. Schwob's telephone number and assured me that she would talk to me. Naturally reserved, Ms. Schwob became particularly guarded when she spoke about her job at Crédit Suisse. Her noticeable discomfort made me wonder whether the bank was somehow implicated in the Kopp affair.

Ms. Schwob noted, "I knew that Rudolf Gerber [the

Swiss Chief Prosecutor] did not inform Mrs. Kopp about the investigation, so I took it upon myself to tell her." Ms. Schwob continued, "I pleaded with Mrs. Kopp to call her husband and ask him to resign. I thought it wise to keep the name Kopp from becoming associated with Shakarchi Trading Company." Mrs. Kopp initially asked Ms. Schwob to call Hans Kopp and warn him, but Ms. Schwob insisted that Elizabeth Kopp make the call herself. The way Ms. Schwob emphasized her insistence made me wonder if she did this at the request of a third party. I asked, "Why did you insist," and she changed the subject. In retrospect, it is this phone call that cast suspicion on Elizabeth Kopp. Had she not made the fatal call to her husband, she might still be Justice Minister, perhaps even president of Switzerland. It was Renate Schwob's advice that precipitated Mrs. Kopp's forced resignation.

While planning the trip to Switzerland, I contacted Alfred Reber, Mohamed Shakarchi's lawyer, hoping he could arrange a meeting with the Kopps. To my surprise, the very next day, I received a handwritten fax inviting me to dinner at their home. Dinner was set for June 10, 1991, the last evening of my week-long visit to Switzerland. An English-speaking lawyer who works for Mr. Kopp was supposed to pick me up at my hotel. Instead, it was the non-English-speaking assistant, Kathrina Schoop, who came to fetch me. The drive to Zumikon, the exclusive suburb of Zurich, took about thirty minutes. The buxom young blonde asked me in German, "Did you achieve what you came for?" I responded in English. This is how we conversed, she in German and I in English. We discussed the drug problem in Switzerland, how bad it was and how little was being done.

When we arrived, Mrs. Kopp, a petite, attractive, well-dressed woman greeted me at the door. With her Slavic features, she did not look Swiss. She seemed sad and made no attempt to veil her emotions. Soon Mr. Kopp joined us. "How was the drive?" he asked. "We had a most interesting conversation," I said. "Aha," he responded, "I knew all along that you are fluent in German." After some small talk we moved to the dining room for dinner.

The dinner featured lots of artfully blended fresh vegetables, a crisp green salad, and a whole salmon baked in phyllo dough that tasted as good as it looked. Mr. Kopp dominated the conversation while I struggled to avoid swallowing the fish bones. The air was tense and there was no doubt that I had been invited to bear witness to the Kopps' innocence.

There was no lighthearted conversation, no small talk, no joking. Mr. Kopp's monologue consisted mostly of his claim that the CIA and the DEA had framed them both. While Mr. Kopp lectured me, Mrs. Kopp made several comments, became more and more emotional, and left the table sobbing. "Perhaps the Swiss banks are behind this?" I suggested. "Ridiculous," replied Mr. Kopp without hesitation. His response did not surprise me because I knew that his brother was a member of the Board of Crédit Suisse and as a businessman in Switzerland his natural inclination would be to defend the banks. As for his association with Shakarchi, "I don't see him, never saw him socially," Mr. Kopp said emphatically.

* * *

Dark, solidly built, rugged-looking, endowed with a friendly face and an easy smile, Mohamed Shakarchi is a shrewd self-assured Arab merchant exuding European sophistication. A Lebanese national, Sunni Muslim, Mohamed Shakarchi was born in 1939 in Mossul, northern Iraq, into a well-to-do merchant family. The Shakarchis moved to Lebanon in 1947 and started doing business there. By 1951 Mohamed's father began to trade in gold and currency. His business grew and expanded into the Gulf States, particularly the United Arab Emirates, Bahrain and Saudi Arabia. By 1954 the father had expanded his operations to Switzerland, where he dealt with the Swiss Banking Corporation (SBC). In 1958 the new Iraqi revolutionary government seized the family's holdings in Iraq. In 1969 the Shakarchis moved to Geneva and in 1983, following his father's death, Mohamed Shakarchi founded his own company in Zurich, the Shakarchi Trading Company. Shakarchi does business in Europe, the Middle East, Africa, and North America, but not in South or Central America, as a commodity trader specializing in gold and currency exchange. In that capacity his name was mentioned in investigations by the *Guardia di Finanza* (Italy's Fiscal Police) in 1986 in connection with the transfer of capital and gold to and from the Middle East on behalf of Yasar Musullulu and Paul Waridel, notorious Turkish drug traffickers, who according to the DEA reports were among "the largest suppliers of morphine base in the world." No direct links between Shakarchi and the Turkish traffickers, however, were ever established. Further, Shakarchi denies that he even knows them. In addition, the *Sonntags Zeitung* obtained and published a confidential report leaked from the Central Bureau of the Police in Berne identifying Mohamed Shakarchi and the Magharians as recyclers of drug money and gold in connection with the Iran-Contra affair.

It was when I met with Mohamed Shakarchi that I understood how deeply Crédit Suisse was involved in the Kopp affair. Shakarchi said that he learned that $2 million in small bills had been confiscated by U.S. agents at the Los Angeles International Airport in November 1986. As mentioned in the preceding chapter, the money was identified as drug pay on its way from the Andonian brothers in Los Angeles to the Magharian brothers in Zurich. Shakarchi knew the Magharian brothers—they had worked for him as traders when they first arrived in Zurich. He knew that they had bank accounts in Crédit Suisse dating back to 1985 and also kept money in Union Bank of Switzerland (UBS) and in Société de Banque Suisse (SBS). In its April 11, 1989, report on the Kopp affair, the Swiss Federal Commission of Banks confirmed that Shakarchi called UBS twice, first in 1987 then in April 1988. Shakarchi advised UBS not to do business with the Magharians. "Their money is no good," he said, "don't touch it." UBS has recently been in the news for accepting $11 million from General Noriega *after* his well-publicized indictment for drug trafficking and drug money-laundering in the United States. The money was disguised as the Republic of Panama's account. Shakarchi also called Crédit Suisse with the same message. Crédit Suisse alerted the Magharian brothers of the investigation and suggested that, instead of having individual accounts with an address in Zurich, they should change their account to "Magharian Frères Sarl., Beirut." Crédit Suisse did not call the authorities nor did they freeze the Magharian account. Instead, two years later, in November 1988, when the "Lebanon Connection" story broke in *Tages-Anzeiger* in Zurich, Crédit Suisse froze the Shakarchi accounts. Mohamed Shakarchi called the bank to ask why his money had been blocked. The bank replied that "the recent publicity made it a necessary precaution." Shakarchi complained repeatedly to the bank and to the Swiss authorities that his warnings about the Magharians had been ignored. The bank claimed that no one could remember such warnings.

This is not the first time Crédit Suisse was rumored to be involved in shady dealings. Its name came up in the Pizza Connection trials. The Pizza Connection was a billion-dollar drug conspiracy that moved Turkish morphine base to Sicilian laboratories where it was transformed into high-grade heroin and then shipped to the United States where it was sold in pizza parlors, restaurants, and cafés throughout the country. The profits were laundered in Miami, The Bahamas, Rio, Zurich, Palermo, Istanbul, and Sofia. The FBI busted the network on April 9, 1984. Crédit Suisse transmitted letters of recommendation to the Swiss Consulate in Sofia, Bulgaria, enabling Lebanese and Turkish nationals employed as couriers to transit through Bulgaria to Switzerland. It was further revealed that some of these nationals were known crime figures making as many as two trips a week from Bulgaria to Switzerland. This was pre-Perestroika Bulgaria when transiting in this staunchly pro-Soviet Balkan nation was difficult and required approval not only from consulates but also from Bulgarian immigration. By writing those letters of recommendation Crédit Suisse made it easier to transfer money and gold through Bulgaria and it wasn't bothered by the telltale fact that the couriers were not Bulgarian. Crédit Suisse even wrote letters on behalf of the couriers transiting gold and money in Sofia on assignment for the Magharians.

Denying all allegations against him, Mohamed Shakarchi claimed that he had helped the U.S. Government transfer money to the Afghan rebels. Between 1981 and 1988 the Argin Corporation, a CIA-owned bogus company, purchased $25 million worth of "rare" currencies from Shakarchi. The payments were transferred through the Schroeder International Bank in New York to Shakarchi's account at the Swiss Banking Corporation in Zurich. The American ambassador to Switzerland, Philip Winn, issued a press release in the summer of 1989 confirming Shakarchi's business relations with the U.S. Government. According to a DEA report, Shakarchi also deposited in a Zurich bank money known to have been paid in connection with a Middle East aircraft hijacking. The report provided no details and there was no further investigation. In fact, Shakarchi claims he helped U.S., Swiss, and other Western governments in their struggle against terrorism. Hans Kopp, by then, was on the Shakarchi company board of directors.

Mohamed Shakarchi boasted that his company has the most sophisticated currency exchange and commodity trading operations in Switzerland. His offices occupy two floors in a highly secure building in the business district near Zurich's airport. The offices have a communications center that looks like Dr. No's headquarters in the James Bond movie. Before the Kopp affair, Shakarchi employed twenty-two people and grossed a revenue of SF8 billion or more per year. Ultimately, the publicity generated by the Kopp affair proved bad for business. He had to fire many of his staff and his profits decreased substantially. I doubt this diminished his standard of living, but it surely affected his social life. Life had become so unpleasant for the Shakarchis in Switzerland that Shakarchi sent his Swiss wife and two children out of the country to live in an undisclosed location.

Shakarchi survived the media's negative publicity, but complained about the Swiss, "they are not easy to make friends with."

Shakarchi hired the Magharian brothers in his Zurich office in 1984—according to them for only six months. In statements to the Swiss press, however, Shakarchi said he broke relations with the Magharians in the spring of 1987. By the time I interviewed him in June 1991, he denied that the Magharians had ever worked for him. Both Shakarchi and the Magharians admitted that they had known each other in Lebanon through their fathers. Shakarchi refused to elaborate. More talkative, the Magharians alleged that Shakarchi had become a major arms dealer in Damascus by the time the Syrian Government seized his office in 1975. The Syrians discovered $5 million in cash and a quantity of arms and ammunition. Shakarchi went to Syria to reclaim his property. Oddly, he was not arrested by Syrian authorities. The Magharians mentioned that Shakarchi's regular business partners included several well-known arms and drug dealers, including Armenians and Turks, as well as the Bulgarian Government.

Shakarchi made the interesting admission that he was

doing a brisk business in Turkey and Bulgaria. U.S. law enforcement sources have alleged that Shakarchi and the Magharians had in fact conspired with the Bulgarian Government to launder drug money. The former Communist government in Sofia had been involved in drug trafficking and drug money-laundering for years. Opium paste and heroin from Turkey and hashish from Lebanon pass through Bulgaria on their way to Switzerland and other European countries, and the Bulgarian Government helped Turkish smugglers launder their proceeds. A DEA report dated January 3, 1989, stated "the Bulgarian government takes a percentage of the value of goods whether it be illegal cash, drugs or weapons, and guarantees safe passage of the material through Bulgaria." The same report documented the drug connections of Globus, a Bulgarian trading company run by Ivanoff Tochkov and Stoyan Paunov, Bulgarian secret police operatives. Globus, said the DEA report, was "formerly known as Kintex and Korekom," two former government agencies notorious for brokering arms for drugs. "Globus," continued the report, "transmitted Middle Eastern drug money to Switzerland through Shakarchi." By 1988, estimated law enforcement sources, the Magharian operation was laundering at least $2 billion a year, of which the Bulgarian cut was over $10 million annually. As we talked, Shakarchi admitted that he held unusually good standing with Bulgarian officials.

"Have you ever done business with Kintex and Globus?" I asked him. "I never heard of them," he replied.

The DEA report notwithstanding, this was a curious statement from someone who flew back and forth to Bulgaria on his private jet at a time when Bulgaria's own iron curtain was nearly impenetrable. He said, "I traveled to Bulgaria many times to hunt game with friends. They *happened* to be Bulgarian high officials."

Our conversation took a strange turn. Shakarchi told me that he had learned from *his agent* in Bulgaria on November 28, 1986, that an alert Pan American employee had discovered three suitcases filled with drug money addressed to the Magharians at the Los Angeles International Airport. It is astounding that he learned about it the same day the discovery occurred. Sent by the Turkish drug-money launderer, Dikran Altun, the money belonged to the Colombian Medellín cartel and constituted the Swiss end of the trail uncovered during the American Polar Cap money-laundering investigation. The undercover operation led to 127 arrests in Los Angeles and other American cities in February 1989.

I facetiously wished Mohamed Shakarchi *Mazal Tov*—good luck in Hebrew—and said I had heard that he was Jewish; he winced defensively and went to great lengths to reiterate his Arab Muslim background. I later learned that the Swiss media and the Magharians have suggested that like Elizabeth Kopp, Shakarchi too is "Jewish." He insisted that he was quite proud to be an Arab Muslim and expressed dismay that anyone would "accuse" him of being Jewish. I suddenly remembered Hans Kopp telling me that "the Jews control the world's finances and manipulate the media in the U.S." When I had asked Kopp to name Jewish bankers and Jewish media moguls in America or elsewhere, he quoted Lyndon LaRouche, the head of a U.S. extreme right wing organization, and cited his publications. Considering that billions of dollars in Arab money, legal or other-

145

wise, keep the Swiss banking industry afloat, and given the blatant anti-Semitism in Switzerland, I was not surprised to hear that Shakarchi had been labeled a "Jew." Shakarchi believes that the Swiss and U.S. authorities were actually seeking to indict Edmund Safra, the owner of National Republic Bank, who is Jewish. He went on to explain that because he holds bank accounts at Safra's bank the investigators used him in their attempt to catch Safra. As it turned out Shakarchi was exonerated and Safra and his bank received a clean bill of health.

Switzerland has a long history of selectively protecting its "secret" bank accounts. Many drug barons, organized crime chieftains, and terrorist groups have received "most favored" account status in Swiss banks. The case that triggered the long-awaited changes in Swiss banking regulations was the Kopp affair.

If there is one thing that the Kopps, Mohamed Shakarchi, and the Magharians share, it is a loathing of Dick Marty, a handsome, intelligent, bearded man in his late thirties who was the district attorney in Ticino, the southern Italian-speaking canton of Switzerland, at the time of the Kopp affair. Dick Marty took his job too seriously. He wanted to stop money-laundering and drug trafficking in Switzerland but he soon discovered that such zeal was not politically expedient; for apparently drug money was reaching deep into the Swiss establishment. His prosecution of the Kopp affair had swiftly disabused him about the Swiss banking industry's integrity. He entered politics, hoping to exert more influence and thus change the status quo.

The Swiss began to investigate the Magharians in connection with Polar Cap, following the discovery of drug money at Los Angeles International Airport in suitcases addressed to the brothers in Lugano, Switzerland. Barkev and his brother Jean Magharian worked out of offices at the Novapark Hotel in Zurich but their legal residence was in Lugano, in the canton of Ticino. This southern enclave of Switzerland borders Italy and traditionally has served as a tax haven for Italians. It has been often implicated in international money-laundering. Not surprisingly, this small canton has one bank for every five hundred citizens.

The Magharian brothers did not enjoy Swiss residency permits nor was their business registered in Switzerland. More seriously, they and their employees never paid taxes. According to their lawyer, Tuto Rossi (whom they fired at the end of the trial and before their appeal), their currency exchange and transfer business had reached "sizable proportions" by the mid-1980s. By then, he said, "they had already taken away about 10 percent of Shakarchi's business and one or two of his major clients." It was Shakarchi, said Rossi, who introduced the Magharians to Mehmet Yldirim and Celal Dahabi, money changers from Istanbul.[3] By the time the Magharians were arrested, they laundered at least SF620 million for the two Turks. Packed in small denominations, the money would arrive in Zurich in suitcases and boxes. The Magharians then deposited it in one of the many accounts they held at three leading Swiss banks. In the three years prior to their arrest in July 1988, they deposited SF1.4 billion in Crédit Suisse, SF1.2 million in the Swiss Banking Corporation, and SF130 million in Union Bank of Switzerland. Depositing the money was the

first and most important step in their operation. Once the
money was in the banking system, it was successfully laundered. In the next step, cash was withdrawn and transferred
back to the drug dealers. A significant portion was used to
purchase gold bullion either from the banks or from
Mohamed Shakarchi, who was a major bullion dealer in
Zurich. Shakarchi claims he did not know at the time that
he was receiving drug money.

Dikran Altun, a Turkish drug dealer, laundered drug
money on behalf of the Colombian Medellín cartel. He
worked with the Andonian brothers in Los Angeles and
began doing business with the Magharians in June 1985.
Following the discovery of the suitcases in 1986, he was
recruited by the DEA as a confidential informant (CI). At
the beginning of their business relationship there was nothing wrong with the money Altun was sending to the Magharians. This changed in February 1986 when Altun met
Carlos Pineda, a Columbian drug dealer, in Los Angeles.
Pineda arranged for Altun to go to Colombia and launder
drug money on behalf of the Medellín cartel. Court files
from the Polar Cap investigation revealed that Altun
skimmed off a 7 percent commission from the cash he
transported to Switzerland, while the Magharians took one
tenth of a percent as their commission when they transferred the money from Switzerland to Panama. In Switzerland the Union Bank and Crédit Suisse wire-transferred the
money to the Colombia-based branch of the Panamanian
Banco de Occidente and to a Panamanian branch of Banco
Cafetero, a state-owned Colombian bank that had exten-

sive holdings in the scandal-ridden Italian Banco Ambrosiano, whose late chairman, Roberto Calvi, was found hanging from Blackfriars bridge in London in 1982.[4] Court files in New York and in Lugano proved beyond doubt that the Magharians knew the money was drug money and that this was not the first time they had engaged in drug money-laundering. They were also indicted for laundering the proceeds of heroin that entered the United States via a Turkish drug-trafficking organization. In my interview with them, they denied all such charges.

No sooner were the money-packed suitcases discovered at the Los Angeles airport, than Dick Marty, the Ticino prosecutor, was alerted and asked to investigate. Then, on February 22, 1987, the Swiss seized eighty kilograms of heroin and twenty kilograms of morphine base with a street value of SF7 million near Bellinzona near the Italian border. The Swiss suspected that Haci Mirza, a Turkish Kurd, owned the shipment. He and an associate were promptly arrested in their room at the Hotel Excelsior in Lugano. The investigator in this case was also Dick Marty. Upon Mirza's arrest, Marty discovered that at least five more companies were involved in drug trafficking and money-laundering with the Turkish drug dealer, among them the Magharians and the Shakarchi Trading Company. According to Swiss reports, Mahmoud Kassen Shakarchi, Mohamed's father, had had business and social connections with Mirza dating back to the early 1980s, as did the son. Mohamed Shakarchi denies it.

Mirza and his Italian partner, Nicola Giulietti, confessed to the Swiss that as far as they knew the proceeds of the drug deal were supposed to pay for weapons needed by Iran in the war against Iraq. This was not the first time law enforcement agents heard that the pair was involved in drugs-for-arms deals on behalf of Iran but now it was learned that the contact in Tehran was none other than Hashemi Rafsanjani, Iran's president.

Based on information provided by Mirza, Dick Marty issued a warrant for Jean and Barkev Magharian. They were arrested in Zurich on July 7, 1988. They were indicted in California on March 8, 1989, for conspiracy to launder drug money and on March 10 in New York for selling cocaine. It was in August 1988, after the Turkish media reported on drugs, money, and gold smuggling activities between Turkey, Bulgaria, and Switzerland that Shakarchi made his phone call to Kopp and suggested he resign. It is difficult to understand why Kopp did not distance himself from the Shakarchi Trading Company at that time. Unharmed by previous brushes with the law he had perhaps become arrogant or careless.

By early September 1988, Jacques-André Kaeslin, the Swiss federal public prosecutor, had gathered evidence linking the Magharians and the Shakarchi Trading Company in their illegal activities. Elizabeth Kopp, then Minister of Justice, first learned about this investigation on October 27 when she was coaxed into making the fatal phone call, six weeks after her husband had heard from Shakarchi. By November the *Tages-Anzeiger* carried banner headlines about the "Lebanon Connection," claiming that over SF1.5 billion in drug money had been laundered in Switzerland. The article also implicated the Shakarchi Trading Company and the Magharians, and gave as its sources the DEA and its Swiss counterparts. The media blitz that ensued led to Elizabeth Kopp's resignation on January 12, 1989.

Another casualty of the Kopp affair was Swiss Chief Prosecutor Rudolf Gerber. A parliamentary inquiry into the Kopp affair revealed that Gerber and his chief aides had been lax in their investigations of drug trafficking and money-laundering. With this publicity Gerber's past resurfaced and came back to haunt him. In 1976 he had been implicated in the yet-unsolved murder of a woman. The woman, an acquaintance of the Kopps and a resident of fashionable Zumikon, was frequently seen in Gerber's company. He was the last person to see her alive. The case was freshly aired when Gerber went into "early retirement" following the Kopp affair investigation. Gerber was asked for comments by the media. He replied he had "nothing [to say], but if you have evidence to the contrary, verify it." Gerber, reportedly, is a good friend of Hans Kopp but Hans Kopp denies it. All these revelations and publicity led to Gerber's dismissal on March 6, 1989, and to the reorganization of the Attorney General's office.

While this was taking place in Switzerland, U.S. law enforcement agencies continued their Polar Cap investigations. In early January 1989, Shakarchi was reportedly seen meeting Wanis Koyomejian in Zurich.[5] Shakarchi denied ever meeting with Koyomejian, the owner of Ropex, a gold refining and jewelry company in Los Angeles with which Shakarchi was doing business "on behalf of an Italian client." On March 8, 1989, in Los Angeles, the Magharians were indicted for laundering $32 million to $60 million. During March 1990 the prosecutor in Zurich opened a formal investigation of Mohamed Shakarchi. And on March 10, 1990, the U.S. Attorney in the Eastern District of New York subpoenaed Shakarchi's bank account from the National Republic Bank in New York via registered mail. Two U.S. postmarks dated the sixteenth and the twenty-second of March are clearly visible on the envelope. However, according to the Swiss postmark, Shakarchi received the subpoena in Switzerland on the twenty-eighth. The subpoena directed him to respond within twenty days but delay in delivery left him with only two days to comply. Other extraordinary details surrounded the subpoena: it said that Shakarchi exported $693 million from the United States while importing only $159 million. In fact, he exported $205 million from this account and imported $886 million to the United States. According to U.S. government documents, these wire transfers dated back to 1977; Shakarchi, however, had founded his Zurich company in 1983. This discrepancy made it very easy for Shakarchi to have the subpoena dismissed in the United States less than a month after it was issued. Wire transfer experts assure me that the entries and amounts shown in the subpoena could not have been the result of computer error. The only possible conclusion is that the information in the subpoena was falsified by someone in the United States to ensure Shakarchi's exoneration. This is a rare but welcome example of cooperation among U.S. government law enforcement agencies. When I confronted an important U.S. law enforcement official who took part in the investigation, he expressed relief that the inaccurate data were not the result of computer error. "We have invested a great deal of money in our system," he said.

In August 1990 the drug money-laundering laws went into effect in Switzerland and by the end of February 1991 all proceedings against Mohamed Shakarchi in Switzerland were dropped. The Magharians were released from their Lugano prison on July 7, 1991. In Los Angeles, at the other corner of the Polar Cap investigation, the Andonian brothers were sentenced to 505 years each in August 1991. Wanis Koyomejian still awaits trial.

At the Zurich airport, on my way to interview the Magharians in Lugano I had to go through Passport Control. The flight takes about half an hour and, on arriving in Lugano, passengers again go through Passport Control. As an Israeli, aware of the stringent security surrounding travel in and out of Israel, I was struck by the unusual security measures governing a short domestic trip. With such tight security, I thought, it should not be possible for drugs and drug-money couriers to come and go so freely. When I asked Swiss officials about these measures, I was reassured on five separate occasions that "this was not especially for you." In fact, I had never thought that it was.

When I met Barkev and Jean Magharian on June 7, 1991, in a conference room at Hotel Montalbano outside Lugano, they were out of prison on work release. I was accompanied by a Swiss reporter, a friend whom I had asked to join me. I felt I needed a witness. Barkev and Jean Magharian are in their late thirties, but they look much older. Maybe serving time in Swiss correctional facilities has aged them. The brothers, Syrians of Armenian descent, born in Aleppo, look like stockbrokers or investment bankers. They lived and worked in apartment No. 3499 rented from Novapark Hotel in Zurich. Both are married with families in Syria. Their wives and children resided in Aleppo but visited Zurich on occasion. Unaccompanied by a lawyer, Barkev and Jean were friendly but cautious. Both had learned Italian in La Stampa Prison, outside Lugano. Barkev also spoke fluent French and English. Jean spoke Arabic and Armenian; he appeared to understand English but professed not to speak it. It was Barkev who presented their case. Jean occasionally interrupted in Armenian to clarify certain points. The meeting lasted over three hours during which the brothers attempted to convince me that they were simply the victims of Swiss xenophobia. They admitted that they were in business to launder money—"Yes, we were laundering money, nothing unusual in Switzerland," they said, "everybody does it"—but they denied any knowledge that the source of the money was from the sale of drugs in the United States or elsewhere. They also suggested that they had been investigated, tried, and convicted because Shakarchi now viewed them as stiff competitors. The Magharian brothers were sentenced to four and a half years but were released on good behavior after serving just over three years. They were also fined SF50,000 but almost all of their $5 million that had been seized by the Swiss authorities was returned. I asked them whether they intended to remain in Switzerland. They said they were anxious to leave Switzerland as soon as possible, never to return. Syria was not on their itinerary.

As part of the Polar Cap investigation, the Magharians were also wanted in New York and Los Angeles for laundering $32 million to $60 million in the case implicating Dikran Altun and the Andonian brothers. They were never extradited, however, because they had already served time in Switzerland for the same offense.

When we parted, they presented me with an autographed color Xeroxed portrait of the two and with Barkev's home phone number in Aleppo, Syria.

At this writing, as the Bank of Credit and Commerce International (BCCI) and the Banca Nazionale del Lavoro (BNL) scandals were just breaking, no information was available connecting Hans Kopp and Mohamed Shakarchi to either or both banks. Yet Dr. Alfred Hartmann, dubbed "the Swiss Clark Clifford," and popularly known as "rent-a-face,"[6] was the chairman of Banque de Commerce et de Placements (BCP), a partly owned subsidiary of BCCI in Switzerland. He was also the director of Lavoro Bank in Zurich, a fully owned BNL subsidiary. BNL's branch in Atlanta, Georgia, was implicated in the unauthorized $4 billion agricultural loans to Iraq and other fraudulent activities discussed elsewhere in this book. Hartmann is on the board of at least sixteen other companies registered in Switzerland. He is said to be a close friend of the Kopps and a frequent guest at their home. Hartmann, I was told in Luxembourg, sold BCP to a Turkish conglomerate, Çukurova, without authorization of the holding company of BCCI (in Luxembourg) fourteen days after BCCI was ordered to close down by the Bank of England. When I asked Shakarchi about his connections to Çukurova, he replied, "I have none, but Mehmet Emin Karamehmet [president of Çukurova group] is the most honest banker

I've ever known." Are these prime figures—Shakarchi and Kopp—somehow involved in the BCCI/BNL affairs? As events unfold, the importance of Switzerland and its banking industry in this international scandal may become evident.

Punctuality is no longer a proverbial Swiss trait. Trains do not run on time in Switzerland but the banking industry continues to operate like a well-oiled clock movement. Perhaps, too well oiled. Although money-laundering legislation allegedly promulgated to keep "dirty money" out of Swiss banks was passed in 1990, and regulations were altered to allow banks to break the veil of secrecy surrounding their clients, there is little inclination to enforce these edicts. Modeled after U.S. laws that target the assets of drug traffickers and other organized crime figures, new legislation is now being drafted in Switzerland and other countries around the world. Echoing the steadfast clarion calls for a thorough cleansing of the banking industry, the press is filled with reports on summits and international meetings proclaiming cooperation and pledging a host of new regulations designed to combat money-laundering. But don't hold your breath. Enacting laws is one thing—enforcing them is another—as recent events in Switzerland demonstrate.

On Sunday evening, June 9, 1991, I was invited by a high-ranking Swiss military official to dine at his home with his family. He is a friend of a friend, whom I had first met a week earlier during lunch. He had expressed interest in my research and concern about my safety, particularly in relation to the Kopp affair.

When he picked me up at my hotel he seemed anxious and rushed. It was a gray rainy evening in Zurich and the roads were empty. As we drove toward his home he frequently checked the rearview mirror. Suddenly, he pulled over, came to a stop, and waited until a car he thought was following had passed us. I felt as though I was taking part in a B-movie. Scenes of Cold War oppression and surveillance in Eastern Bloc countries came back to haunt me. I had to remind myself that I was in Switzerland, land of chocolate and pristine Alpine peaks and "holey" cheese.

Late in August 1991 I dialed Barkev Magharian's home phone in Aleppo, Syria. The line had been disconnected.

Bank of Credit and Commerce International (BCCI):

THE ROBIN HOOD OF THE THIRD WORLD

BCCI was operated as a corrupt, criminal organization, throughout its entire nineteen-year history. It systematically falsified its records. It knowingly allowed itself to be used to launder illegal income of drug sellers and other criminals and it paid bribes and kickbacks to other public officials.

—ROBERT M. MORGENTHAU, District Attorney, County of New York, July 29, 1991

CAST OF CHARACTERS

Robert M. Morgenthau, District Attorney, County of New Yor[k]

Zulfikar Ali Bhutto and Zia ul-Haq—former presidents of Paki[stan]

Agha Hasan Abedi—Pakistani banker who founded the Bank [of] Credit and Commerce International (BCCI) in 1972

Sheik Zayed bin Sultan al-Nahayan—the ruler of Abu Dhab[i], Abedi's friend and business partner in BCCI

Abdur Sakhia—former Director of Global Marketing for BCCI

Swaleh Naqvi—a friend and close associate of Abedi, chief exec[u]tive of BCCI

Kamal Adham—Saudi Arabia's former head of intelligence and large stockholder in the parent company of First American

Clark Clifford—Washington lawyer and power broker, adviser t[o] Democratic presidents from Truman to Carter, former secr[e]tary of defense during the Johnson administration and pres[i]dent of First American and lawyer for BCCI

Robert Altman and his Hollywood star wife, Lynda Carter— Clifford's protégé and partner and president of First America[n]

Ghaith Pharaon—prominent Saudi financier, front for BCC[I], owner of banks in Atlanta, Georgia, and Encino, California[,] and BCCI stockholder

Dr. Abdul Qader Khan—in charge of Pakistan's nuclear progra[m]

Prince Mohammed Bin-Faisal-al-Saud, Saudi Arabia—owner [of] Faisal Islamic Bank and Dar-al-Maaral Islami

Rita and Arnold Mandel and Hong Kong businessman Leung Y[.] Hung—smugglers of nuclear technology to Pakistan

160

Brigadier Inam ul-Haq—Pakistani intelligence officer, and Ashad Pervez—Pakistani-born Canadian smuggler

Ghassem Qassem—former manager of BCCI's Sloan Street branch in London, handled Abu Nidal's accounts

Bertram (Bert) Lance—Director of the Office of Management and Budget (OMB) for the Carter administration. Introduced Abedi to Carter.

Andrew Young—former U.S. Ambassador to the UN, consultant to BCCI

John Kerry—Democratic senator from Massachusetts whose persistence uncovered BCCI's illegal activities

Bill Clinton—Democratic presidential candidate, governor of Arkansas, 1992

Masihur Rahman—former chief financial officer of BCCI

David Paul—chairman of failing Centrust Bank in Florida

Robert Magness, president, and Larry Romrell, vice president, TCI and founders of Capcom

Syed Ziauddin Akbar—head of BCCI's Treasury. Assisted Noriega in hiding $23 million.

Gokal brothers, Hussein, Mustafa, Abbas, and Murtaza—Pakistani shipping magnates

Sani Ahmad—head of BCCI's lobbying firm in Washington, DC

Christopher Drogoul—manager of BNL Atlanta branch and his assistant, Paul Von Wedel, funneled $4 billion in U.S. agricultural subsidies to Saddam Hussein

Ishan Barbouti—Iraqi businessman who fronted for Iraqi and Libyan illegal acquisitions of weapons and technology

Mohammed Hammud—Shiite Lebanese businessman, BCCI financier, and HizbAllah activist

Immam Mussa Sadar—deceased leader of HizbAllah in Lebanon

Colonel Muammar Qaddafi—Libya's leader

Mussa Hawamdah—operator of Manara Travel Agency

Anwar Khan—former manager of the Ottawa branch of BCCC

Louis Farrakhan—leader of Nation of Islam

Lenora Fulani—1988 and 1992 presidential candidate of New Alliance Party

Mian Faruq, Mr. Arshad, Mr. Amjad and Mr. Abid—Pakistani businessmen who conducted the illegal procurement efforts in the U.S.

Sabri al-Banna—Abu Nidal Organization (ANO)

Carlos Zarouk—front man for PLO in Nicaragua

George Hallak—a Lebanese con man operating on behalf of the PLO

Salem Azzam—General Secretary of the London-based Islamic Conference

Mohammed Bakir Sayid Fadlallah and his brother Ayatollah Mohammed Hussayn—leaders of the Shiite militants in Lebanon

Mohammad Reza Narachan—Iranian ambassador to London

Sheik Hussayn Shiachadin—Khomeini's representative in West Africa

Mehdi Hashemi—Khomeini's representative in Sierra Leone

Saamir Najmeddin—Abu Nidal's representative in London

Joseph Momoh—president of Sierre Leone

Shabtai Kalmanovitch—KGB mole

Qasser brothers, Ghassan, Haytham, and Mazin—Syrian terrorists and arms dealers

Alan García—former Peruvian president

Asaf Ali—Lebanese arms dealer and good friend of Abedi, brokered arms through Peru

Hussein Bouzidi—an Abu Nidal operative arrested in Peru

PAUL ERDMAN, in *The Crash of '79*,[1] described how the Arabs offered to bail out the failing banks of America—in exchange for weapons. His tale was shocking but it pales next to the real story of the Bank of Credit and Commerce International, S.A. (BCCI). While Erdman was writing his fiction, BCCI was already well on its way to becoming the most important Islamic bank in the world. On July 5, 1991, at 1 P.M. Greenwich time, BCCI was shut down by the Bank of England.

The balance of economic power shifted when industrial nations became dependent on Arab oil. By the mid-seventies, OPEC emerged and Arab control of the world's oil supply was largely dictated by Arab/Muslim nations employing terrorism and economic blackmail. Quick to exploit the situation, and anxious to recycle petro-dollars, the West pandered to the Third World by selling it both its technology and its conscience. In return, oil-producing countries deposited their newly reaped riches in eager Western banks. The Western banks gladly accepted the funds Third World leaders had stolen from their governments and reloaned them, thus earning profits from both sides. In 1972 banks in Pakistan were nationalized by President Zulfikar Ali Bhutto. One such bank was the United Bank, Ltd., whose president was Agha Hasan Abedi.

Abedi, a Pakistani banker and financier, was born in 1922 in northern central India. During the partition of India in 1947 Abedi and his family joined other Muslim refugees in Pakistan. Abedi went to work as a clerk in a bank and later joined the United Bank. Following the bank's nationalization, Abedi, helped by his friend, Sheik Zayed bin Sultan al-Nahayan from Abu Dhabi, founded BCCI. The timing was fortuitous and the bank prospered. The marketing BCCI practiced brought more customers and bought more people than any Western company would dare to do. With $10 million in capital—$625,000 from the Bank of America (BOA), $2.5 million from Abedi himself, and the balance from Sheik Zayed—BCCI opened its doors to international business. BOA shares in BCCI were sold by the end of 1980. In an internal memorandum BOA declared a lack of trust as its reason for pulling out of BCCI.[2]

Sheik Zayed, an illiterate multibillionaire and an early patron of the Palestinian Liberation Organization (PLO), was the first Arab leader to use oil as a political weapon following the Yom Kippur War with Israel in 1973. He contributed millions of dollars to the cause of the PLO and just before the war with Iraq in 1991, he branded the United States "our number two enemy" (after Israel).

In order to prevent nationalization of the newly established bank, BCCI was chartered in Luxembourg in 1972. Within a year it had opened five offices, in London, Beirut, Dubai, Sharjah and Abu Dhabi, the Gulf Emirates. In the beginning its operational center was in Abu Dhabi. The bank grew fast. By 1975 it counted 146 branches in 32 countries. It then split into two separate entities, one in Luxembourg, the other in the Cayman Islands. The latter, as was later discovered, operated "a bank within a bank" through which billions of dollars were stolen by BCCI management. By the time the bank was shut down in July 1991, it ran 430 branches in 73 countries. At first, BCCI appeared to be functioning as a major financial institution catering to Western and Third World interests. Only upon closure and ensuing investigations has public attention focused on the bank's criminal character. This was the bank that "would bribe God."[3] For too many years BCCI was left unregulated, pretending to be a legitimate enterprise. It was the disingenuous complacency of many governments and political leaders who used the bank to their own ends that ruined many small depositors. Although BCCI was headquartered in London, the real power behind BCCI rested in both Saudi Arabia and Pakistan, acting as the representatives of the Muslim world. Pakistan has long been known as a crossroad for drugs, money-laundering, and illegal arms sales.

Abedi structured BCCI so as to avoid basing the bank in any major country—it was offshore everywhere—thus avoiding scrutiny by regulators. "We were . . . an international bank with a worldwide network. And since we were not carrying any specific flag . . . we were a purely international bank,"[4] said Abdur Sakhia, former Director of Global Marketing for BCCI. New York County District Attorney, Robert Morgenthau, offered a more straightforward description: "The corporate structure of BCCI was set up to evade international and national banking laws so that its corrupt practices would be unsupervised and remain undiscovered," he said in a press conference announcing the indictment of the bank in July 1991. He added "this indictment spells out the largest bank fraud in world financial history."

Swaleh Naqvi, a friend and close associate of Abedi, was appointed chief executive of BCCI from its inception. Kamal Adham, Saudi King Faisal's most trusted adviser, joined a group that acquired Financial General Bankshares (FGB) in Washington, D.C. Following the bank's acquisition, its name was changed to First American. When the BCCI scandal broke, First American was promptly dubbed by the press "First Arabian." Clark Clifford, the president of the newly acquired bank, later mentioned that one of the first people to ask him for a favor was Kamal Adham, the "informal chairman" of the shareholders. The approach came in 1981 as Abedi and Adham hosted a lunch in London celebrating Clifford's successful negotiations with the old FGB management. Adham took Clifford aside and asked if he would run their new bank. Clifford always emphasized his impression that Adham ran the show, especially when he was rebutting the charges of secret BCCI control. At the lunch and the handful of other times he saw them together, Clifford noticed how Abedi deferred to Adham, to the point of fawning on him. "It seemed plain to us that Mr. Abedi was an agent of the investors, not a principal."

Clifford also revealed that Adham was one of the founders of BCCI, one of the first bankers, who along with Sheik Zayed, made it possible for Abedi to realize his dream. The genial Adham, his round face trimmed by a fluffy white cotton-ball beard, spent the seventies directing intelligence and external influence-buying for Saudi Arabia's King Faisal. Adham was the ultimate royal insider. He owed his position to his half-sister Iffat, King Faisal's favorite wife and a remarkable person in her own right. (Iffat did more than any one else to open opportunities for women in puritanical Saudi society.) Iffat came from the al-Thunayan branch of the al-Saud family and had been raised in Istanbul under the Ottoman Empire. Her mother remarried a Turk of Albanian extraction, the father of Kamal Adham, and throughout his career in Arabia, Adham was known as "the Turk." Iffat and Faisal raised Adham like their own son, and he became the closest foreign policy adviser to the dour, hard-working King.

It was an open secret in Saudi Arabia that Adham attended the CIA training school at Langley, Virginia, along with the head of Israel's foreign intelligence service, the Mossad. He came home to handle sensitive missions for Faisal, which often included substantial payments to other Arab leaders. He acted as paymaster to the Royalists during the North Yemen civil war in the early sixties and in 1972 brokered a major foreign policy coup, Egyptian President Anwar Sadat's expulsion of his Soviet advisers. Adham was considered pro-Western, both in politics and business. Along the way he amassed a personal fortune through brokering contracts. His other nickname in Saudi circles was "Mr. Two-Percent."

Adham's influence at court faded after the assassination of King Faisal in 1975. His résumé states that his government service ended in 1979. But his business reputation flourished. The UAE ambassador to London, a notorious fixer in the Gulf, was once asked about a story that he had paid $30 million to Adham to settle a border dispute between the Saudis and Abu Dhabi. "I think Adham is worth more than $30 million," the ambassador replied.

Adham's name popped up in American business deals

before the FGB takeover. *The Wall Street Journal* reported that he earned commissions from the Boeing Company, which was later charged with making "questionable foreign payments." (Both the SEC and the Federal Trade Commission brought suits against Boeing, which were settled in 1978 by consent arrangements.) Adham also owned a large part of the First Arabian Corporation, which backed another prominent Saudi financier, Ghaith Pharaon's purchase of Detroit's Bank of the Commonwealth. Pharaon, also a BCCI shareholder, acting on behalf of Abedi, secretly purchased the National Bank of Georgia in Atlanta from Bert Lance and, later, the Independence Bank of Encino in California.

Assume, as most of the U.S. press hasn't, that Clifford was right about Adham's role. The specter arises of a double penetration. Did Adham use BCCI in the seventies to further his intelligence duties or to extend Saudi economic influence in the United States? Or, on the other hand, did the CIA (or other spy outfits) work through BCCI for their own ends? Answers are still lacking and the questions have scarcely been asked.

The Bank of Credit and Commerce International was instrumental in the acquisition and transfer of military nuclear technologies and equipment from Western Europe to Third World countries. Abedi was openly committed to the creation of an "Islamic bomb" and he often conveyed this in speeches and meetings with Third World leaders. Abedi's support for the Islamic bomb did not fade even after BCCI's debacle. In a public address on October 22, 1991, Dr. Abdul Qader Khan, head of Pakistan's nuclear program, thanked Abedi for donating 500 million rupees for the establishment of the Gulam Ishaq Research Institute for nuclear development. A day earlier Khan had acknowledged that "it is a fact that Pakistan has become a nuclear power, and it is at present concentrating on manufacturing sophisticated arms to fulfill its requirements."[5] On February 7, 1992, Pakistan admitted to having the capacity to produce nuclear weapons.

BCCI's origins were primarily ideological. Abedi wanted the bank to reflect the supra-national Muslim credo and serve as "the best bridge to help the world of Islam, and the best way to fight the evil influence of the Zionists."[6] He planned for BCCI to become the most important full-fledged Islamic bank, with enough political clout to compete with and even dominate Western financial institutions. Abedi's aim was to enhance the power of Islam through Third World countries. He echoed anti-Western and anti-imperialist slogans to stir up support. It is not surprising, therefore, that when BCCI was shut down, Abedi and the bank were viewed in Pakistan and other Muslim nations as victims of Western—particularly United States—anti-Islamic fervor.

Abedi, a Sufi mystic, shares the same political views and commitment to the expansion of Islam as do the other members of BCCI's board. Aided by Sheik Zayed al-Nahayan and the Gokal brothers, Pakistani shipping magnates, Abedi established BCCI as an Islamic financial institution in all but name. The bank was geared to operate in the West, but its constituency lay in the Third World, particularly in Islamic nations and communities around the globe.

It was Abedi's unswerving goal to see BCCI become the world's largest bank by the turn of the century. His mission was to revive Third World economies by spurring on Islamic tenets and business practices. Abedi claimed that BCCI was created with "goodness and equality" as its motto and he often portrayed himself as the Robin Hood of the Third World. In practice, however, he and his bank stole from the poor and gave to the rich. He eventually came to be known as the "Rasputin" of the Middle East.[7] BCCI's success was not all that Abedi yearned for. "He wanted to be bigger than the bank, he wanted to control countries and heads of state, obliging them with jobs for relations, balances of payment assistance, and gifts according to Abdur Sakhia a former BCCI employee."[8] Feigning modesty, Abedi observed, "I created the philosophy, and the bank grew by itself."[9]

BCCI's policy was determined by Muslim interests and ideals, and anchored in the desire to increase the economic power and political leverage of local Muslim communities by exploiting their lucrative and sometimes illicit activities. By 1984, BCCI had set up an Islamic banking unit in its London branch to solicit deposits for Muslim investors. By 1989, deposits were estimated at $1.4 billion. The real concern of Western central banks then began to focus on institutions such as Faisal Islamic Bank and Dar-al-Maaral Islami, both headed by Prince Mohammed Bin-Faisal-al-Saud of Saudi Arabia. Based in Egypt, the Faisal Islamic Bank is 51 percent owned by the Egyptian Government and 49 percent by the Saudi Government. An estimated 25 percent of its assets are said to be with BCCI. The strength of BCCI in Muslim communities stemmed from its Islamic banking practices, which do not permit interest payments. The Koran forbids "usury" (interest), therefore the law of the land in both Pakistan and Iran follows the Koran. BCCI followed suit. They call their fixed-interest payments something else. BCCI became the conduit for approximately $1 billion of unrecorded Islamic banking deposits to be used under contractual stipulation for commodity investments according to Islamic law. Such massive infusion of unrecorded deposits from Arab, primarily Saudi, investors provided BCCI with a distinct advantage over its Western counterparts.

Throughout the eighties, BCCI expanded and attained a unique status in the Third World. By the end of the decade, the "special services" provided by BCCI included access to Western humanitarian and international development funds, as well as methods for skimming and safekeeping those funds; easy cash; "creative" accounting for illegal business practices such as bribes, overpricing, money-laundering; smuggling cash across borders and creating a "bank within a bank," thus making secret transfers easy for intelligence services and terrorist organizations. One of its more unusual courtesies was the instantaneous provision of cash. A Pakistani client who fancied a car he saw on a short visit to London said, "I wanted it immediately, so I called BCCI and a man turned up carrying £25,000 in a plastic bag."[10]

The bank's "special services" also lured criminals, drug lords, and corrupt politicians. BCCI's services on their behalf included falsification of documents and "shell game" transactions to siphon off financial resources from central banks. Its involvement with government financing enabled BCCI to manipulate and control officials in many countries. BCCI held accounts for central banks in Jamaica,

Barbados, Peru, The Bahamas, Trinidad, Suriname, Aruba, Curaçao, Belize, Morocco, Panama, Zimbabwe, and many others. BCCI's access to new countries was usually preceded by hefty "charitable" donations to high governmental officials or prominent public figures. These favors were returned to BCCI with interest. A reciprocal relationship was also nurtured where BCCI opened secret and offshore accounts, thus facilitating the purchase of arms and restricted technologies, and encouraging drug money laundering. In return, many governments deposited their central bank funds into BCCI. A "Black Network" (a special "enforcement unit") was reported by a former Arab employee of the bank to operate from Pakistan. He alleged that the network supported logistically by Abu Nidal and other terrorist organizations, helped BCCI blackmail, threaten, and punish disobedient clients. BCCI was also a major catalyst in the transfer of strategic weapon sales including nuclear military technology from the West and ballistic missiles from China to Third World countries, especially Pakistan and Saudi Arabia. The following vignettes offer a glimpse into such activities:

· In 1983 a Dutch court convicted Dr. Abdul Qader Khan, head of Pakistan's nuclear program, on charges of stealing the blueprints for a uranium enrichment factory. A similar plant was begun soon after in Kahuda, Pakistan. Khan's lawyer, a former Pakistani justice minister, was paid by BCCI.

· In 1984, three Pakistani nationals were indicted in Houston for attempting to buy and ship to Pakistan, high-speed switches designed to trigger nuclear weapons. The trio offered to pay in gold supplied by BCCI.

• In 1987 two Americans, Rita and Arnold Mandel, together with Hong Kong businessman Leung Yu Hung, were indicted by the U.S. Attorney in Sacramento, California, on charges of illegal exportation of $1 billion worth of oscilloscopes and computer equipment for Pakistan's nuclear program. Fifteen shipments were made between July 1982 and August 1983 through Leung's Fortune Company in Hong Kong to Oftah Brothers, a company in Pakistan. BCCI facilitated some of these transactions.

• In 1987 in Philadelphia, Ashad Pervez, a Pakistani-born Canadian, was indicted for conspiring to export restricted specialty steel and metal used to enhance nuclear explosions. Pervez was fronting for Brigadier Inam ul-Haq, who acted as senior buyer in Canada on behalf of obscure Pakistani companies. Pervez, on ul-Haq's instructions, established a company in Willodale, Ontario, and began purchasing diversified equipment, including such items as beryllium and tens of tons of specialized maraging steel. In all his deals Pervez had excellent letters of credit from several branches of BCCI in Luxembourg, London, and Toronto. He promptly paid high prices with money delivered to the Toronto BCCI branch from BCCI London.[11]

Some Islamic nations and organizations oppose Western ethics and political values. When Palestinian Liberation Organization (PLO) activists in the United States claimed that Saddam Hussein was fighting for the values espoused by Abraham Lincoln, they were using the English language and Western rhetoric to their advantage, not to promote democracy. The outbreak of the Gulf War may be attributed to

Saddam Hussein's misreading of Western values, or perhaps to his megalomaniacal obsession to become the leader of the Arab world, as Gamal Abdel Nasser had once yearned to be. To his supporters, Saddam Hussein was often touted as the modern Saladin who reclaimed Islamic holy sites from the infidel Crusaders. Saddam had successfully fueled anti-Western sentiments among Islamic fundamentalists, Pan-Arabists, and Palestinian radical organizations. After the war Saddam's status had risen to mythical proportions, owing to his ability to survive the West's merciless onslaught. The confrontation was subsequently perceived in the Islamic/Arab world as a contest between Islam and the heretic West.

The Gulf War devastated more than Kuwait and Iraq; it also signaled the end of BCCI's influence. Revelations that followed the collapse of the bank uncovered a web of corruption and fraud that was characteristic of BCCI's global operations. Third World countries, Arab and Muslim, have rightfully blamed the West for the demise of BCCI. No longer able to ignore the bank's criminal activities, the United States and England pulled the plug and finally exposed it. The sums of money involved were too vast for Price Waterhouse, the auditors of BCCI, to ignore. In addition, the District Attorney of New York County, Robert Morgenthau, was well along in his investigation and about to make the information public. The reaction in the Third World was that the U.S. and U.K. governments closed BCCI to curtail the growing fiscal power of the internationally based Arab/Muslim bank. A ridiculous argument that ignores the reams of evidence of mega-fraud.

In much of the Third World, where corruption, favoritism, and nepotism are common, BCCI's failure was perceived as a Western conspiracy. A large gap lies between Western banking law and Islamic/Arab political and economic culture, where corruption plays a structural role. As the English writer David Pryce-Jones explained, "Force and favors, as determined among individuals through corruption, are the fundamentals of Arab and inter-Arab politics. Corruption among Arabs is nothing more nor less than a daily functioning among everyone of the power-challenge dialectic, and it is registering individual advances and retreats everywhere and at all times. Corruption plays a role approximating competition in a democracy. At the top of the social scale, corruption represents the power of the strong over the weak; at the bottom, however, it may soften the caprices of power and so promote tolerance."[12]

Most Arab/Islamic states do not give high priority to improving the people's welfare and standard of living. Instead, they view arms procurement as essential to maintaining the government's power base. Democracy and economic development in these countries do not necessarily translate into progress and innovation. Since radicalism and fundamentalism are "in," anti-Western activities become a "must." Events in Algeria in December 1991 demonstrate this optic: In the first round of parliamentary elections, Algerian fundamentalists, funded by Iran, won 188 out of 231 seats and were certain to win the majority of the Parliament's 430 seats in the second round. The Islamic Fundamentalist party used the club of anti-Western sentiment to achieve a major political majority. The second round never found range, preempted by a military coup engineered to crush Arab fundamentalism.[13] Violent demonstrations by fundamentalists continued and in February 1992 the new military government declared a one year "state of emergency."

Following the steady expansion of Islamic fundamentalism since the mid-seventies, we have witnessed the spread of violence and human rights abuses, factors that have led to political instability. Violence has become the voice of political and religious conflicts among the Muslims. "Terrorism stems from cultural violence rooted in a perversely callous attitude to human life, and a general disregard for the worth of individual rights."[14] To paraphrase Karl von Clausewitz, the famous Prussian general and strategist, terrorism for Islam is the extension of both war and diplomacy by other means. Arab and Islamic regimes traditionally use terrorism as a political weapon to enhance their security domestically and externally.

Thus, support of terrorism is a crucial element in Islamic political culture. The absence of democracy and the use of terrorism are the reasons behind state sponsorship for all terrorist organizations in the Middle East. It is not surprising, therefore, that the founders of BCCI saw in the Islamic fundamentalist opposition to the Shah of Iran an opportunity to undermine Western influence in the Gulf. They were willing to assist the revolution financially and in every other way. In this manner they reinforced their position within the leadership of the Iranian revolution. The Ayatollah was given all support in anticipation of his success. This was not charity. BCCI's contributions to the Ayatollah later provided BCCI with an Iranian foothold that greatly extended BCCI's reach toward its ultimate objective to become the most important Islamic bank in the world.

Iran, the ideological leader of Islamic revivalism, carries the torch of "jihad"—or holy war—and is followed by radical states such as Libya and Syria. Iraq, also a radical and terrorist state, first carried the message of Pan-Arabism. Before the outbreak of the Gulf War, Saddam Hussein added jihad to Pan-Arabism in order to gain more support in the Arab/Muslim world. But "moderate" states such as Algeria, Tunisia, and Yemen are also known for sponsoring terrorism. Saudi Arabia and the Gulf States continue to enlist everyone to their cause, in the name of Islam. The distinction between moderate and radical Arab/Islamic nations is often a hypocrisy kindled by the West and incorporated into Western foreign policy.

International terrorism peaked in 1985 with 792 incidents. It was also in 1985 that the CIA reportedly linked BCCI with the funding of terrorism. According to Richard Kerr, then Acting Director of the CIA, "as early as 1983, 1984" the agency began investigating BCCI's money-laundering activities. Kerr further stated that in 1985, "the CIA disseminated that intelligence . . . through the intelligence and law enforcement communities."[15] At about the same time the British intelligence service (MI6) also linked BCCI with the funding of terrorism. They learned about those connections from the former manager of BCCI's Sloan Street branch in London, Ghassem Qassem, who handled Abu Nidal's accounts.[16] But the Bank of England first learned about this in "about March 1988."[17]

Contrary to Kerr's testimony, other U.S. government agencies denied ever receiving these reports. It remains unknown why the CIA failed to disseminate this information; however, it seems that MI6 apparently followed suit. What was it that prevented them from putting an end to BCCI's activities? It took six more years of arms sales, drug trafficking, money-laundering, embezzlement, and fraud for BCCI to be shut down. It took many more terrorist acts and the lives of many victims worldwide before BCCI was stopped.

The CIA eventually admitted it kept accounts with BCCI, but claimed it used the bank legally to fund covert operations. Despite denials from the CIA about any relationship with Abedi, Kamal Adham's close ties with both Abedi and the CIA imply otherwise. It has already been established that the CIA was investigating BCCI's operations as early as 1983. BCCI's drug connections were first reported in 1984, yet no action was taken against them. The National Security Council reportedly also used BCCI accounts for nine years to fund the Afghan *mujahadin*. In 1985 the CIA entered into an arms deal with Iran through Adnan Khashoggi and BCCI. Arthur Liman, who served as a chief counsel in the Senate's Iran-Contra investigation, claimed that ''BCCI accounts were used to pay for the sale of TOW anti-tank missiles to Iran in 1985. The Iranian go-between, Manucher Ghorbanifar, wrote checks on BCCI's accounts to pay Richard Secord, the supply-master for the missile shipments.''[18]

The religious convictions of the founders of BCCI coincided with those of the Muslim and Arab leaders who sponsor terrorism. The Iranian revolution was an initial victory for Islamic fundamentalism. It was also the extension of this belief that led Agha Hassan Abedi to immerse BCCI in terrorist activities. Funding revolutions, terrorism, and other subversive activities is expensive and difficult. An Iranian web of international financial institutions was created, with BCCI as one of the most prominent strands. The bank not only facilitated direct contact between terrorist networks, it also provided cover and deniability for the sponsoring states. After all, "Islam is moving across the earth . . . nothing can stop it from spreading in Europe and America,"[19] said the Ayatollah Khomeini.

In order to penetrate the United States, BCCI used Saudi financier Ghaith Pharaon, among others, who had the advantages of a Harvard education, Western manners, and contacts with the Saudi royal family. Pharaon established high-level contacts with members of the Carter administration, including Bertram (Bert) Lance, the Director of the Office of Management and Budget (OMB), Andrew Young, U.S. Ambassador to the UN, and Clark Clifford, former Johnson administration Secretary of Defense and an established Washington influence peddler. The white-haired eighty-five-year-old patrician-looking and impeccably dressed adviser to five presidents, Clark Clifford, and his young, dynamic, social-climbing partner, tabloid headliner Robert Altman, and his Hollywood star wife Lynda Carter were some of the individuals who helped create BCCI's high-flying image. Morgenthau noted that, "The defendants created the appearance of respectability by persuading world leaders to appear with them and defraud their thousands of depositors, both small and large, who relied on that appearance of respectability."[20] It is alleged that BCCI had a list of politicians they bought off in the United States and elsewhere. Abedi spread BCCI's influence by cultivating politicians and inveigling national leaders to spread his bank's influence. The BCCI debacle made its first intrusion into the U.S. presidential race in 1992 and may be more damaging to the Democratic presidential candidate Bill Clinton, governor of Arkansas, than his alleged extramarital affair. Clinton's fund-raiser and confidant, Jackson Stephens, a billionaire from Little Rock who owns the controlling interest of Worthen National Bank in Little Rock, was the person who introduced Bert Lance to Abedi. While Stephens might not have known back in 1977 that BCCI was a criminal bank, Bill Clinton had full knowledge of Stephens's involvement with BCCI when he accepted hundreds of thousands of dollars from the Stephens family for his campaign. On the eve of the New Hampshire primary Robert Morgenthau was looking into the BCCI/Stephens/Clinton link.[21] In December 1991 *The Wall Street Journal* reported that Stephens and his bank invested in Harken Energy, a small Texas investment company of which George Bush, Jr., is a board member. The money Stephens invested came through the Swiss BCCI subsidiary.

Manuel Noriega (Panama), Mohammad Zia ul-Haq (Pakistan), Willy Brandt (West Germany), Indira Gandhi (India), Julius Nyerere (Tanzania), Lord Callaghan (Britain), Javiér Pérez de Cuéllar (the UN and Peru), Alan García (Peru), Carlos Menem (Argentina), and President Jimmy Carter (U.S.) were among BCCI's best promoters. Masihur Rahman, former chief financial officer of BCCI, boasted that while on a visit to Ghana with Abedi, Carter praised BCCI on national television. Rahman said, "It was a wonderful endorsement and it certainly helped us to get more business." Rahman further described how Lord Callaghan, a former British Prime Minister, "would take us to lunch to meet members of Parliament."[22]

Using BCCI funds, Ghaith Pharaon was able to gain control of several American financial institutions on behalf of BCCI. Officially he borrowed the money from BCCI but the Federal Reserve alleges that he was acting as Abedi's agent. He secretly bought the National Bank of Georgia and owned it from 1977 to 1982. By the mid- to late eighties, Pharaon was in financial trouble. His Saudi construction company, REDEC, was bankrupt, and he needed quick and large infusions of cash. In 1987, First American bought the National Bank of Georgia for at least $220 million, of which $150 million went directly to BCCI and helped Pharaon stay afloat. In 1986, Pharaon had been used by BCCI to purchase yet another bank. Using the Banque Arabe Internationale d'Investissements as its financial base, Pharaon bought the California-based Independence Bank of Encino for $23 million. Pharaon claimed to be the sole owner. However, U.S. government investigators claim that BCCI owned at least 25 percent of the bank. In 1987, Pharaon, acting again as BCCI's covert agent, purchased 20 percent of common stock of Centrust Bank in Miami, Florida, for $12 million. Centrust collapsed eventually in the S&L scandal but Pharaon's investment was fully redeemed. Other investors lost at least 50 percent of their holdings in the bank. Centrust chairman, David Paul, contributed $30,000 to the Democratic Senatorial Campaign Committee (DSCC) at the time (1987) that Senator John Kerry's subcommittee began investigating BCCI. BCCI worked in tandem with leading figures in American cable television. In 1984 Robert Magness, the founder and chairman of the board of TeleCommunications, Inc. (TCI), the largest cable company in the United States, together with Larry Romrell, vice president of TCI, joined a small group that launched Capcom Financial Services, Ltd., an affiliate of BCCI. Capcom was an offshore investment trading company based in London with a desk at the Chicago Futures Exchange. According to an audit by Peat Marwick McLintock, Magness and Romrell borrowed $500,000 from BCCI. The audit revealed that "the funds were used to purchase interests in a futures-market brokerage concern that Capcom controlled in Chicago." In October 1989 Capcom was expelled from the Chicago market for "reckless and unbusinesslike dealings" and for laundering drug money for the Colombian Medellín cartel. BCCI gave more than $3 million through "artificial transactions" to a business associate of Romrell. The contact between Capcom and TCI was Kamal Adham, the former chief of Saudi intelligence and a BCCI principal. One of the founders of Capcom, Syed Ziauddin Akbar, a BCCI trader, boasted "we have got very good connections, very good people . . . we don't want to spoil or play with the name of these big people like Romrell . . . or Bob Magness of Denver, Colorado . . . No one has ever asked anything because they knew Romrell will not do anything wrong."[23] Romrell and Magness resigned after BCCI and Capcom were indicted in 1988 in Tampa, Florida, on money-laundering charges. They issued a public statement insisting that they were duped into investing into Capcom.

BCCI and Pharaon broke U.S. antitrust and banking regulations. They engaged in criminal activity by laundering drug money and participating in and funding illegal arms sales. The case of the Cayman Island branch of BCCI is particularly interesting, having receipted multimillion-dollar deposits from First American corresponding with the dates during which some of these activities took place.

In 1976, U.S. bank regulators turned down BCCI's attempt to buy the Chelsea National Bank in New York City. BCCI used the Gokals as a "front." Even then, rumors about BCCI's "dicey" operations were circulating.[24] In 1978, Pharaon began to acquire Bert Lance's National Bank of Georgia, for a mere $290 million. In 1979, U.S. regulators denied BCCI's request to purchase Financial General Bankshares (FGB) in Washington, D.C.

Clark Clifford, introduced by Lance, was retained by Abedi to assist BCCI in refiling its application for FGB to the Federal Reserve. Following the successful purchase in 1981, FGB was renamed First American, with Clifford as chairman and Robert Altman as president. This had been BCCI's intention all along. By secretly owning an American bank, BCCI could implement its financial strategy in the United States. Through First American and other fronts they purchased other banks and other businesses in the States. BCCI established its own lobbying arm in Washington, D.C., to influence government officials and politicians, including executives of organizations such as the International Monetary Fund and the World Bank. Located on K Street in northwest Washington, D.C. and headed by Sani Ahmad, a naturalized Pakistani, the office employed twenty-two people, mostly Pakistani. Ahmad was arrested on bribery charges in Washington, D.C., in January 1992.

Through First American, as well as independently, BCCI forged alliances with banks such as the New York Inter-maritime Bank in Geneva and Banca Nazionale del Lavoro (BNL) in Atlanta, Georgia. Christopher Drogoul, BNL's branch manager, and his assistant, Paul Von Wedel, were responsible for funneling $4 billion of U.S. agricultural subsidies into Saddam Hussein's war machine and they used BCCI and its affiliates in the process. BNL, like BCCI, issued letters of credit to facilitate the transfer of money and arms to Iraq. Iraqi officials used BCCI channels to deposit loans and kickbacks they received for military contracts at branches in Grand Cayman, Switzerland, and Luxembourg. Some of the money was siphoned off into the pockets of Saddam Hussein and his coterie of trusted foot soldiers.

BCCI also played a vital role in financing nuclear technology and chemical weapons development programs on behalf of Iraq and Libya. These programs were headed by Ishan Barbouti, an Iraqi businessman with interests and businesses in Western Europe and the United States. In the past few years Barbouti has been twice reported dead, most recently in 1991. Rumors abound that he is well, doing business as usual, traveling from Amman to London and from Tripoli to Baghdad.

A crucial part of BCCI's tactics was "to make an impact in the marketplace, to have contacts or relationships . . . with all the people who matter, whether in business circles, in academia, political circles, the administration, high net-worth individuals, you name it. We would develop relationships with everyone of consequence," testified Abdur Sakhia, former BCCI official, during hearings in the summer of 1991.[25]

Agha Hasan Abedi was introduced to former President Jimmy Carter in 1981 by Bert Lance, who brought Abedi to Plains, Georgia, to meet Carter and his wife, Rosalynn. Abedi and Carter became friends and Abedi arranged an $8 million donation to Carter's Global 2000 project. Abedi made his personal jet available to Carter on at least four occasions during which he accompanied the former President to Thailand, the Soviet Union, Hong Kong, Tibet, and other destinations. Carter, in turn, introduced Abedi to other heads of state, including Chinese leaders Deng Xiaoping and Zhao Ziyang, the King of Thailand, and James Callaghan, the former British Prime Minister. In an interview published in early August 1991, after the scandal broke, Abedi boasted, "All the top politicians and heads of state were my friends . . . I knew them all. . . . In [the] Caribbean . . . I knew the heads of state, I knew the Finance Ministers, I knew the governors of the central banks, I knew heads of all the major banks in the area, the heads of foreign banks, I knew the people in various official agencies like the Caribbean Development Bank, the Inter-American Development Bank, and the Organization of American States."[26] Deposed Panamanian leader Manuel Noriega, the late Philippine President Ferdinand Marcos, and Iraq's Saddam Hussein are but a few of BCCI's long list of clients.

In February 1979, at the height of the Iranian revolution, Andrew Young prophesied in the UN that "Khomeini will be somewhat of a saint when we get over this panic."[27] By the end of that year, Young had to resign as U.S. ambassador to the UN after his unauthorized meetings with the PLO leaked to the press. Apparently, Andrew Young's support for the Islamic revolution, the Arab cause, and Third World countries did not diminish with his resignation. He moved to Washington, D.C., where he opened a lobbying firm on behalf of his new constituency, the Third World. In 1980, to expand his business, he received a line of credit from the National Bank of Georgia (secretly owned by BCCI). However, in 1981, Young's credit line was transferred to BCCI directly. Abedi personally retained Young as a consultant for BCCI for $50,000 annually and in 1990, BCCI forgave a $150,000 loan given to Young while he was mayor of Atlanta.

Meanwhile, Iran began to settle terrorists into Europe. They were members of the so-called Strike Units (Goruh Zarbat). The Iranian fundamentalists also put in place an import-export network funded through BCCI. Mohammed Hammud, a Shiite Lebanese businessman who became a BCCI financier, provided important assistance for the network. For instance, Iran secretly owned the Qirtas Conserve Company in Shtura, Lebanon. The company shipped explosives concealed in food cans from Qirtas to Alissar, another import-export company the Iranian Shiites owned in Spain. The operation was sponsored by the Hammud family. The Hammuds were also mentioned in the United States in connection with BCCI investigations linking them to Orrin Hatch, Republican senator from Utah. Mohammed Hammud reportedly died in 1990, under mysterious circumstances. Many key operatives within the Iranian terrorist organizations were Lebanese Shiites; Mustaffah Hamad/Hammud, Mohammed's brother, coordinated Libyan covert operations in France. Consequently, all Iranian Shiite international organizations, officials, bankers, and international transportation companies took their orders directly from Tehran.

Following the Iranian revolution the activities of the official Iranian banks—Bank Sepah Iran and Bank Melli—were curtailed, and BCCI among others stepped in. By then, Agha Hasan Abedi, whose commitment to Islamic revivalism was well known, had already established BCCI in the West with headquarters in London. The Gokal brothers, Abedi's associates, had proved their support for Iran. Back in 1969, Hussein Gokal, the eldest, was hanged in Baghdad as a spy for Iran, and the surviving brothers—Mustafa, Abbas, and Murtaza—went on to become the owners of Gulf Shipping Lines in 1969. Funded by BCCI, their company was the major player in delivering strategic and nuclear weapons from the West to Iran and other Muslim countries. Mustafa Gokal served as Zia ul-Haq's adviser until the Pakistani president died in a plane crash orchestrated by the KGB and the Gokals fled to Europe.

During the sixties and early seventies Immam Mussa Sadar, a Lebanese Shiite educated in Iran, conducted missionary work among the long oppressed Shiite minority in Lebanon. He organized the "disadvantaged on earth" later known as the HizbAllah. In the beginning the HizbAllah centered their efforts at the Lebanese border against Israel and Israeli targets. Despite repeated Israeli warnings that this brand of terrorism would spread worldwide if not stopped, the West chose to ignore the warnings. Before long the HizbAllah were carrying out suicide bombings, such as the 1983 attacks on the U.S. embassy in Beirut and the U.S. marine headquarters building, killing hundreds of people; hijackings; hostage taking; and other spectacular acts of terrorism around the world. The ensuing fame created a problem for the Shiites in Tehran because it focused world attention on Iranian-supported terrorism. Iranian companies, organizations, and Shiites previously available openly to promote those activities were suddenly suspect.

The success of Iranian terrorism in Europe whetted Colonel Qaddafi's appetite. By June 1984, he stepped up his European activities. In addition to "eliminating" his opposition, he offered Iran unlimited funds in return for the cooperation of the Iranian terrorist network. Thus, Libya joined the campaign against the West. Qaddafi joined the Iranian-led campaign against the West with money and access to local assets and agents. He supported Islamic associations throughout Western Europe, in countries such as France, Italy, Belgium, and Germany, which served as fronts for dormant terrorist networks.

In his book *Unholy Alliance*,[28] Warren Kinsella, a Canadian investigator for the Canadian Parliament's Finance Committee, describes how BCCI funneled money to Libyan terrorists and front groups in the United States and Canada. Anwar Khan, former manager of the Ottawa branch of Bank of Credit and Commerce Canada (BCCC), testified that during 1987 and 1988 the bank transferred deposits ranging from $200,000 to $1.7 million from Libya. The funds were wired from Libya via other Canadian banks for the account of Manara Travel Agency, Inc., a company incorporated in Washington, D.C., and established by Mussa Hawamdah in 1980. Manara later opened a branch in Ottawa. First American branches in New York and Washington were used as conduits. The money, according to the U.S. Attorney's Office, was disbursed by the People's Committee for Libyan students in McLean, Virginia. The People's Committee was established to support Libyan Students in the United States and was exempt from the economic embargo against Libya. A special license from the Treasury Department's Office of Foreign Assets Control allowed Libya to maintain accounts at First American Bank in Washington, D.C. The bank limit for checks not requiring special approval was restricted to $2,000. Although the license was given only to First American, Mr. Khan testified that Riggs National Bank in Washington, D.C. also received funds. In July 1988 officers of Manara Travel and the People's Committee were arrested and charged with being fronts for Libyan intelligence. The U.S. Attorney in Alexandria, Virginia, charged that they funneled thousands of dollars to "dissident American groups and Libyan intelligence gathering activities." Manara provided free trips to Libya, financial support, and training in armed struggle against "American Imperialism and Zionism." Three hundred and fifty American citizens were taken by the Libyans to a "peace gathering" in Tripoli in April 1987 to commemorate the first anniversary of the U.S. bombing of Libya, among them delegates from Louis Farrakhan's Nation of Islam, the American Indian Movement, Hispanic and other antiwar groups, and the New Alliance Party, whose leader, Lenora Fulani, was a presidential candidate in 1988 and is running again in 1992. This was revealed in detail at hearings in late 1991 in Ottawa before the

Canadian Parliament's Finance Committee. The BCCI and Libyan connection was widely covered by the Canadian media whereas it received scant attention in the U.S. press. Christoph Halens of the Southam News Organization was also at the gathering in Tripoli. Under mysterious circumstances, he fell from his third-floor hotel window and died. At the time he was researching neofascist Libyan connections in Canada.[29] This happened during the time that the BCCI and First American were under investigation in relation to Libyan money transfers in Canada and Virginia. The BCCI branch in Florida was also under investigation for drug money-laundering and other illegal activities. Upon learning about the U.S. Customs investigation in Florida, Canadian investigators came to the United States in search of cooperation. They encountered a surprising lack of interest.

An even more interesting role that Manara played for the Libyans was as a cover for Neutron International Trading Co., a web of Libyan-owned companies formed for the illegal acquisition of equipment used in the development and production of chemical and biological weapons. Neutron had branches in Edmonton, Alberta, Canada, and in Brussels and Luxembourg. BCCI expedited many of their transactions, including false end-user certificates and credit lines, a habitual business practice for BCCI. Following the Libyan example, with Qaddafi's assistance, Iran began building a similar facility for the development of biological and chemical warfare in Gashwin. Its production line is expected to become operational by 1994. In addition to Libya, Iran is also actively cooperating with China and Pakistan in the development of the "Islamic bomb." BCCI and other banks and front-companies have facilitated the acquisition of needed materials. In late January 1992, Israel publicly exposed Iran's nuclear and other unconventional warfare plans and denounced European and especially German involvement.

Muammar Qaddafi is the most overtly radical leader committed to the acquisition of unconventional weapons, nuclear and chemical. Qaddafi knew that Libya lacked scientific and technological expertise but had an abundance of petro-dollars. In the early seventies he boasted, "a few years ago we could hardly manage to produce a squadron of fighter planes; tomorrow, we shall be able to buy an atom bomb and all its component parts." In January 1972 Bhutto expressed his opinion about the Islamic bomb: "this is a very serious political decision, which Pakistan must take, and perhaps all Third World countries must take one day . . ." In February 1974, Qaddafi and Pakistan's Zulfikar Ali Bhutto signed an agreement which promised massive Libyan support for the Pakistani military efforts in return for full access to the "Islamic bomb," and soon after Libya flooded Pakistan with money. It is reported that a plane carrying $100 million in cash landed in Islamabad to secure the procurement of illegal nuclear technology from the West.[30] Qaddafi also arranged to supply Pakistan via Libya with large quantities of uranium from Niger and other African countries in return for Libyan oil and cash. When Zia ul-Haq, the new Pakistani leader, came into power in the late seventies, he was reluctant to honor the former agreement with Libya. Instead he focused on the development of a *Pakistani* nuclear bomb. In July 1978 Zia stated, "China, India, the USSR, and Israel possess the atomic arm. No

Muslim country has any. If Pakistan had such a weapon, it would reinforce the power of the Muslim world."[31] Since then Zia has spoken of a "Pakistani bomb." But Qaddafi continued his pursuit of a nuclear bomb and in the mid-1980s, North Korea became Libya's most promising source of nuclear weapons. At the time, North Korea was a surrogate of both China and the Soviet Union, and its military nuclear program began in the fifties when then Premier Kim Il Sung sought to balance the U.S. nuclear presence in South Korea. In the beginning the nuclear program was sponsored by the U.S.S.R. and China. Both countries supplied technology, facilities, and training for the North Korean scientists. By the mid-seventies China had become the more prominent sponsor. In 1980 North Korea began construction of a 30-megawatt gas-cooled reactor to produce plutonium. The reactor was activated in February 1987. Strategic cooperation between North Korea, Libya, Syria, and Iran gradually increased over the past twenty years. All shared a commitment to confrontation with the United States. They were able to use Iranian Western-educated scientists, the existing North Korean nuclear program, and the Libyan clandestine procurement infrastructure to enhance the development of nuclear weapons.

What makes all of this significant is that Libya used front men and companies funded by BCCI and its branches throughout the world. BCCI was not the only bank involved in supporting these activities but it certainly was the most important.

"Most prominent among these businessmen were Mian Faruq, a Karachi businessman, and three individuals working under the assumed names, Mr. Arshad, Mr. Amjad, and

Mr. Abid, who conducted the procurement efforts in the U.S., Canada, UK, Switzerland, West Germany, Italy, France, and Holland. They concentrated on equipment and materials on export-control lists and sent the equipment first through Turkey, and later through more complex routes. For non-listed yet sensitive equipment, such as specialized machine tools for production of re-engineered equipment already in Pakistan, the Pakistanis established several front companies in Pakistan. The most important material was purchased in the name of the Karachi Textile Mills and the Machinery Coils Factory. BCCI Holdings of Luxembourg provided the required letters of credit directly and through several front institutions."[32]

BCCI was not only involved in criminal and clandestine activities. A large part of its holdings originated in normal banking business involving many small depositors, especially in Third World countries. BCCI maintained a vast network of personal and other contacts throughout the Third World available primarily to the Shiite and the fundamentalist community. It is only recently, with the ongoing investigations of BCCI and the political changes in Eastern European countries, that we have been allowed a glimpse into the intricacies of the Islamic/Arab conspiracy against the West and learned about mutual ventures between Communist regimes and Arab and Muslim radical states and organizations. In a 1987 White Paper prepared by the State Department Office of Counter Terrorism and released in the summer of 1991, the Abu Nidal Organization (ANO) and its connections with Eastern European government-owned companies were detailed. Among them was a commercial network for gray-arms transactions (SAS Foreign

Trade and Investment) operating from the INTRACO building in Warsaw, Poland. They brokered arms sales on behalf of the Polish Government, the ANO, and other similar organizations. An East German company, Zibado, exported arms and other commodities from East Germany to foreign buyers. Strangely enough, nothing was heard regarding the involvement of the founder of modern terrorism—the former U.S.S.R.

The Palestinian Liberation Organization (PLO), one of the Soviet Union's protégés, had bank accounts with BCCI from the start. Usually the PLO received loans, but in 1981, assisted by BCCI, the PLO lent $12 million to the Nicaraguan Government. Early on, the PLO started buying partnerships in airlines in Africa, Latin America, and other parts of the Third World with financial backing from Libya and other Arab countries, handled mainly by BCCI. In 1979, the PLO gave a Boeing 727 to the Nicaraguan national airline, Aeronica. Their investment in Aeronica grew until they owned 25 percent of the airline by the end of the Sandinistas' regime. They also invested in the duty-free store at Aeropuerto Internacional Las Nercedas, the international airport in Managua, Nicaragua. Most of their transactions were handled by BCCI. Their front man in Nicaragua was Carlos Zarouk (a Palestinian), then Nicaraguan Minister of Transportation.[33] The PLO's scheme for purchasing airlines and duty-free stores around the world was the result of George Hallak's strategems. It was with Hallak, an experienced Lebanese con man who was famous for obtaining illegal airline tickets and forged travel documents, that the PLO formed Caledonian Airlines in Beirut and Maldive Airways;[34] they were partners in Nigeria Airways and owned the duty-free shop at the Muritala Mohammed International Airport in Lagos, Nigeria. The PLO also had controlling interests in Air Zimbabwe at Harare International Airport in Zimbabwe and Kenya Airways and the duty-free shop in Jomo Kenyatta Airport in Nairobi. Owning airlines and duty-free stores in many places made it easier for the PLO and their affiliates to move arms and terrorists inconspicuously. SAMED, the arm of the PLO dealing with economic development, was established in 1970 and by 1973 was international in scope. SAMED had joint venture business agreements in agricultural farms, shoe factories, food processing plants and oil refineries with governments in Poland, Romania, Hungary, People's Republic of the Congo, Mali, Syria, the former German Democratic Republic (East Germany), the Sudan, Somalia, Yemen, Zaire, Uganda, and Jordan to name a few. SAMED worked closely but not exclusively with BCCI.

When Khomeini was in exile in Paris during the early seventies, members of the traditional Shiite families rallied around him. After his rise to power, he rewarded their support with lucrative Iranian-controlled smuggling businesses in locations such as West Africa. Simultaneously, the "cosmopolitan" Shiite commercial elite, already committed to the Shiite cause, sought closer ties with Khomeini and his allies.

During the early eighties, the Islamic infrastructure in Western Europe expanded dramatically. By the mid-eighties, there were Shiites everywhere in Western Europe, quietly infiltrating local Muslim communities. Their aim was to subvert them from the inside and eventually to gain control. A myriad of legal and quasi-legal institutions, including religious, cultural, and economic groups, concealed the dormant HizbAllah networks and served as a source of manpower for future recruitment of European-based terrorists. Led by Saudi Arabia, conservative Arab states pumped millions of dollars into these Islamic institutions, mainly through two banks: the Islamic Development Bank (IDB) and the Dar-al-Mal-al-Islam (DMI). Currently the bulk of the Sunni Muslim activities is under the supervision of Salem Azzam, the General Secretary of the London-based Islamic Conference, ostensibly Riyadh's closest ally. However, he has been part of the Iranian-controlled network since 1986.

Meanwhile, the Muslim Brotherhood, under the dynamic leadership of Hassan al-Turabi from Sudan, expanded its international operations. Although the HizbAllah and the brotherhood share the same commitment to establish an Islamic state worldwide, they differ in their approach to implementation of this idea. The HizbAllah insists on centralized leadership to promote the Islamic revolution while the Muslim Brotherhood acknowledge a phase for local movements to take responsibility for the promotion of Islam. By the late eighties the brotherhood had gained influence over several major Islamic financial institutions operating in the West, such as the Islamic Holding Company, the Jordanian-Islamic Bank, the Dubai Islamic Bank, and the Faisal Islamic Bank in Egypt. Subsequently, by early 1991, the brethren saw, in the establishment of Taqwa Bank of Algeria, the beginning of "a world bank for fundamentalists," designed to compete with Western financial institutions.

This idea also bore Iran's stamp. Indeed, Salem Azzam had been working on such a scheme since the mid-eighties. In addition, virtually all Iranian-support institutions such as student associations, humanitarian foundations, scholarships, international organizations and officials, bankers, and international transport companies received formal instructions from Teheran.

Under the cloak of these front groups, Iran and its allies formed a solid network for the conduct of international terrorism. Currently, Iranian headquarters in charge of European operations as well as the key organizational and transit bases are based in France. Terrorist activities are funded through international companies established by the Shiite international commercial elite, which are controlled by HizbAllah leaders who recycle the funds through Western banks. They also assist with venture capital for the establishment of small local businesses, like shops and restaurants within the émigré community. These, in turn, serve as fronts and centers for the recruitment of terrorists. For instance, the Ahl al-Bayt (the House of the Prophet) Islamic cultural center in France serves as a meeting and recruitment place for the HizbAllah. Mohammed Bakir Sayid Fadlallah, the brother of Ayatollah Mohammed Hussayn Fadlallah, leader of the Shiite militants in Lebanon, is in charge. In addition, he operates a religious bookstore used for covert communications and coordination with the HizbAllah. Bakir's activities are funded by Lebanese import-export companies run by his brother, and managed in Beirut and France by Lebanese Shiites who often use pseudonyms. The Fadlallahs have a monopoly on grain importation to Iran. They use the same channels to move large amounts of money to their network in France. A precondition for the success of these financial activities are banks with flexible services permitting the laundering and the transfer of unrecorded cash. The Hammuds from Lebanon were directly involved in these activities. One of the main Islamic fund-raising centers in France was in Evian where, according to BCCI documents, Mohammed Hammud had a large real estate holding mortgaged to BCCI's partially owned subsidiary in Geneva, Banque de Commerce et de Placements (BCP).

Some of the initial organization of Iranian intelligence and terrorist networks in the United Kingdom was led by Mohammad Reza Narachan, Iran's ambassador to London. By the early 1980s, the Iranians had succeeded in establishing a network in London. When the HizbAllah threatened British government buildings in early November 1984, a HizbAllah member explained: "We have people in place. They are just waiting for orders."

Subsequently, by 1985, London had become the SAVAMA's (the Iranian security services) primary center for intelligence collection and oversight of clandestine activities. Ayatollah Shahabadi, of the Islamic University, established London as an Iranian espionage center and carried out subversive activities on behalf of Tehran. BCCI supported his activities through its Western European branches.

In 1979 another company, "The International Metro," also established headquarters in London with a transportation office in Geneva. "The International Metro" was owned 51 percent by SAVAMA and 49 percent by Agha Hasan Abedi. This organization secretly established front companies throughout Europe, disguised as ordinary businesses. By August 1981 the Council of Ministers in Iran appropriated 1 billion rials to send HizbAllah members as students to the West, supervised covertly from London by the Shiites and BCCI.[35]

But Europe was not the only field of operation. The Shiite fundamentalists also increased their activities among Muslim communities in Africa. The Iranians were assisted by the large Lebanese Shiite community in the West African nation of Sierra Leone. Sheik Hussayn Shiachadin, the leader of that community, was Khomeini's representative in West Africa while Mehdi Hashemi traveled from London to Freetown, Sierra Leone's capital, to establish a SAVAMA center for all sub-Saharan operations. Sierra Leone became the hub for Shiite terrorism when the KGB conveniently stepped in.[36] Libya and Eastern European countries also joined, providing diplomatic fronts and commercial, financial, media, cultural, educational, and religious networks. Just how important West Africa is to the new system of international terrorism and to the intelligence services sponsoring it can be learned from recent events in Sierra Leone. By the mid-1980s Sierra Leone was riddled with corruption. The illegal smuggling and financial systems were safely in the hands of its 25,000-strong Lebanese community. Sierra Leone fronted for the acquisition of sophisticated weapon systems and electronic equipment for Middle Eastern terrorist organizations and East European intelligence services cooperating with them. Most of these acquisitions and supply operations were organized, financed, and supervised by Abu Nidal's people, led by Saamir Najmeddin through London's Park Lane branch of

BCCI, as reported in the Task Force on Terrorism and Unconventional Warfare, Fall 1991.[37]

The transformation of heretofore peaceable Sierra Leone into an international terrorist center began before Joseph Momoh seized power in 1985. Momoh promised swift eradication of the then prevailing corruption. His rise to power was allegedly supported by a Soviet émigré to Israel, international businessman and KGB mole, Shabtai Kalmanovitch, who had major business interests in Sierra Leone. While still maintaining close relations with the Lebanese community and Iran to ensure the flow of cheap oil, Momoh approached Israel for help in stabilizing the country's economy.

In Israel, Kalmanovitch[38] used his close ties with Israel's Labor party leadership to launch an intense lobbying effort to obtain contracts to assist Sierra Leone. He had come to Israel in 1971 after a lengthy "struggle" to emigrate. Armed with unlimited Soviet funds, Kalmanovitch developed successful businesses throughout the world and within ten years managed to insinuate himself into Israel's Labor party elite. He made friends at the highest levels of government and in military circles. Kalmanovitch exploited his political connections within the KGB and the Israeli Labor party, as well as his friendship with Momoh, to obtain contracts in Sierra Leone. His agenda, however, was to establish Sierra Leone as a base of operations for terrorists and the KGB. This heralded the beginning of his undoing.

LIAT,[39] the ad hoc company established by Kalmanovitch in Sierra Leone in 1986, engaged in a vast range of activities, including the establishment of a security network for Momoh and his aides and the promotion of various public sector development programs. Despite a promising beginning and Momoh's resolve in the face of rising political violence from Lebanese factions, the situation worsened—with an apparent assist from Kalmanovitch. By the end of 1987, some 90 percent of Sierra Leone's gold and diamond production and exports were controlled by illegal networks from the Lebanese Shiite community. BCCI was one bank that serviced this community. There were others. BCCI provided false end-user certificates for Abu Nidal's operatives and for other terrorist organizations. Reminiscent of scenes in Miami, Florida, individuals carrying shopping bags and cardboard boxes filled with money were frequently seen entering BCCI's branch in Freetown. No records were kept. Pretending to be traveling on behalf of Sierra Leone, Kalmanovitch traveled extensively to Eastern Europe, the Soviet Union, and other countries where he was spotted in the company of KGB operatives. LIAT ceased operations in January 1988 when the Israeli Secret Service in Tel Aviv announced the arrest of Kalmanovitch as a Soviet spy. He was tried behind closed doors and in December 1988 was sentenced to nine years in prison. Kalmanovitch, who successfully penetrated the Israeli political establishment, became the sacrificial lamb to enable the KGB to continue to maintain its stronghold in Sierra Leone. Kalmanovitch's end had no effect on the expansion of Shiite and other terrorist organizations in the sub-Saharan state.

The State Department White Paper, released in autumn 1991 at the BCCI hearings, confirmed the bank's involvement in aiding and abetting the Abu Nidal Organization

(ANO), headed by Sabri al-Banna' and its commercial front companies worldwide.[40] This documentation followed earlier revelations of Abu Nidal's account in BCCI London. On August 2, 1991, from Nicosia, Cyprus, the ANO issued a statement denying ties to BCCI. The group declared the bank closure "a swindle aimed at stealing Arab money."[41] Following the demise of Communist regimes in the Soviet Union and its Eastern Bloc surrogates, details revealing their support for Middle Eastern and other radical terrorist organizations have come to light. Information provided by the new governments in the area and BCCI's own documents have also revealed that Hungary, the former German Democratic Republic (East Germany), Romania, Poland, Bulgaria, Czechoslovakia, Yugoslavia, the People's Republic of China, North Korea, Cuba, and Nicaragua acted in cahoots with the ANO and other terrorist organizations.[42] For instance, ANO's commercial front in Warsaw, SAS Foreign Trade & Investment, was serviced through BCCI. The bank by then was heavily involved in the ANO and other Arab and revolutionary movements. SAS fronted mainly for illegal arms deals. It dealt heavily in arms trading in the Middle East and Africa and worked closely with the official Polish arms exporter CENZIN to broker arms transfers for the Polish Government.[43] The State Department White Paper provided evidence for the growing threat of narcoterrorism as "an international and frequently state-sponsored phenomenon."[44] In addition to the ANO, the Syrian Qassar family, headed by Munzir and his three brothers Ghassan, Haytham, and Mazin, dealt in guns and drugs out of Poland, Austria, and Spain with the knowledge of those governments. The Qassar brothers also dealt with Abu

Nidal's front company in Warsaw. When the Austrian police raided their Austrian office, the Qassar brothers moved their headquarters to Damascus but their office in Warsaw continued to operate. Their bank of choice was BCCI.[45]

BCCI's activities and those of the ANO covered much ground. Their goal was to establish a foothold in the Western Hemisphere. They found Peru to be a suitable host country. BCCI's expansion in Latin America and especially in Peru was motivated by the same Islamic anti-Western ideologies as those of Iran, Libya, and Syria. Peru, the major source for coca paste in the world, became the focal point of BCCI's drug-trafficking network and a major distributor of weapons originating in Eastern Bloc and Arab countries to local terrorist groups. Eventually, it was BCCI that cemented the symbiotic relationship between Peruvian terrorists and drug traffickers, setting the stage for the emergence of narco-terrorism in Peru. The Partido Communista del Peru por el Sendero Luminoso del Pensamiento de Jose Carlos Mariategui (Shining Path), the Peruvian Maoist terrorist organization, had taken over the upper Huallaga Valley, the major coca-growing area in Peru where it controlled the campesinos and the drug business. The Task Force on Terrorism and Unconventional Warfare reported, "Since the mid 1980s, BCCI had played a crucial, if primarily supportive role, in the expansion and consolidation of Peruvian narco-terrorism, and in solidifying its connections to international terrorism."[46] Led by Alan García, the Peruvian Government helped BCCI become a major force in the Peruvian economy during his 1985–90 administration. The Peruvian Government also assisted in BCCI's international arms deals. False end-user certificates were made readily available for BCCI by Peruvian officials. Ironically, BCCI's activities complemented one of the goals of the Shining Path—the "demoralization of the Yankee Imperialists."

By failing to acknowledge BCCI's involvement with Abu Nidal and the Shining Path in the early 1980s, the U.S. Government indirectly helped strengthen narco-terrorism in Peru and elsewhere. Isolating drug trafficking from terrorist activities was and still is one of the major foreign policy errors in the West.

BCCI's role in Peruvian narco-terrorism was significant and ranged from influencing presidential policies to educating terrorists. BCCI's banking procedures also played an important role in supporting the economic policies of President Alan García from 1985 through 1990. In return for his benevolence, President García was able to live well beyond his official means. In August 1991 the former president was officially accused by the House of Representatives of looting the country of as much as $50 million and moving that money from the Bank of Credit offices into foreign bank accounts. In late 1991 the Peruvian Supreme Court declared the charges unfounded.

During the Peruvian internal investigation $50 million were traced to Panamanian bank accounts maintained under the name of the former President's wife but the extent of Alan García's personal wealth is unknown. Approximately 25 percent of Peru's national hard currency reserve was on deposit with BCCI between 1985 and 1987, despite legal constraints limiting such deposits to not more than 10 percent with any one bank. According to the Manhattan District Attorney, two Peruvian officials were paid

$3 million to expedite the transactions and to overlook the transfer of reserve funds to a BCCI branch in Panama. The investigation failed to prove that Alan García had knowledge of both the bribes and the illegal deposits. He, together with BCCI, used these funds as collateral to obtain "favorable loans" from the International Monetary Fund (IMF) equivalent to half the amount on deposit. The loans from the IMF carried 1.5 percent more interest than standing rates. When President García announced that Peru would be unable to repay its debt as scheduled, BCCI stepped in and helped García conceal Peruvian assets overseas through a web of bogus companies and bank accounts. Reports in 1987 of BCCI's financial troubles forced the central bank to withdraw all the national reserves from BCCI. In December 1991, the Peruvian Supreme Court threw out the government's case against García for lack of evidence.[47]

The relationship between Peru and BCCI had other ramifications involving international arms deals. For example, Peruvian officials provided false end-user certificates to BCCI employees acting as arms brokers for major weapons deals. Asaf Ali, a Lebanese arms dealer and a good friend of Abedi, used those certificates in his acquisition of Dassault Mirage combat aircraft and related equipment for customers in the Gulf States, Libya, and Pakistan.[48] BCCI also played an important role in Peru's internal policies, undermining the internationally supported antidrug policy. Its connections with Peru's Shining Path on the one hand and Alan García on the other helped transform the Huallaga Valley, the center for the production of coca, into a state within a state. With BCCI acting as consultant, Shining Path introduced a fixed payment schedule for drug traffickers who came to Peru to purchase planeloads of drugs. They charged the traffickers $10,000 per landing and $15,000 for drug purchase permits. In return, Shining Path offered security and guidance to the drug traffickers. The illegal monies earned were deposited in accounts at BCCI for hefty commissions. The rest was used by Shining Path in the following proportions: 50 percent was devoted to the Shining Path national budget; 40 percent was for the expansion of the local infrastructure; the balance was divided between the local forces and the population.[49] The Department of Economic Works in the Armed Struggle was in charge of money transfers and transactions for the Shining Path. Based on BCCI's advice, Shining Path insisted that "all business must be conducted in U.S. dollars."[50] In 1988, the estimated revenue from the production of coca amounted to $28 billion, primarily funneled through BCCI. Economic hardship and declining earnings in foreign exchange made the narco-dollar the only commodity available to Lima's business community. By the end of 1991 at least 20 percent of Peru's legitimate GNP was generated from drug money. Legal exports generated only 1.4 percent of the GNP. BCCI provided its services in Peru for a sizable fee and high profits on exchange rates. To secure their money the corrupt Peruvian officials also kept it in BCCI's Panama branch. One of the consequences of BCCI's relationship with Shining Path was the expansion of urban warfare tactics and terrorism. Beginning in 1987, the Abu Nidal Organization (ANO) advised and trained Shining Path members in urban guerrilla warfare tactics. With logistic support from the ANO, Shining Path evolved from a rural revolutionary movement into a sophisticated urban army. It divided its forces into the Revolutionary Movement of the People's Defense (in charge of terrorist activities in urban areas) and the Revolutionary Front of the People's Defense (in charge of narco-terrorism in rural areas). International law enforcement agencies had no difficulty in seeing Abu Nidal's hand in the techniques and tactics used by Shining Path. Hussein Bouzidi, a senior Abu Nidal operative, and two of his aides were arrested in Lima in 1988 following the bombing of the U.S. embassy. Atif Abu-Bakr, one of Abu Nidal's ex-deputies, stated that, "in 1989 he [Abu Nidal] made more than $4 million in Peru."[51] This drug money was transferred to BCCI's London headquarters.

Hussein Bouzidi and his acolytes were released from prison in the spring of 1990. A few months later they led an assassination attempt on Yaacov Hasson Ichab, the executive director of human relations for the Jewish community in Peru. When arrested for the attempt Bouzidi had a hit list in his possession, which included Hasson's name.

The Shining Path terrorist campaign went into high gear before the 1990 presidential elections. Alberto Fujimori, Peru's new president, promised to fight terrorism and to improve the defunct economy. But to obtain U.S. financial support his policy had to include a program to eliminate coca production. With this plan in place, a bilateral antidrug accord between the United States and Peru was signed on May 14, 1991. The UN joined in an agreement to supervise Peru's antidrug campaign in July 1991. Narco-terrorism and corruption had distorted the Peruvian economy to the extent that it was impossible to implement Fujimori's plans without taking the necessary steps to change Peru's social and economic infrastructure. One year after Fujimori took office, Hernando de Soto, his top adviser, resigned. His letter of resignation carried a stinging attack on the new government's continuing involvement in drug trafficking. On April 6, 1992, following Fujimori's dissolution of the Peruvian congress, the U.S. condemned his actions as "unjustified" and "unconstitutional" and suspended its aid to Peru. In the meantime, murder, kidnapping, and bombings by the Shining Path have continued to plague Peru along with an outbreak of cholera. A French research institute in Paris reported that cholera first appeared in the Huallaga Valley and spread along the drug-trafficking trail. Over a period of eleven years 22,000 Peruvians, mostly campesinos, were killed in the political strife. During the Gulf War, Shining Path led virulent anti-West, pro–Saddam Hussein demonstrations during which it bombed U.S. and other Western diplomatic and commercial facilities. Investigators concluded that the bombing techniques were those commonly used by Abu Nidal. The ANO took advantage of drug-trafficking routes to the United States and used BCCI and its branches to launder money and transfer funds. The ANO, the Shining Path, and BCCI shared the same goal, combating imperialism, although their ideology was different. Abu Nidal's cooperation with drug traffickers in Peru and other Latin American countries helped set up a dormant terrorist infrastructure in the Western Hemisphere and more specifically in the United States.

The unfolding of the BCCI scandal exposed the bank's unique role in supporting myriad Iranian and other anti-

West terrorist states and organizations' clandestine activities ranging from the illegal acquisition of weapons to international terrorism. In the aftermath of the Gulf War and the release of the hostages, rapprochement between the United States and Iran is well underway. Yet just before the war the House Republican Research Committee, for the Task Force on Terrorism and Unconventional Warfare, issued the following warning: "The Iranian threat is expressed not only in terrorism but also in the decay caused by the pursuit of profits and double dealing that undermines and destroys the political life of Western democracy."[52] Acting through the Lebanese cosmopolitan Shiite elite, which rallied to the HizbAllah flag, BCCI made it all possible.

Although the U.S. and British governments were aware of banking fraud, irregularities, and other illegal activities of BCCI, nothing happened until the Bank of England shut it down in July 1991. It was only in the aftermath of the Gulf War that BCCI became the centerpiece of the biggest banking scandal to date. BCCI's illicit activities, such as secret takeover of U.S. banking institutions, fraud, and money-laundering, were not the motivating factors behind the American and British banking establishments when they decided to close BCCI. They took advantage of the victory in the Gulf to diminish the influence and power of BCCI in Third World countries and to dismantle its network in the West. The threat posed by BCCI lay in the unique banking structure that effectively fused Saudi capital and Islamic banking institutions.

It didn't take long for BCCI's activities to raise a few eyebrows in the international banking community. But the temptation for quick and easy money was irresistible to a few non-Muslim leaders in various nations who deposited their central banks' funds with BCCI. The bank took advantage of the situation to effectively control those communities—often through blackmail. This control enabled the bank to implement the Muslim fundamentalist "agenda" in a particular locality. The Muslim fundamentalist agenda is very clearly expressed in *The Chapter of Allah, The Platform of the Islamic Resistance Movement* (Hamas): "Under the wings of Islam, coexistence is possible with members of other faiths. When Islam does not prevail then bigotry, hatred, controversy, corruption and oppression prevail."[53]

Since the collapse of the bank, BCCI's Abu Dhabi subsidiary continued trading under a different name as the central bank of the UAE. It has been estimated that deposits held at BCCI's UAE branches are as high as $2 billion. The central bank of the UAE is back on its feet and steps for paying depositors of the failed BCCI are now being negotiated.

What Abedi put in place through BCCI was allowed to continue for nineteen years while the world banking community and many governments sat back and watched and sometimes contributed to its nefarious schemes. BCCI was not the only bank involved in such wide-ranging corruption and evil deeds but it was the largest and the most obvious. The closing of BCCI does not mean an end to the prevailing corruption, lack of supervision, and disinterest of international regulatory agencies. Although capitalism and the free market economy system have been declared winners, the international monetary system must accept regulation and control to prevent another BCCI.

The Colombianization of the United States:

ABDICATING TO THE NARCOCRACY[1]

Once widespread corruption in both civic and personal affairs
becomes established, reestablishment of the necessary
equilibrium in affairs of state is nearly impossible because the
rise of corruption means that the [republic] already is lost when
both its leaders and its ordinary citizens lack civic virtue.

—MONTESQUIEU, *Spirit of the Laws*, 1748

Cast of Characters

Fidel Castro—Cuba's dictator

Fernando Ravelo-Renedo—Cuba's ambassador to Bogotá

Belisario Betancur—former president of Colombia (1982–1986)

Virgilio Barco—Betancur's successor (1986–1990)

César Gaviria—current president of Colombia (1990–)

Luís Carlos Galán—Liberal Party vice-presidential nominee who was murdered in August 1989

José Gonzalo Rodríguez Gacha—one of the leaders of the Medellín cartel, also known as "the Mexican"

Antonis Navarro Wolff—leader of M-19

Carlos Ossa Escobar—member of the Monetary Council of the Bank of The Republic

Retired Colonel Augusto Bahamon—former commander of the Fourth Brigade in Medellín, author of *My War in Medellín*

Tomomitsu Oba—Japanese financial adviser

William von Raab—former U.S. Commissioner of Customs

Herman Siles Zuazo—former Bolivian president

Garcia Meza and Luis Arce Gomez—former Bolivian military men and notorious drug traffickers

Klaus Barbie—infamous Nazi living in Bolivia was employed by drug traffickers to manage security and extradited to France during Reagan administration. Tried and convicted in France and died in prison in 1991.

José Blandon—former consul general of Panama to the United States

General Manuel Noriega—deposed Panamanian dictator convicted in the United States on drug-trafficking and money-laundering charges

Guillermo Endara—lawyer and Noriega's successor

Tomas Cabal—brave local reporter in Panama

Augusto Falcon and Salvador Magluta—Cuban-American drug traffickers based in Miami

Henry Gonzalez—chairman of the House Banking Committee

Alan Greenspan—chairman of the Federal Reserve

Pietro Banas—American correspondent for *Il Mondo*

THE AMERICAN PUBLIC has ceased to believe that law enforcement can regulate and control the drug problem. To wit: even those assigned by the government to investigate money-laundering shrug their shoulders in utter discouragement. Even high-level officials admit, "looking too closely into this issue will threaten the economic stability of the U.S. and other countries."[2] In other words, government officials merely denounce money-laundering, but do little to stop it. What Colombia and other drug-producing countries "matter of factly" argue is that so long as there is a demand for drugs, they will continue to supply them. However, the argument can be made that Latin American governments helped create the markets.

During 1990 and 1991, corruption and fraud seemed to reach epidemic proportions. In addition to the S&L scandal, large-scale fraudulent activities and embezzlement were discovered in workers' compensation systems, insurance companies, and brokerage houses. Violent crimes increased 10 percent in the first half of 1991, according to the FBI, and the United States was labeled "the most violent and self-destructive nation on earth."[3] More than 24,000 people were murdered in the United States during 1991, and Washington, D.C., continued to be the per capita murder capital of the United States. The United States has the highest known incarceration rate in the world: 426 prisoners per 100,000. Cocaine users rose from 1.6 million in

1990, to 1.9 million in 1991, according to the National Household Survey on Drug Abuse (December 18, 1991). Drug-related emergency room visits jumped 12 percent, and the number of unemployed drug users went from 2.9 million to 3.8 million. Drug users are also notably younger than before (starting between the ages of twelve and seventeen) and the number of weekly cocaine users has grown by one third, mainly among those aged thirty-five and older. Altogether, the FBI reported that 37 percent of the U.S. population used illicit drugs at least once!

Another factor contributing to the money-laundering problem in the United States is the presence of 294 foreign banks from over sixty countries, operating in sixteen different states. The regulatory system apparently does not function well owing to a shortage of qualified examiners. A good example is the Atlanta branch of Italy's Banco Nazionale de Lavoro (BNL), charged in 1991 with funneling $2 billion to Saddam Hussein's war machine. The money was originally intended for agricultural loans. "After news of the scandal broke, federal examiners, looking at BNL's operations in Atlanta, gave the office the lowest possible rating, and reported that they would have given a lower rating if there had been such a thing."[4] Henry Gonzalez, the chairman of the House Banking Committee, wrote in a letter to Alan Greenspan (chairman of the Federal Reserve): "Given the magnitude of the criminal activities involving BNL and BCCI, the Banking Committee is seriously troubled by the continuing revelations of misdeeds by foreign banks operating in the U.S., and the apparent lack of oversight by the Federal Reserve and the states responsible for regulating foreign banking entities."[5] As Pietro Banas, from

Il Mondo speculated, "Often during crises such as BNL-Atlanta, and BCCI, the Federal Reserve has given the impression of being very slow to act. It remains to be seen how much prudence demonstrated by the Fed is attributable to the pressure imposed from above for reasons of 'National Security,' a vague term which encompasses everything from the political interests of those in office to the clandestine agenda of the CIA."[6]

The mid-seventies were the turning point both for Colombia's drug cartels, and for drug money-laundering activities in the United States. The state of Florida was the center of both activities. "Since the mid 70s, money laundering has become an entrenched feature of the state's economy. It is almost as if a financial network arose in tandem with the consolidation of the Colombian cocaine and marijuana cartels."[7]

The Florida/Caribbean Drug Enforcement Task Force indicted 773 offenders in 1990. The prediction that California or Texas would become prime drug-trafficking markets did not materialize. Florida continued to be the major drug-importing state, as well as the center for drug money-laundering; Miami had a $5.7 billion cash surplus in its banking system by the end of 1991.[8]

The magnitude of the drug problem in the United States, the enormous profits from drug trafficking combined with economic hardships, have created a fertile ground for declining moral values, escalating crime, growing public apathy, and corruption. The police, the courts, prosecutors, lawyers, mayors, city councilmen, and the entire political legal system of cities and governments alike have been affected. Many are suffering from a "double corruption," when the "corrupt official becomes a user and has a double stake in protecting the drug traffickers."[9] This is frightening and seems uncomfortably familiar. It has striking parallels to the decline of democracy in Colombia. "If somebody wants to go bad, there is nothing you can do to stop him."[10]

The greatest strategic difficulty for drug traffickers continues to be moving huge sums of money. The necessity to hide the source of the money has created many innovative ways to launder it. As I have illustrated throughout this book and in the following case histories, money laundering relies on an elaborate infrastructure within the international banking system itself, a network that includes bank accounts, trust companies, financial institutions, dummy corporations, and other "fixers" along the way.

Since the passage of drug money-laundering legislation in 1986, over 290 accountants, 151 CPAs, and 225 attorneys have been charged with laundering drug money. Most were convicted.[11]

The following examples illustrate how prevalent money laundering has become in the United States.

. . . To the Last Drop

One of the first major money-laundering cases in the United States, in 1983, well before the anti-drug money-laundering laws were enacted, was that of Eduardo Orozco-Prada. Assisted by partners in Seattle, Washington, and Boston, Orozco, the owner of Cirex International, a Colombian coffee-importing company in New York, successfully laundered $150 million in four years. The case drew public attention because John Z. DeLorean, the automobile entrepreneur, was implicated in the case—and later exonerated. Satchels filled with twenty-dollar bills were delivered to Orozco's New York offices on Wall Street where the bills were counted. The money was then deposited in a New York Citibank branch and subsequently transferred to eighteen different bank accounts in Colombia, Panama, and Switzerland. The bank manager, Fred Gamble, knowingly assisted Orozco with these transactions. He was later arrested and cooperated with the government. Orozco was found guilty.[12]

Housewarming Party

Timothy Brumlik, a multimillionaire from Seminole County, Florida, made his fortune in television stations and real estate. In September 1990, following a two-month investigation by law enforcement agents, Brumlik was arrested for scheming to launder $12 million in drug money using the sale of a condominium he owned to conceal the source of the money. He cooperated with the government and was fined $500,000.

Pot Luck

William Dean "Wig" Barrow, former Florida state senator (1968–72) and former president of the local bar society, was charged with transferring the proceeds from the sale of marijuana from Florida to Texas banks in return for a percentage of the profits. He was also charged with structuring deposits so as to avoid filing currency transaction reports.

The Secret Aerie

Robert B. Anderson, former Treasury Secretary, Navy Secretary, and Deputy Secretary of Defense in the Eisenhower administration (1957–61), was sentenced in June 1987 to one month in prison, five months house arrest, and five years' probation for tax evasion and for operating an illegal offshore bank, the Commercial Exchange Bank and Trust in Anguilla. The bank lost $4.4 million of its investors' money and laundered large amounts of cash on behalf of drug traffickers. Like Clark Clifford, the former Secretary of Defense in the Johnson administration who turned power broker in Washington, Anderson, upon retiring from government service, advised and sat on the board of major corporations. He also lobbied for and was a consultant to the Reverend Sun Myung Moon's Unification Church. Anderson blamed alcoholism for his downfall. Jim Wright, the former Speaker of the House, was one of the more influential political colleagues who wrote to the court on his behalf. Jim Wright resigned in 1989 following a House Ethics Committee investigation stemming from charges of ethical misconduct.[13]

Babes in Toyland

Only twenty-four years old when he was arrested in New York, Thomas Mickens already owned a fleet of expensive cars, including a Rolls-Royce, twenty real estate holdings, among them houses, stores, and condominiums, and a yacht anchored in a secluded California cove. In January 1990, Mickens was sentenced to thirty-five years in prison for drug trafficking, money-laundering, and tax evasion. Mickens laundered the profits of his thriving drug business not through Swiss banks or offshore corporations, but by burying cash in legitimate investments. Mickens could not have amassed such wealth without the complicity of lawyers, accountants, merchants, and real estate agents. The Rolls-Royce was purchased for $165,000 cash, no questions asked. The dealer justified his action to the IRS by saying, "I'm not a cop. My business is to sell cars." Mickens had a flair for the dramatic. He had diamonds, sapphires, and emeralds implanted in his teeth. Had his tastes been less ostentatious, the police conceded, he may probably have gone on undetected.

Research and Development

Slight and self-effacing, bespectacled Bruce Perlowin enjoyed a "joint" or two on occasion. He did not look like the successful businessman he really was. When arrested in November 1985, he was on board an airplane headed for a "Yoga course in Detroit." Perlowin was charged with illegal sales of marijuana totaling $120 million during a ten-year period. What makes Perlowin's case interesting is how he operated. He retained a research firm in Berkeley, California, commissioning it to "determine what mistakes major drug dealers made and [reveal] the weak spots [of] law enforcement tactics." Using the results, he erected a counterintelligence barrier with state-of-the-art electronics, including antennas, beepers, and radar to evade detection. He even built a $3 million fortress in northern California's Mendocino County, complete with bulletproof walls, an electrified stairway, and a sophisticated communications center connecting him to his drug businesses around the world. Like most drug traffickers, Perlowin was helped by lawyers and accountants. The money was laundered through Las Vegas casinos, Panamanian corporations, banks in the Cayman Islands, and a trust in Luxembourg. Perlowin attributed his downfall to "an addiction to greed . . . [I] wanted to own everything." Perlowin told investigators how he handled large quantities of small bills. To avoid electronic detection at airports, five-, ten-, and twenty-dollar bills were packed in carry-on luggage. The money was flown to casinos in Las Vegas and, for a 4 percent commission, changed into one-hundred-dollar bills. From there the money was taken to Luxembourg, deposited in trusts, wired to Panamanian corporations and banks in the Cayman Islands, and put into legitimate nontaxable offshore bank accounts. Perlowin then borrowed against his own accounts for investment in the United States. Perlowin was paroled in 1992 and, looking for a job, sent around his résumé, in which he advertised his experience as a manager of "a fleet larger than most countries' navies . . . and a money-laundering ring that extended from Las Vegas to banks in the Cayman Islands." This experience helped him land a $25,000-a-year job with California-based Rainforest Products, Inc., an inporter of nuts from the rainforests of South America.[14]

Horsepower

Breeding racehorses offers Kentuckians one level of risk.
Laundering money, although more profitable, is far riskier.
Delmus "Bunt" Gross, an Irvine, Kentucky, car dealer,
learned the difference the hard way. He was convicted in
September 1989 for laundering drug proceeds through his
car dealership.

Vault Face

The first drug money-laundering case involving a bank's
central cash vault employee ended with an easy victory for
the government in April 1990. José O. López, the former
supervisor at the Los Angeles branch of Security Pacific
National Bank, agreed to launder $364,000 through the
cash vault for a 5 percent commission. The money, however, was clean. It had been given to him by undercover IRS
agents. Unaware, López opened fictitious bank accounts on
behalf of his clients, thus enabling the "drug traffickers" to
withdraw their profits at will. López and four of his bank
associates pleaded guilty and were convicted.

The Rubber Band

On a rainy day in November 1989 federal agents raided two
jewelry stores on Canal Street in New York's Chinatown
and arrested the owners, Richard So and his wife Nancy. At
the same time the Thai police raided two shipping companies in Bangkok and seized over 1,000 tons of heroin hidden in bales of rubber destined for a warehouse rented by

the Sos in Elmhurst, New York. This smuggling operation yielded at least $2 million a year from heroin sales in Chinatown. The Sos were caught when Nancy So, approached by an undercover agent, offered to transfer money from New York to Hong Kong in forty-eight hours without leaving a paper trail; her fee: a 5 percent commission. The Sos' arrest followed the nabbing of other businessmen in Chinatown, including restaurant owners.[15]

Snow Job

Even G-men are not immune to temptation. Three DEA agents led by Darnell Garcia were convicted of drug trafficking, money-laundering, theft, and tax evasion in Los Angeles in 1991. Beginning in 1983 Garcia, Wayne Countryman, and John Jackson, who turned state's evidence, began looting money and drugs confiscated in raids in the Los Angeles area. In his testimony Jackson revealed that Garcia had explained his operation and persuaded him to join in. "Garcia told me he preferred 'to steal money rather than drugs' because he could claim it was his. I told him I would rather steal money too." Together they looted heroin, cocaine, and millions of dollars. For a fee, Garcia also smuggled gold jewelry on behalf of Oro Aurora, an Italian jeweler who had a branch in Los Angeles. By 1986 the former DEA agents had accumulated so much money that they traveled to Switzerland and deposited $2 million in personal bank accounts. Garcia then moved the money to the Luxembourg branch of the Swiss Bank Corporation and continued to maintain a bank account at Union Bank of Switzerland. When Jackson and Countryman were arrested, Garcia fled to Europe. Garcia was arrested in the summer of 1989 in Luxembourg. He was extradited to the United States in February 1990. Garcia was also charged with leaking intelligence information to drug dealers and money launderers. During his trial, Garcia claimed that the charges against him had been fabricated in retaliation for an earlier dispute with the DEA during which he was fired, then reinstated. He further charged that he, Jackson, and Countryman were unfairly singled out because they were black. Garcia was unable to explain how he happened to have millions of dollars in bank accounts in Luxembourg and Switzerland. The jury convicted him on the evidence.

The Panama Canard

Linda Leary and her sons Richard and Paul Heilbrunn, of Indianapolis, were arrested in December 1989 for running drugs and laundering money. Fiftyish, Linda Leary, the former president of the Indianapolis League of Women Voters, was led in chains to court after she and her sons were extradited from Austria where they had sought refuge. Thirty-four other people were charged in connection with the same case for distributing at least 250,000 pounds of marijuana in Indiana, California, Connecticut, Washington, Alabama, Mississippi, Georgia, South Carolina, Florida, Michigan, and Virginia. Linda Leary's younger son, Paul, a commodity broker and columnist for a local business paper, was the ringleader. His brother Richard and their mother helped run the family cottage industry by setting up dummy corporations registered in The Bahamas and Panama where the money was laundered.[16]

All the President's Men

Another family business that spread from Brooklyn, New York, to Detroit and the Midwest involved Marann Hanna, her niece Liala Farah, and her nephews Elias Farah and Michael Latouf, who were arrested for laundering money for a multimillion-dollar heroin ring. The heroin was imported from Lebanon and Syria. The money was laundered by small banks in the United States, turned into cashier's checks, and carried back to Lebanon by courier where they were cashed at a local bank. The ringleader was a relative of Soloiman Franjiyeh, a former Christian president of Lebanon. The Franjiyehs are well known in the Middle East for their involvement in drug trafficking. The lingering war in Lebanon, now reduced to tenuous cease-fires by the Syrian takeover in October 1990, was in part fed by a feud over drug production and export in Lebanon's Bekáa Valley. In fact, "the war for the drug trade began within the 'Christian family': In 1978, under the direction of Bashir Gemayal, a small detachment of soldiers assassinated Tony Franjiyeh, son of the former Lebanese president. . . . This agreement between the Christian factions over equitable divisions of drug revenues soon followed."[17] The Franjiyehs did not limit their business to Lebanon. According to Australia's *Sydney Morning Herald*, "a link existed between the heroin importing racket and the Zgharta militia, headed by Soloiman Franjiyeh who was Lebanon's president from 1970–1976. This link was identified when 1.4 kilos of heroin were discovered by the New South Wales police."[18]

Soloiman Franjiyeh lost a libel suit in Paris in 1987. He

225

had sued Rémi Favret, a reporter, and the French magazine *Actuel* because of an article documenting his involvement in the drug trade. Franjiyeh's family scheme fell apart when Mohamad Damouri, another relative, was arrested at New York's JFK airport with 1.5 kilos of heroin in his possession. Damouri cooperated with the police and the ring was broken. Hanna was sentenced to twenty-four years in prison in May 1989.

Big Wheels

Fifteen people representing five major New York car dealers—Mercedes-Benz, Manhattan Gidron Ford, Manhattan Nissan, Bronx Acura, and Manhattan Mazda—were arrested in late 1990 for laundering drug money. Several bank accounts and thirty-one cars were also seized. The dealers accepted cash without filing the required IRS form (Form 8300). All except one were willing to accept false names and false I.D.s on papers. The deals were not made with floor salesmen but with the owners. Despite lingering government suspicion it took an undercover operation to set the indictments in motion.

By the end of 1991, almost 60 percent of the Massachusetts car dealerships failed to comply with IRS requirements to report cash transactions exceeding $10,000. None of these dealers was charged, although failure to report such transactions is common practice for laundering drug money.[19]

The following examples illustrate the international flavor that money-laundering brings to the United States.

Art Depraisal

In March 1991, on a sun-drenched street in the heart of Beverly Hills, the police confiscated the contents of an art gallery alleged to have been involved in an international drug ring. The seizure and the arrest of the gallery's Armenian owners stemmed from Operation Polar Cap, the largest drug money-laundering investigation ever conducted in the United States. The owners distributed cocaine from the gallery and laundered the proceeds by overvaluing the art in the gallery. For example, a painting for sale with a $60,000 price tag was later appraised by art experts to be worth only $800. Drug money made up the difference.

The Syrian Connection

Edmund Hurley, a prominent lawyer from Boston, laundered $5 million in drug money through The Bahamas on behalf of Salvatore Michael Caruana, a member of New England's Patriarca organized crime family. The March 1990 indictment uncovered schemes Hurley had devised to help his client evade taxes. Kendal Nottage, one of Bahamanian Prime Minister Lynden Pindling's "bagmen" and Nottage's wife Rubie were included in the indictment. Both the Nottages and Caruana are fugitives. The Nottages are safe in The Bahamas. Caruana's whereabouts are unknown. Caruana imported drugs from Syria and Lebanon reportedly in cooperation with a relative of Youssef Haider, a senior Syrian intelligence officer in charge of narco-terrorism on behalf of the Syrian Government, and used Hurley, the Nottages, and others to invest the money in corporations they had formed in The Bahamas.

All in the Family

In December 1990, Jorge Roca Suarez, the reputed Bolivian drug kingpin, and twenty-seven confederates were indicted in Los Angeles for running the "Santa Ana cartel," a multi-million-dollar cocaine-trafficking network, as well as for tax evasion, money-laundering, bank fraud, and conspiracy to export millions of dollars in U.S. currency. The organization was mostly composed of Roca's family, including his mother, sister, wife, and brothers, all of whom were permanent residents of the United States. In his late thirties at the time of his arrest, Roca's California assets were worth many millions of dollars, all of which were confiscated by the government. A DEA spokesman compared Roca's importance to the cocaine industry with that of U.S. Steel as a prime supplier to General Motors and Ford. Roca also supplied cocaine paste to Pablo Escobar in Colombia. His mother, Blanca Suarez, played a major role by shipping millions of dollars in drug proceeds from Los Angeles back to Bolivia. The money was usually moved through many different bank accounts, some located in Panama. Large sums were also packed and carried from the United States to Bolivia.

Hail Colombia

A former Colombian judge and senator, Luis Alfonso Pinto-Buitrago came to the United States in 1980 to seek a better life. He was shot and killed in 1985 after serving twenty-three months of a ten-year sentence for drug trafficking and money-laundering. Pinto's wife and their son, Alvaro, were also indicted but the charges against them were later dropped. Alvaro was killed soon after, presumably for turning state's evidence, as his father had done. The senior Pinto had laundered money for José Gonzalo Rodriguez Gacha, one of Colombia's drug kingpins, receiving a 2 to 3 percent commission for his efforts, which he promptly deposited in a Kentucky bank. He then converted the cash into checks, cashier's checks, and bank drafts, and transferred the money to different accounts in the United States, Panama, Canada, and Colombia. The Pinto investigation revealed a curious lack of cooperation between Canadian banks and the Royal Canadian Mounted Police (RCMP). In fact, the Montreal branch of the Royal Bank of Canada denied the RCMP permission to seize Pinto's accounts despite the evidence that the money was tainted. Canada's Supreme Court ruled in favor of the bank.

How many other S&L failures can be attributed to drug money-laundering activities is left to conjecture. It was disconcerting to hear representative John Conyers, Jr. (D-MI), saying in the summer of 1991 that, "the drug crisis is no longer on the front pages . . . drug use has gone down," only to compare U.S. ghettos to Andean villages where cocaine is produced. He might be right, on this last score, for the parallels between this nation's underclass and the poor in Third World, drug-producing countries become more evident. As for the leaders, it's business as usual. Major crimes in the United States are rising steadily, with more than 60 percent unreported to the police. Robbery, being the most prevalent crime, is usually drug-related.[20]

Americans tend to blame others for their problems and politicians nurture this attitude by invoking lofty moral values and principles while financial scandals erupt all around them. Although the United States has the harshest drug-trafficking and money-laundering laws and regulations, drug consumption is soaring and major crimes continue to rise. A comparison of all criminal activity in the United States suggests that corruption of the kind and measure innumerated in these pages is far from being episodic or incremental.

U.S. and Colombian history differ but there are alarming similarities in the consequences of a decade of drug trafficking on the moral fiber and democratic process in both nations.

Colombia, the oldest Latin American democracy, lost its independence in 1991. The driving force behind this metamorphosis was greed, and the vehicle, cocaine. Armed with untold financial resources, drug cartels have penetrated and corrupted the government, subverted commerce and industry, and torn apart the nation's social fabric.[21]

Colombia declared its independence in 1819. Throughout the nineteenth century it suffered fifty-two civil wars, most of them ignited by rivalries between the pro-clerical and the anticlerical and federalist pro-free trade forces. Personal animosity also contributed to the violence. Two of the bloodiest conflicts were the "Thousand Day War" (1899–1902) and "La Violencia" (1948–58) in which over

200,000 people lost their lives. The latter culminated in a new national front in which Liberal and Conservative parties shared government control. Democratically established, the coalition drew from as many different factions inside government as outside, a recipe derived of an easy compromise that engendered widespread discontent.

Colombia has had four constitutions. The first, in 1821, unified the country. The second (1886) revised the Río Negro Constitution of 1863 and marked an era of conservatism. Subsequent constitutional amendments contributed to an imbalance in political power, at times strengthening and at times diminishing the central government's authority. An artifact of an earlier constitution was the 1888 extradition treaty with the United States; the terms of the treaty made enforcement possible without separate rulings for each case by the judiciary. Ironically, this loophole would be later used as an excuse to nullify the very same treaty.

The current constitution, ratified in December 1991, canceled the extradition treaty with the United States and turned things around yet again. A striking feature of the new constitution gives blanket approval to the legalization of the drug trade. This surrender did not occur in a vacuum but was preceded by the murders of thousands of citizens, law enforcement personnel, reporters, politicians, even presidential candidates and judges. The violence was the result of thirty years of strife between the central government and leftist terrorist organizations, including Fuerzas Armadas Revolucionaries de Colombia (FARC), Movimiento 19 de Abril (M-19), Ejército Popular de Liberación (EPL), and Ejército de Liberación Nacional (ELN). In the late

231

seventies yet another violent force emerged in Colombia: the drug cartels.

In the early eighties an alliance between terrorists and drug traffickers began to solidify and take hold. At first the terrorists provided mostly physical *protection* to the drug traffickers, for which they were handsomely rewarded. The matchmaker in this marriage was Fidel Castro. Castro actively supported the revolutionary movements in Colombia and elsewhere. Always the pragmatist, he understood the important role drugs could play in funding insurgency. And it was with the help of the Cuban ambassador in Bogotá, Fernando Ravelo-Renedo, that Castro brought drug traffickers and terrorists together. For a fee, Castro allowed drug traffickers to use Cuba as a safe haven and a transit point between drug-producing Latin American nations and the United States. In return for his benevolence, he requested that the traffickers carry arms for the terrorist organizations he supported, such as the FARC and M-19. Despite Castro's support and political weight, the relationship between drug cartels and terrorists was volatile at best. With huge amounts of money at stake, greed would often temper or, equally as often, subvert both political and economic alliances. Infighting and jockeying for control soon convinced the terrorists that they could handle the drug business by themselves. This called for war, and violence soon spilled into the streets of Colombia. Political and economic destabilization combined to erode Colombia's social fabric and to corrupt its democratic institutions. The growing cocaine trade and rampant violence led to civic unrest, lawlessness, political and public apathy, and economic decline. It also led to increased government intervention, abuses by agents of the state, and escalating human rights violations.

The money that began to pour into Colombia in the early eighties was typically spent on personal luxury items, while some was reinvested in the production and distribution of cocaine. But it didn't take long for drug traffickers to indulge in political bribery and influence peddling. Policemen, politicians, and judges were bought off or killed. Many Colombians lost their lives. For even the most civic-minded, death was too high a price to pay. The choice between bribes and bullets further contributed to public lethargy and the growing power of the cartels, bolstered by the international community's indifference, helped drugs become the most widely traded commodity in the world. To paraphrase Carlos Lehder, the notorious drug trafficker who was sentenced in 1988 to 135 years in prison in the United States, "drugs are the atomic weapon of the Third World."

Colombia's drug cartels thus gained political influence through their enormous wealth and through raw intimidation. It was their economic clout that convinced regional and national politicians—including presidents—to legislate in their favor. Corruption and drugs spread throughout Colombia and spilled over its borders, contaminating its neighbors. The plague widened worldwide, and the United States became deeply infected.

Colombia's booming cocaine trade brought with it sudden riches, giving rise to a new class of rich and infamous who, unlike the traditional landowning elite, came from the lowest rungs of society. Seemingly inexhaustible, drug money fed the black market, augmenting Colombia's gross national product by a whopping one third. This, in turn, weakened Colombia's commercial and industrial infrastructure by giving drug production and export precedence over traditional means of economic expansion. Housing, schools, stadiums, and roads were developed in areas where traffickers lived and fastidiously kept up. Other neighborhoods were neglected. This blatant political favoritism sent clear signals to the constituency about the frailties of Colombian democracy.

As the drug commerce increased and more cocaine flooded the United States, several traffickers were extradited under heavy diplomatic and economic pressure from the States. At first, Colombian politicians and the media supported extradition to the United States as a way of diffusing the violence and weakening the traffickers. Over the years, however, many backers of the treaty were assassinated and support for extradition soon faded.

The first president to negotiate with terrorists and drug traffickers was Belisario Betancur (1982–86). He tried to produce "a political settlement . . . through amnesty and reincorporation in the political process." Negotiations broke down, however, when M-19 took over the Palace of Justice in Bogotá.[22] Betancur's successor, Virgilio Barco (1986–90), overwhelmed by a rising tide of violence and intimidation, and weakened by the growing complicity and corruption of public officials, continued to kowtow to his nation's criminals. Chaos ensued, and the government surrendered to drug traffickers and terrorists. The negotiations for the surrender were carried out secretly, while actual agreements were finalized after the election of César Gaviria, the current president.

Fortyish, the boyish-looking Gaviria holds degrees in economics. He likes rock music and tennis. A member of the very small Colombian middle class, his lack of ties to the ruling class was viewed as an asset by the elite who supported him. A Barco protégé, Gaviria was considered the best possible compromise candidate. His supporters hoped he would be able to negotiate with drug traffickers and terrorists, put an end to violence—and keep the drug trade intact. Not everyone was aware of this, not even some of the drug traffickers, and it took more deaths before negotiations culminated in the repeal of the extradition treaty with the United States.

In Colombia, one of the largest populations in Latin America, the gap between the rich and the poor, as in most Latin American countries, is wide and conspicuous. The wealthy upper class is small and influential. The poor make up the rest of Colombian society. The middle class, composed of bureaucrats, is small, and lacking in political clout. Socialism was the best thing to happen to the bourgeoisie in Latin America: it sired it. When the Liberal Gaviria was elected president, he was already well known in Colombia. He had held two cabinet posts during the Barco administration, first as Finance Minister, then as Minister of the Interior. He was also a vice-presidential candidate under Liberal party nominee Luís Carlos Galán.

By the time Galán was murdered in August 1989, the situation was already out of control. Forced to react, Barco's government launched an all-out war on drug traffickers. Many were killed on both sides. A major blow to the drug cartels was the killing of José Gonzalo Rodríguez Gacha in December 1989. Gacha, also known as "the Mexican," was one of the leaders of the Medellín cartel, and the first to be killed by the government. When President Gaviria took office in August 1990, the winds of change had begun to blow. In his inauguration speech, Gaviria made the distinction between narco-terrorism and the drug trade itself. The first spread violence and chaos and, therefore, had "to be fought without concessions." The drug trade was another matter. According to Gaviria, "drug trafficking is not a Colombian problem, it is an international problem." Although he did not call for the legalization of drugs, Gaviria argued that as long as there is a market for cocaine, it will be hard to convince the Colombian people that they shouldn't benefit from this commodity. He conveniently made a distinction between terrorism exercised by the revolutionary movements and the violence that follows drug trafficking. While not publicly endorsing the drug trade, he placated terrorist groups, acknowledging their existence as political entities but never challenging their activities.

Gaviria continued the negotiations Barco had begun with the terrorists. He was able to persuade most terrorist organizations to turn from violence to political advocacy, and to participate in the political process. And so they did—with a vengeance. Antonis Navarro Wolff, the leader of M-19, was elected to Parliament and became a cabinet minister. Wolff, who had been on Colombia's Most Wanted list, now stands a good chance of becoming the next president of Colombia. Like other reformed Communists elsewhere, Wolff now embraces capitalism and the free market system. He was instrumental in pushing through many changes including the repeal of Colombia's extradition treaty with the United States. But Wolff could not have acted alone nor could he be such a strong advocate in a vacuum. Many members of the Constitutional Assembly had been financed by Pablo Escobar and other cartel members. Drug fortunes bankrolled Colombia's constitutional backsliding. A videotape documenting a payoff by the cartel to members of the Constitutional Assembly was presented to Gaviria just days before the assembly voided the extradition treaty with the United States. Gaviria did nothing.

In reality, the extradition treaty has seldom been enforced. Claiming that the *gringos* were interfering in Colombia's domestic affairs, drug traffickers fomented demonstrations and sponsored a massive media blitz to enlist public support against the treaty. Their efforts succeeded. The treaty was declared null and void in June 1991. This spelled the end of democracy in Colombia, a nation now devoured by "narcocracy."

Colombia's cartels control about 80 percent of the world's cocaine market and have recently expanded into heroin.[23] In round figures, this represents more than $1 trillion a year wholesale. Conservative estimates put Colombia's drug revenues in 1990 at about $6 billion,[24] on a wholesale basis, much of which was converted to pesos.[25] However, by the end of 1991, the DEA's estimate of Colombia's revenue from the drug trade was up to $30 billion. Was this increase the result of the growing global drug trade or was this the result of the legalization of foreign bank accounts in Colombia? A five-fold increase in one year![26] Colombia is one of the few countries in Latin America able to repay its foreign debt. Recent changes in monetary laws have eliminated regulations controlling foreign exchange—including the disclosure of the source of the money—thus allowing Colombian nationals to maintain U.S. dollar or other currency accounts in Colombian banks. It is now more profitable to exchange U.S. dollars at banks than on the black market. Naturally, this has caused the black market to shrink. In January 1992 1 U.S. dollar was worth 220 pesos at the official bank rate of exchange whereas it bought only 400 pesos on the black market. The currency law changes bring more dollars than ever into the Colombian government coffers and make it easier for drug traffickers to launder money. Colombian government officials claim that only pittances of drug money enter Colombia's economy. But in December 1991 a brave Colombian, Carlos Ossa Escobar, member of the Monetary Council of the Bank of The Republic, issued a public warning that Colombia's economy has become "drug dependent."[27]

In the meantime, the kind of egregious spending that drug money now affords Colombia is in strong evidence. It is common to see Baccarat chandeliers worth hundreds of thousands of dollars and castles in Spain, Swiss chalets, and Caribbean hideaways worth many millions of dollars advertised in Colombian newspapers and magazines. Colombia has become a major international market and a showcase for luxury items from furs to automobiles, jewelry to high-tech appliances. Much to the consternation of DEA and Colombian agents, drug traffickers have also contributed to the development of the most sophisticated telecommunications system in Latin America.

The first benefactor of the extradition treaty repeal was Pablo Escobar-Gaviria. No longer in fear of government sanctions, he and many of his colleagues negotiated a deal and turned themselves in. They were promised suspended or very lenient sentences. Six months later—in early 1992—they were still awaiting trial at a comfortable hacienda built by the government on land Escobar had purchased. Handpicked by Escobar, guards patrol adjacent acreage also bought by Escobar to further ensure his security. The Colombian Government never opposed any of these arrangements. While under house arrest, Escobar continues to monitor his global drug empire, enjoys his mother's cooking, and receives visits from his many girlfriends.

Retired Colonel Augusto Bahamon, the former commander of the Fourth Brigade in Medellín, published a book in December 1991 entitled *My War in Medellín*. In it, Bahamon tells how Escobar bought everything he wanted in Colombia. Bahamon claims to have written the book because he was "no longer interested in contributing to . . . lies . . . when I know that drug traffickers continue to run their business from prison." Bahamon and his family fled Colombia.[28]

Since Escobar's surrender, rumors about the Medellín cartel's demise and the growing power of the Cali cartel have flourished. Considering that money-laundering operations on behalf of both cartels have been led by the same organizations, it is doubtful that there is much difference between them. Despite the arrest of a few drug traffickers, and the confiscation of millions of dollars, Colombian drug cartels continue to ply their trade with impunity. During 1991, there were 9,714 Colombians arrested in twenty-four countries for drug trafficking, equivalent to 27 a day, or 1 every fifty minutes. Reportedly, the couriers are paid $10,000 for smuggling two kilos of cocaine.[29] Even U.S. law enforcement officials admit that there is little they can do about Colombia's drug trade: "We can disrupt the hell out of the cartel here, but if they are not under pressure in Colombia, then we have done nothing more than be bothersome."[30]

If drug trafficking is vilified and punished, the proceeds of this crime—drug money—are welcomed with open arms everywhere. Where have all the dollars gone? Dependent primarily on U.S. dollars, this commerce has created an artificial worldwide shortage of U.S. currency because the dollar has supplanted local currencies in many Third World countries. Most countries are able to track down about 80 percent of their national currencies at any given time. The U.S. Treasury can account for only 18 percent *at best*.[31] According to Tomomitsu Oba, a former Japanese financial adviser who addressed the annual meeting of the Asian Bankers Association (ABA) in Kuala Lumpur on December 10, 1991, this situation "leaves a projected financial gap of over $100 billion by 1992. This shortfall is traditionally financed by what the IMF [International Monetary Fund] calls 'errors and omissions' which is thought to include a high proportion of laundered drug money."[32]

Current estimates place the amount of drug money being laundered annually at $150 billion in the United States and $500 billion worldwide. Probably more accurate is an estimate of $1 trillion worldwide, of which 40 percent, or $400 billion, is laundered in the U.S.[33] This amount represents almost twice France's GNP. These drug revenues are either physically carried out or wire-transferred from the United

States to banks in Switzerland, Liechtenstein, Luxembourg, Austria, Hungary, Panama, Colombia, Argentina, The Bahamas, Austria, Nigeria, Pakistan, and Hong Kong. All of this is laundered money. Where is this money? Why is the United States drowning in oceans of red ink with so much money flowing in its veins? Why doesn't this money shore up the economy? Unlike the early 1980s when much of the laundered money was invested by drug cartels in U.S. real estate, industry, and automobiles, the lion's share of drug proceeds in recent years appears to have left the United States. U.S. banks do not have enough capital reserve to meet international banking regulations.[34] Since the biggest market for drugs is the United States, the dollar continues to be the most desirable currency and therefore the most sought-after commodity. Advanced technology enables the rapid transfer and exchange of dollars into local currencies. This empowers U.S. drug suppliers and traffickers with enormous economic resources that readily translate into political influence. This huge amount of money could not be channeled without political intervention.

In 1982 William von Raab, then U.S. Commissioner of Customs, attended a bankers' conference in Miami, Florida. By then drug money-laundering had become a serious problem in the United States, especially in Miami, and the banks had much to do with it. Not known for his tact, von Raab got the bankers' attention: "I am ashamed of all of you," he snapped. "You and your banks are engaging in sleaze." A sudden rustling and buzzing rose from the audience and the meeting was abruptly adjourned. That was just the beginning. The bankers were furious with this Washington bureaucrat who dared confront them. They complained to the Treasury Secretary and to the senators from Florida. The bankers wanted von Raab removed from his post. But the White House and the Senate decided to keep him on. His initiative resulted in antidrug money-laundering legislation now adopted worldwide.

In addition to bankers, von Raab's main focus should have been the lobbyists and policymakers in Washington and elsewhere. While bankers are responsible for returning as much profit as possible to their stockholders and investors, the rules and regulations governing banking business practices are dictated by politicians who are coddled by well-connected and solidly funded influence peddlers. So long as politicians have hidden political agendas and priorities, crime will prevail. Crime often requires money, large sums of money not readily available through legitimate channels. The largest pool of cash available in the world today is generated through drug trafficking. The second-largest money-making business is weapons. Arms deals are known to be an extension of foreign policy, and through terrorist and even legitimate governments such as Cuba and Syria, drug money has been used to fund these deals. As Antonio Farach, a Nicaraguan defector noted: "In the first place, drugs did not remain in Nicaragua; the drugs were destined for the U.S. Our youth would not be harmed, but rather the youth of our enemies. Therefore, the drugs were used as a political weapon against the U.S., the drug trafficking a very good economic benefit which we needed for our revolution. We wanted to provide food for our people with the suffering and death of the youth of the U.S."[35] This demonstrates how drugs have become a foreign policy tool to promote political objectives.

Since the late seventies, drug money has become an important feature in the local economies of many countries. With the expansion of the drug trade, drug money has become the world's most powerful commodity. Colombia and Panama exemplify the stranglehold of drugs on nations forsaken by the international community. In 1980 Bolivia was taken over by General Garcia Meza and Lieutenant Colonel Luis Arce Gomez, a cousin of the country's leading coca paste producer, Roberto Suarez Gomez, both notorious drug traffickers. Reverend Sun Myung Moon reportedly offered money in support of the coup, while the Nazi war criminal Klaus Barbie provided security.[36] Initially, the United States was unresponsive and it took tons of cocaine, many lives, and a lot of political pressure in Latin America for the U.S. Government to relent and assist in the hunt for drug traffickers. In May 1981, when Meza officially announced that Bolivia would eliminate its action against coca growers "because of the poor reception given its efforts by the consuming countries,"[37] the United States finally responded. The American pressure resulted in yet another military coup. However, within a year a new civilian coalition government headed by Hernan Siles Zuazo was established with international support. Garcia Meza and Arce Gomez escaped to Argentina and Klaus Barbie was extradited to France.[38] During the Reagan administration, a new procedure was enforced. It certified producing or intermediary countries for cooperating with the United States in drug eradication and interdiction programs. Decertification meant the reduction of foreign aid by 50 percent, and no help for debt relief. When the world tin market collapsed in 1985, the United States and international efforts for crop substitution programs in Bolivia completely failed, and cocaine production increased dramatically. Today, Bolivia is the second-largest supplier of coca paste in the world. The proceeds, which are estimated to be between $300 million and $400 million, could easily pay its annual debt bill, which, in 1988, was $360 million. Even Bolivian officials acknowledge the situation: "We have a successful crop substitution program; coca plants have been substituted for everything else."[39]

In Panama, drug trafficking and money-laundering continued for a much longer period of time. The U.S. invasion of Panama and the capture of Manuel Noriega have not helped matters.[40] Drug trafficking and money-laundering continue unabated. In his testimony before the House Subcommittee on Terrorism, Narcotics and International Operations in April 1988, José Blandon, the former consul general of Panama to the United States, described his country's money-laundering activities as follows: "The Panamanian Banking System, which was conceived precisely to make full use of our geographic position, lends itself, if the officials are corrupted, to such operations . . . Cash is transported by plane from the site where it is generated, say Miami or New York, to Panama . . . shipped in small denominations, the money is transferred to banks. . . . In the Republic of Panama, the National Bank acts as a clearing house for all cash transactions. Banks that have cash deposits exceeding their daily needs must send [it] to the National Bank. The National Bank then issues a note of credit to the corresponding bank, and the cash, if not used in the system, is sent by the National Bank to the U.S. Federal Reserve. In this process, when the National Bank sends the cash to the U.S. Reserve and it is deposited there, *then it is clean. . . .* During the period from 1980 to 1984, $3.5 billion in small denominations circulated from the National Bank of Panama to banks in Miami and New York and the U.S. Federal Reserve Bank to Panama."[41]

Noriega's successor, Guillermo Endara, has made things worse. Tomas Cabal, a local reporter, colorfully described the situation when he wrote: "They took Ali Baba, and left us with the forty thieves."[42] In January 1992, Endara's law firm was implicated in the largest drug-trafficking case in U.S. history. Endara and members of his law firm allegedly fronted for two Cuban-American drug traffickers, Augusto Falcon and Salvador Magluta, who had imported seventy-five tons of cocaine into the United States. Panamanian-registered companies laundered $2.13 billion. Endara's response was, "I never knew them, they never called our office." The DEA stated that at that time it could not find any connection between Endara's law firm and Falcon and Magluta. With such pervasive government corruption and drug trafficking on the rise, how much money is being laundered in Panama is anybody's guess.

No one has a monopoly on money-laundering. The huge sums of money made from the worldwide sale of drugs attest to the relative ease with which this commerce can be pursued. The U.S. dollar, and not drugs, has become the commodity of choice. The vast amounts of dollars flowing through the international pipeline, as well as the dramatic increase in U.S. currency counterfeiting, particularly in Southeast Asia, Africa, Eastern Europe, and Latin America, have created an omnipresence for the U.S. dollar that the Federal Reserve and the U.S. Treasury could never have anticipated or desired. Bankers in these parts of the world claim that it is exceptionally difficult to detect counterfeit dollars, harder yet to control their circulation because theirs are "cash societies," where anyone can "come in and make cash deposits of $200,000 or $800,000," with no questions asked.[43]

Money-laundering has come to be considered not only legitimate but respectable. But selling drugs is deemed criminal. Nothing has compromised the well-being of America as much as drug money. Neither forty years of Cold War nor Vietnam has had such a corrosive effect on the people and institutions of the United States as has drug trafficking. And money-laundering could not occur without the complicity of banks, accountants, and lawyers. When Sir Thomas More described Utopia, there were ". . . no lawyers among them for they considered them as a sort of people whose profession it is to disguise matters."[44]

Drug proceeds, like those from tax evasion, gambling, prostitution, S&L fraud, and embezzlement, also require a corruptible financial structure. The volume of laundered money has increased immensely in recent years, facilitated by the speed and flexibility of electronic banking. Almost everyone has a price and drug money can meet that price. The Clark Cliffords of the world are not alone in promoting special interest groups. "If you were to get BCCI's Rolodex for its influence peddlers, you would have the blue-chip list of Washington influence peddlers," according to William von Raab, former U.S. Commissioner of Customs.[45] Influence peddlers are generally bereft of moral allegiances, and often promote criminals and drug overlords who can afford to buy their way up to the top with calculated indifference.

In turn, those who are bought profoundly influence their country's legal system and economy. Colombia and Panama, among others, are virtually dominated by the drug trade. What happened to Colombia—rampant corruption of the oldest democratic society—may now be taking place in the United States.

Dirty money is ubiquitous, subverting corner grocery stores, local pharmacies, neighborhood auto dealers, banks and cambios, brokerage houses, factories, real estate, the entertainment industry, law enforcement, accountants, lawyers, judges, legislators, and eventually government itself. Never has so much money been available to so many criminals, supporters and protectors. What inspires the New York coffee importer, the Chinatown jeweler, the Beverly Hills art dealer, and the Florida multimillionaire, all of whom simply want to get richer, is greed. Contrary to popular belief, peddling drugs is not the exclusive domain of the poor seeking a way out of their poverty. Nor is it an activity restricted to ghettos or minorities. All too often it is the privileged and the well heeled who promote, distribute, and launder the profits from this illegal trade. Their motive is not necessity but avarice. White middle-class and Middle America are awash in drugs, from the Blue Mountains to Montana's big sky country, from Niagara Falls to the plains of Texas.

After two years of proclaiming success in the war on drugs and alleging declining drug use, the United States has been forced to face a reality that is quite different. By the end of 1991, according to NIDA's annual Household Survey, there were almost 2 million users of cocaine in the United States, a substantial increase from 1990.

While drug addiction, narcotics trafficking, and money-laundering are now an international phenomenon, the implications for the United States—politically and ethically—are enormous. Devoured by corruption, willingly seduced by easy money, the United States is rapidly changing from the "land of opportunity," prosperity, and freedom to a symbol of crime and degeneracy in the eyes of the world. Turpitude, violence, social alienation, unemployment, homelessness, apathy, inertia, and family dysfunction all contribute to undermining American institutions and may transform the United States from a superpower and a robust trading partner into a weak, unreliable, and thoroughly corruptible third-class nation.

While an ineluctable aspect of any free society, corruption by means of drugs and ultimately drug money has taken advantage of capitalism. Adam Smith's "invisible hand," a metaphor for enlightened self-interest in a free market society, is now stabbing itself in the back.

Appendix

Drug-Trafficking Routes

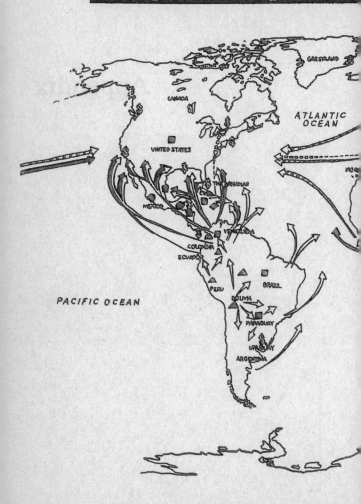

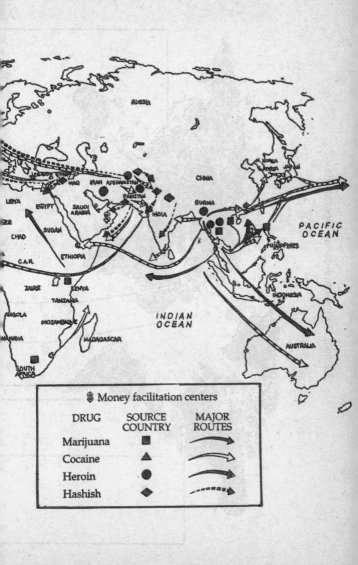

§ Money facilitation centers

DRUG	SOURCE COUNTRY	MAJOR ROUTES
Marijuana	■	→
Cocaine	▲	→
Heroin	●	→
Hashish	◆	→

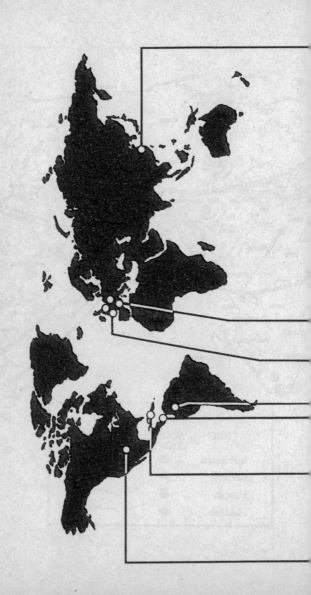

Gacha's Money-Laundering Operations

$2,000,000
- Xayar International
- Haverstock
- Gambia S.A.

$6,000,000
- Watford Investments
- Worcester Park Corp
- Xayar International
- Transcontinental Traders
- Hagar International
- Importadora Slavia
- Fiducorp
- Desarrollo e Inversiones Continentales

$39,400,000
- Transcontinental Traders
- First Interstate Ltd.
- Importadora Persico
- Union Enterprises
- Moorgate Securities
- Xayar International
- Comercial Rasero
- Desarrollo e Inversiones Continentales
- Watford Investments
- Haverstock
- Preston Trading
- Fiducorp
- Lynchburg Corp.
- Importadora Slavia
- Yaichi Corp.
- Continentales

GERMANY
- Transcontinental Traders
- Haverstock
- Fiducorp
- Desarrollo e Inversiones Continentales

SWITZERLAND $10,300,000
- First Interstate Ltd.
- Fiducorp
- Moorgate Securities
- Haverstock

ENGLAND $4,200,000
- First Interstate
- Fiducorp
- Importadora Slavia
- Xayar International
- Haverstock
- Watford Investments
- Desarrollo e Inversiones Continentales

AUSTRIA $5,900,000
- Lynchburg Corp
- Transcontinental Traders
- Xayar International
- Haverstock

ISLE OF MAN
- First Interstate
- Haverstock
- Pinner Investments

West Shore Corp.
- Grupo Latino de Inversiones
- Xayar International
- Fiducorp
- Transcontinental Traders
- Godavari Investments
- Desarrollo e Inversiones Continentales

PANAMA $22,000,000
- Pinner Investments
- Okito Investments
- Kayama Inc.
- IBD Investigations
- Gerencia Financiera
- Infinity Inc.
- Gambia Inc.
- Belize Trading
- Haverstock Ltd.
- Fiducorp

COLOMBIA $42,000,000
- Coordinadora Empresarial
- Inmobiliaria Andina
- Vehiculos Urbanos y Rurales
- Agricola Casa Nueva
- Agrolacteos de Antioquia
- Alianza de Inversiones
- Agropecuaria Santa Claudia
- Administradora de Muebles y Vehiculos
- Circuito Radial 2000
- Comercializadora Ganadera del Magdalena
- Inversiones Macib
- Union Comercial del Valle
- Construcciones y Disenos Urbanos
- Coordinadora Inmobiliaria
- Criadero La Chihuahua
- Ganaderia de Cria y Levante
- Automotores y Maquinaria SA

Gonzalo RODRIGUEZ Gacha

Transaction from the La Mina Case (Polar Cap) — I

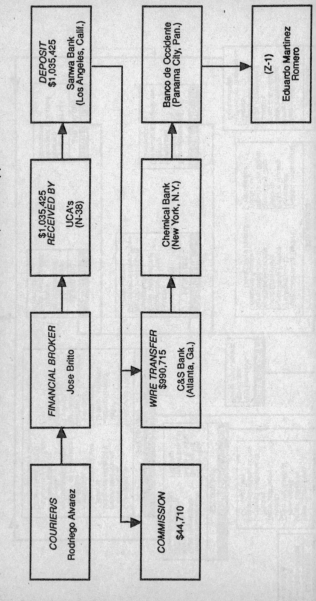

Transaction from the La Mina Case (Polar Cap) — II

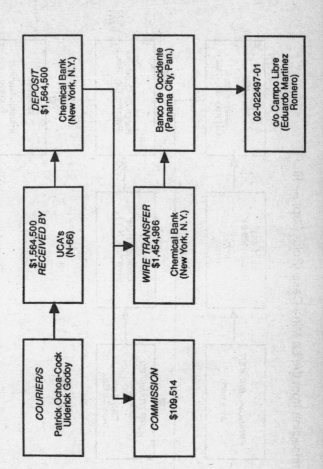

Transaction from the La Mina Case (Polar Cap) — III

COURIER/S	FINANCIAL BROKER	$271,458 RECEIVED BY	DEPOSIT $271,458	
Antonio Campos	Jose Britto	UCA's (N-76)	Sanwa Bank (Los Angeles, Calif.)	

| COMMISSION $12,216 | | WIRE TRANSFER $259,242 C&S Bank (Atlanta, Ga.) | Chemical Bank (New York, N.Y.) | Banco de Occidente (Panama City, Pan.) | $259,242 Eduardo Martinez Romero |

How Drugs Become Money

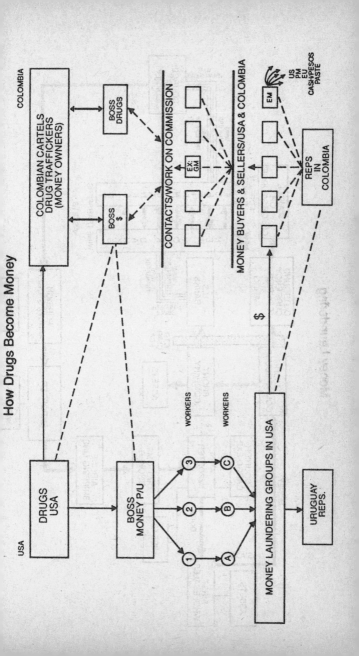

Money Laundering

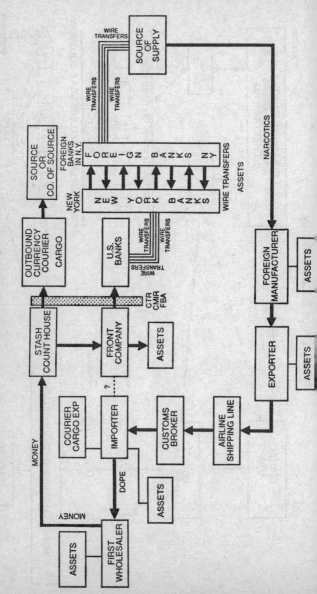

Notes

The Lansky Legacy: "It's Better in The Bahamas"

1. Despite Robert Lacey's claim in his new book *Little Man*, published in October 1991, that Lansky was never involved in drug trafficking or prostitution, there exists reliable evidence to the contrary. In conversation with Phillip Manual, a former congressional special investigator of organized crime, I was reassured that the evidence for Lansky's illegal dealings was ample and that Lacey must have been the victim of his close dealings with Lansky's former associates and family. For details of Lansky's Bahamas operations, see Hank Messick, *Lansky* (New York: G. P. Putnam, 1971), especially chaps. 14–16, pp. 221–277.

2. Athena Damianos, "New Leader Buoys the Opposition," *Financial Times*, July 10, 1990.

3. Messick, *Lansky*, pp. 232–33.

4. Royal Commission of Inquiry, vol. 1, Report, December 1984, p. 172.

5. For an extended examination of the Norman's Cay operation see Paul Eddy et al., "Paradise Lost," *The Sunday (London) Times*, September 29, 1985, especially pp. 34–39.

6. Ibid.

7. Ibid., p. 59.

8. See Royal Commission Report, pp. 123, 127.

9. Ibid.

10. Guy Gugliotta and Jeff Leen, *Kings of Cocaine* (New York: Simon & Schuster, 1989), p. 150.

11. The 1986 Department of State Report on Narcotics, p. 153.

12. Transcript of NBC report, September 5, 1983, pp. 3–4.

13. Ibid., pp. 4–5.

14. Ibid., p. 5.

15. Transcript of "Today" interview, September 12, 1983.

16. Ibid., and on September 7, transcript of "Today" interview, September 7, 1983.

17. Ibid.

18. See Supreme Court of Ontario, Lynden O. Pindling and National Broadcasting Company, Inc., Brian Ross et al. Affidavit of Gloria J. Epstein, Barrister and Solicitor, Municipality of Metropolitan Toronto, January 1986. For other details of the case, see *The Wall Street Journal*, October 9, 1989, p. B-4.

19. "A Call for Action, A Plea for Justice, A Personal Rebuttal and Request for Investigation from the Prime Minister of The Bahamas to the U.S. Attorney General," December 13, 1983.

20. Royal Commission Report, p. 3.

21. Ibid., pp. 2–5.

22. Ibid., p. 9.

23. It is also estimated that in the early 1980s, 85 percent of unemployed youth in The Bahamas had become addicted to free-based cocaine, but as in all of these estimates it must be acknowledged that in The Bahamas reliable statistics are unavailable. See the 1989 Department of State Report on Narcotics, p. 125.

24. See chap. 6 of the commission's report dealing with George Smith, pp. 103–9. See also pp. 32–37 for the effect on Bahamian society.

25. Ibid., p. 108.
26. Carl Hiaasen and Jim McGee, "Corruption in the Bahamas," *Miami Herald*, September 23, 1984.
27. Ibid.
28. Carl Hiaasen and Jim McGee, "Pindling's Friend Accused of Accepting Payoff," *Miami Herald*, September 23, 1984.
29. Royal Commission Report, p. 109.
30. Ibid., p. 53.
31. Ibid., p. 59.
32. Ibid.
33. William Marsden, "How Canadian Banks Are Used to 'Launder' Narcotics Millions: Cash Floods Bahamas Branches," *Montreal Gazette*, December 23, 1985.
34. Ibid.
35. Hiaasen and McGee, "Corruption in the Bahamas."
36. According to my confidential source.
37. Carl Hiaasen and Jim McGee, "A Nation for Sale. In The Bahamas Smugglers Say Everyone Has a Price," *Miami Herald*, September 23, 1984.
38. According to my confidential source, Vesco was pressured into providing the loans to purchase the office building owned by Lady Pindling.
39. Royal Commission Report, pp. 73–75.
40. See *The Sunday (London) Times*, September 29, 1985, p. 30.
41. Royal Commission Report, p. 73.
42. Ibid., p. 190.
43. Quoted in Ibid., p. 180.
44. Ibid., p. 183.
45. Ibid., p. 84.
46. Royal Commission's Minority Report, p. 303.
47. Ibid., p. 305.
48. Ibid., pp. 305–6.
49. Ibid., p. 306; *Sunday Times Magazine*, p. 30.
50. Royal Commission Report, p. 94.

51. Carl Hiaasen and Jim McGee, "Probe Ties Key Aide to Money-Laundering," *Miami Herald*, September 27, 1984.

52. Ibid.

53. Royal Commission Report, p. 98.

54. Ibid., pp. 99–100.

55. Jim McGee, "Bahamian Ex-Official Indicted on Drug-Related Charges," *Washington Post*, March 30, 1989.

56. Royal Commission Report, p. 278.

57. Carl Hiaasen and Jim McGee, "Bimini: Smuggler's Paradise Isle," *Miami Herald*, September 26, 1984.

58. Royal Commission Report, p. 209.

59. Ibid.

60. Marsden, "How Canadian Banks Are Used to 'Launder' Narcotics Fortunes."

61. See Royal Commission Report, p. 199 and p. 204.

62. Marsden, "How Canadian Banks Are Used to 'Launder' Narcotics Fortunes." See also the Royal Commission Report, p. 207.

63. Gray Thomas, "Smuggler Says He Bribed Bahamas Prime Minister," Reuters, February 16, 1988. Reuters tried to contact Pindling but he was not available to comment on these allegations.

64. The Racketeer Influenced and Corrupt Organization Act (RICO) was passed on October 7, 1970, largely the work of G. Robert Blakey, a law professor and a staff member of the McClellan Committee.

65. *The Sunday (London) Times Magazine*, September 29, 1985, pp. 42–43.

66. Hiaasen and McGee, "Bimini."

67. *The Sunday (London) Times*, September 29, 1985, p. 42.

68. Royal Commission Report, p. 13.

69. Marsden, "How Canadian Banks Are Used to 'Launder' Narcotics Fortunes."

70. Ibid.
71. For a background on Canadian economic interests in the Caribbean Commonwealth countries see Karl Levitt and Alister McIntyre, *Canada-West Indies Economic Relations* (Toronto: McGill University, The Centre for Developing-Areas Studies, 1967), especially pp. 24–27.
72. Marsden, "How Canadian Banks Are Used to 'Launder' Narcotics Fortunes." See also William Marsden, "Scotiabank Stonewalled U.S. Drug Smuggling Probes," *Montreal Gazette*, December 24, 1985.
73. Marsden, "How Canadian Banks Are Used to 'Launder' Narcotics Fortunes."
74. Ibid. See also Royal Commission Report, p. 208, and the Department of State 1988 Report on Narcotics, "The Bahamas," p. 152.
75. Quoted in Marsden, "How Canadian Banks Are Used to 'Launder' Narcotics Fortunes."
76. "How Drugs Turned the Tide Against Bahamas' Banks," *Business Week*, May 23, 1988.
77. See "Caribbean Closing the Clearing House," *Daily Telegraph* (London), January 11, 1990.
78. Royal Commission Report, pp. 199–200.
79. Ibid., p. 200.
80. See *The Wall Street Journal*, March 8, 1983, cited in Royal Commission Report, p. 200.
81. Royal Commission Report, p. 201.
82. Ibid., p. 205.
83. Ibid., p. 207.
84. Ibid., p. 210.
85. These sources prefer to remain anonymous.
86. See Don A. Schanche, "Bahamas Leader Denies Drug Ties," *Los Angeles Times*, March 5, 1989.
87. These officials have requested anonymity.

88. See the Department of State 1988 Report on Narcotics, "The Bahamas," p. 151.

89. "Pindling Cancels 'Today' Interview," *Washington Times*, October 10, 1989.

90. Philip Shenon, "Bahamas Leader Calls U.S. Drug Inquiry 'Baseless,'" *New York Times*, September 22, 1988; "Bahamas Asks for Investigation Head of Drug Probe," Reuters, September 22, 1988; Michael Isikoff, "Lobbying Firm to Drop Bahamian Account," *Washington Post*, April 6, 1989. As for Pindling's riposte, see the Department of State 1989 Report on Narcotics, "Bahamas," p. 122.

91. James Forrester, "Bahamas Outlines Plan to Wipe out Drug Barons' Cash Hoards," Reuters, October 23, 1989.

92. Douglas Jehl, "Bahamas Prime Minister Says U.S. Fails to Back Up Drug-War Pledge," *Los Angeles Times*, September 23, 1989; Don A. Schanche, "Caribbean States Want U.N. in Drug War," *Los Angeles Times*, October 23, 1989.

93. The Royal Commission's report released in December 1984 gives an excellent account of those relations. See especially, chap. 18, "Bahamas/United States Relations," pp. 261–73.

94. See, for example, the Department of State 1989 Narcotics Report, "The Bahamas," p. 121.

95. Jim Anderson, United Press International, March 1, 1989.

96. For example, Assistant Secretary of State for Narcotics Affairs Ann Wrobleski made clear in Senate Foreign Relations Committee hearings in 1989 that U.S. "domestic agencies [are] freely operating in the Bahamas . . ." including an "aggressive" U.S. Customs Service station at the Nassau and Freetown airports inspecting "both people and things." Quoted in the *Federal News Service*, April 5, 1989. Also see the 1989 State Department Report on Narcotics, "The Bahamas," p. 121; Jack Anderson and Dale Van Atta, "GOP Loyalty Rewarded," *Washington Post*, November 19, 1989;

and Marjorie Miller, "The Mexico Connection," *Los Angeles Times*, April 13, 1989.

97. In 1983, 363 foreigners were arrested on drug charges; in 1988, that number climbed to 1,261. In 1983 a little more than a ton of cocaine was seized; in 1988 the amount increased nearly fivefold. Schanche, "Bahamas Leader Denies Drug Ties." Also see the Department of State 1989 Report on Narcotics, "The Bahamas," pp. 121–22 and p. 125; and the Department of State 1986 Report on Narcotics, "The Bahamas," p. 158.

98. Michael Isikoff, "Blunt Assessment of Bolivia Ignored," *Washington Post*, March 1, 1990.

99. Elaine Shannon, "Why We're Facing a World of Noriegas," *Washington Post*, October 23, 1988. Also Steve Gerstel, "Senate Rejects Big Push to Punish Bahamas," United Press International, May 11, 1989.

100. Miller, "The Mexico Connection."

101. Royal Commission Report, pp. 263–64.

102. See the 1989 Department of State Narcotics Report, "The Bahamas," p. 124.

103. See the 1988 Department of State Narcotics Report, "The Bahamas," p. 152.

The Treasure of La Mina

1. From the verbatim transcript of videotaped conversations with Martinez, recorded by the government undercover agents.

2. Michael Isikoff, "Los Angeles Bank Surplus Linked to Drug Trade," *Washington Post*, March 19, 1990.

3. Federal Reserve surplus figures, as of March 1992. Baltimore–Washington, D.C., for example, reported a deficit of $851 million in 1989.

4. Evan Lowell Maxwell, "Gold, Drugs and Clean Cash," *Los Angeles Times*, February 18, 1990.

5. Interview with U.S. District Attorney Jean Kawhara, May 13, 1991.

6. Information on the Andonian brothers' holdings is found in the transcript of the United States District Court for the Central District of California, bill of indictment issued by the grand jury in February 1989, *United States of America* v. *Nazareth Andonian et al.*, pp. 3–5. In this indictment eighteen defendants were named, including the two Andonian brothers.

7. Ibid.

8. Ibid. As quoted by Evan Lowell Maxwell, *Los Angeles Times*, February 19, 1990.

9. Ibid.

10. James Ring Adams and Douglas Frantz, *A Full Service Bank* (New York: Pocket Books, 1992), pp. 141–42.

11. Transcript of indictment, *United States of America* v. *Nazareth Andonian et al.*, p. 21.

12. Maxwell, "Gold, Drugs and Clean Cash."

13. "Affidavit of Bruce R. Stephens," pp. 35–36. Stephens is an FBI special agent who assisted in the Polar Cap investigation.

14. Ibid., pp. 38–39 and pp. 41–42.

15. Ibid. Similar invoices with different Canadian and Mexican names were found on April 19 and May 20, indicating other gold purchases, always in cash.

16. Ibid., p. 42.

17. Ibid.

18. Ibid., p. 39.

19. Ibid., p. 11 and p. 14.

20. Ibid., pp. 40–41.

21. Affidavit of Special Agent Michael Orton, p. 41.

22. Ibid., p. 15.

23. Ibid., p. 40.
24. Ibid., p. 42 and p. 44. The surveillance did have a few hitches. On July 11, FBI technicians had to correct technical malfunctions in the camera covering the Andonians.
25. Stephens affidavit, p. 33.
26. Ibid., and Orton affidavit, p. 78 and pp. 84–85.
27. Ibid., p. 85.
28. Ibid., pp. 85–86.
29. Ibid., p. 70.
30. Ibid., pp. 70–71.
31. Ibid., p. 71.
32. Ibid., pp. 72–73, 81.
33. Stephens affidavit, p. 129.
34. Ibid., pp. 61–62.
35. Ibid., p. 98.
36. Ibid., p. 99.
37. Ibid., p. 74.
38. Ferris statement in U.S. District Court for the Northern District of Georgia, Atlanta Division, *United States of America* v. *Pablo Escobar-Gaviria,* "Affidavit of U.S. Drug Enforcement Administration Special Agent David C. Panek in Support of Request for Judicial Orders Seeking Seizure of and Information Relating to Drug Proceeds of the Medellín Cartel," p. 180.
39. Ibid.
40. Ibid., p. 181.
41. In 1987 alone some 20,000 kilos of gold were bought and sold and $250 million was laundered with the help of Ronel Refining. See Affidavit of David Panek about Carlos Desoretz, p. 165.
42. Ibid., pp. 182–183.
43. Ibid.
44. Ibid., pp. 186–87 and p. 189. In one of Ferris's early meet-

ings with Wanis Koyomejian, the Ropex owner proposed that Ronel generate false receipts for nonexistent gold sales. In his statement Ferris said he refused to do that. Later, he would terminate the connection to Koyomejian, but gave no date for this occurrence.

45. Ibid., p. 185.
46. Ibid., pp. 186–88. The Letra account was broken into three parts: Letra N.Y. for New York, Letra H.T. for Houston, Texas, and Letra L.A. for Los Angeles.
47. Ibid., p. 191.
48. Ibid., pp. 192–93.
49. Ibid., p. 196.
50. Ibid., p. 197 and p. 199.
51. Affidavit of David Panek about Carlos Desoretz, p. 178.
52. Nazareth Andonian at one of the meetings with Ferris described his gold trading arrangement in the London market. Affidavit of David Panek about Richard Ferris, pp. 208–10. Also see the statement about Carlos Desoretz in ibid., p. 168.
53. Affidavit of David Panek about Carlos Desoretz, p. 172.
54. Affidavit of David Panek about Richard Ferris, p. 206.
55. Affidavit of David Panek about Sergio Hochman in *United States of America* v. *Pablo Escobar-Gaviria*, pp. 102–3.
56. Ibid., pp. 105–6.
57. Ibid., p. 105.
58. Ibid., pp. 106–7. Vivas told Hochman he had another front company called Omensal, S.A.
59. Ibid., p. 108.
60. Ibid., p. 111.
61. Ibid., p. 108.
62. Affidavit of David Panek about Carlos Desoretz in ibid., p. 175.
63. Affidavit of David Panek about Sergio Hochman, p. 119.
64. Ibid., pp. 122–23.

65. Affidavit of DEA agent David C. Frank about Sergio Hochman, pp. 120–21. See also affidavit of Arthur Donelan, State and County of New York, March 28, 1989. Donelan was at the time a special agent for the U.S. Customs Service. The affidavit appears in *United States of America* v. *Letra, S.A., et al.*, United States District Court, Southern District of New York.

66. Affidavit of Panek about Hochman, p. 109.

67. Ibid., p. 110.

68. Ibid., pp. 119–20.

69. *United States of America* v. *Nazareth Andonian et al.*, United States District Court for the Central District of California, "Trial Memorandum," p. 16.

70. Ibid., pp. 113–14.

71. Ibid., p. 118. Also see affidavit of David Panek about Carlos Desoretz in ibid., p. 153.

72. Statement by DEA agent David C. Frank about Mario Tankazyan, pp. 129–30. See also *United States of America* v. *Nazareth Andonian et al.*, United States District Court for the Central District of California, "Trial Memorandum," p. 9.

73. Statement about Mario Tankazyan, pp. 135–36.

74. *United States of America* v. *Nazareth Andonian et al.*, "Trial Memorandum," p. 16.

75. Evan Lowell Maxwell, *Los Angeles Times*, February 18, 1990.

76. *United States of America* v. *Nazareth Andonian et al.*, "Trial Memorandum," pp. 14–15.

77. Affidavit of Arthur Donelan, Special Agent, U.S. Customs Service, New York, New York, March 28, 1989, p. 20.

78. Affidavit of Arthur Donelan, pp. 24–27; Michael Isikoff, "U.S. Sues Nine Banks in Drug Money-Laundering," *Washington Post*, March 30, 1989.

79. Affidavit of David Panek, p. 22 and p. 24.

80. Ibid., p. 33.

81. U.S. District Court for the Northern District of Georgia, Atlanta Division, *United States of America* v. *Pablo Escobar-Gaviria*, Affidavit of United States Drug Enforcement Administration Special Agent David C. Panek, p. 6 and p. 13. Also p. 45, pp. 48–51, p. 54, p. 64, p. 83, and pp. 93–100.

82. For an account of John Featherly's and Cesar Diaz's adventures see Peter Ross Range, *Washington Post*, August 27, 1989. Also Stephen Labaton, "Fighting the Battle of Dirty Money," *New York Times*, August 27, 1989.

83. United States District Court for the Northern District of Georgia, Atlanta Division, *United States of America* v. *Pablo Escobar-Gaviria* et al., Grand Jury indictment, p. 30.

84. Richard Walker, "Extradited Colombian Appears in U.S. Court over Drug Charges," Reuters, September 7, 1989.

85. "Bookkeeper for a Drug Ring Is Given 6½ Years in Prison," *New York Times*, April 17, 1991.

86. "Money Laundering Case," *Washington Post*, December 29, 1990.

87. Henry Weinstein, "Two Sisters Cleared in Jewelry District Case," *Los Angeles Times*, December 16, 1990.

88. Stephen Labaton, "Bank in Panama to Forfeit $5 Million in Cocaine Case," *New York Times*, August 15, 1989.

The Whip at the End of the Polar Cap

1. Kenneth R. Timmerman, *The Death Lobby* (New York: Houghton Mifflin, 1991), pp. 328–29.

2. Klaus Meienberg from *Woche-Zeitung*, in Zurich, was the first to write about Kopp and the "whip."

3. Interview with Tuto Rossi in Lugano, June 9, 1991.

4. For more information about Banco Ambrosiano, see Nick

Tosches, *Power on Earth* (New York: Arbor House, 1986), and Rupert Cornwell, *God's Banker* (London: Victor Gollancz, 1984).

5. This information was made available to me by a reliable source whom I am compelled to protect.

6. Hearing of the Terrorism, Narcotics and International Operations Subcommittee of the Senate Foreign Relations Committee on Foreign Policy and Narcotics Policy, BCCI Investigation, October 22, 1991, as stated by Abdur Sakhia, former BCCI official.

Bank of Credit and Commerce International (BCCI): The Robin Hood of the Third World

1. Paul Erdman, *The Crash of '79* (New York: Berkeley Books, 1976).

2. Background history of BCCI, Hearing of the Terrorism, Narcotics and International Operations Subcommittee of the Senate Foreign Relations Committee on Foreign Policy and Narcotics Policy, Implications of the BCCI Affair, August 1, 1991, p. 4.

3. "Behind Closed Doors," (BCCI) *Financial Times*, November 11, 1991.

4. Abdur Sakhia, BCCI Hearing, October 22, 1991, p. 13.

5. Task Force on Terrorism and Unconventional Warfare, House Republican Research Committee, U.S. House of Representatives, Washington, D.C., October 28, 1991.

6. "Behind Closed Doors," (BCCI) *Financial Times*, November 11, 1991.

7. Alan Friedman, "B.C.C.I.'s Deadly Secrets," *Vanity Fair*, February 1992.

8. Ibid.

9. Ibid.

10. "Behind Closed Doors," *Financial Times*, November 9–16, 1991.

11. These incidents were described by Senator Alan Cranston, Hearing of the Terrorism, Narcotics and International Operations Subcommittee, Implications of the BCCI Affair, August 1, 1991, pages 133–34, Federal Information Systems Corporation; Federal News Services.

12. David Pryce-Jones, as quoted in Task Force on Terrorism and Unconventional Warfare, *BCCI—An Introduction*, September 4, 1991, p. 3.

13. Youssef M. Ibrahim, "Algerians, Angry with the Past, Divide over Their Future," *New York Times*, January 19, 1992.

14. Y. Carmon, *Securing the Future from the Threat of Terrorism*, paper presented in a conference in Washington, D.C., March 15, 1991.

15. Richard Kerr, Hearing of the Terrorism, Narcotics and International Operations Subcommittee, BCCI Investigation, October 25, 1991.

16. "Behind Closed Doors," (BCCI) *Financial Times*, 1991.

17. "Terrorist Tie of Bank Cited in '88," *New York Times*, July 24, 1991.

18. *BCCI: Issues for Congress*, Congressional Research Service (CRS) Issue Brief, Library of Congress, October 18, 1991.

19. Task Force on Terrorism and Unconventional Warfare, October 4, 1991.

20. Robert M. Morgenthau, Press Release, July 29, 1991, p. 3.

21. Mike McAlary, "Bill Clinton Banker's BCCI Link," *New York Post*, February 7, 1992.

22. Friedman, "BCCI's Deadly Secrets."

23. Thomas Petzinger, Jr., and Peter Truell, "U.K. Audit Points to Large BCCI Role by Two Top U.S. Cable TV Executives," *The Wall Street Journal*, January 17, 1992.

24. Alan Friedman, "Gokal 'Fronted' in Attempt to Buy US Bank," *Financial Times*, July 24, 1991.

25. Abdur Sakhia, Hearings of the Terrorism, Narcotics and International Operations Subcommittee, October 22, 1991, p. 13.

26. "Nightline," ABC News, August 8, 1991.

27. David Butler et al., "Khomeini's Victory," *Newsweek*, February 19, 1979.

28. Kinsella's book *Unholy Alliance* is slated for publication by a Canadian publisher in the spring of 1992.

29. James Ring Adams, "Libya Cash Financing Hate in the U.S.," *Forward*, December 20, 1991.

30. Task Force on Terrorism and Unconventional Warfare, "BCCI and the Nuclear Question," October 28, 1991.

31. General Mohammed Zia ul-Haq, July 1978.

32. Task Force on Terrorism and Unconventional Warfare, "BCCI and the Nuclear Question," October 28, 1991.

33. James Adams, *The Financing of Terror* (New York: Simon & Schuster, 1986).

34. Maldive Airways operates from the Maldive Islands throughout the Third World.

35. Task Force on Terrorism and Unconventional Warfare, October 28, 1991.

36. Ibid.

37. Ibid., "BCCI and Sponsoring Terrorism," October 4, 1991.

38. Dan Raviv and Yossi Melman, *Every Spy a Prince* (Boston: Houghton Mifflin Co., 1990), pp. 232–33, and Israeli daily newspapers from February through December 1988.

39. LIAT does not refer to a Caribbean feeder airline. It was the acronym for the company Kalmanovitch established in Sierra Leone. LIAT is also Kalmanovitch's daughter's name in Hebrew.

40. Department of State, White Paper, July 1987, referred to in Richard Kerr's testimony on October 25, 1991, before the Terrorism, Narcotics and International Operations Subcommittee.

41. Agence France Presse, "Abu Nidal Denies Ties to BCCI," August 2, 1991.

42. Joshua Sinai, "The Next Stage in Middle Eastern Terrorism," *Defense and Foreign Affairs Strategic Policy,* November 1990.

43. Department of State, White Paper, "The Abu Nidal Terror Network," July 1987, p. 15.

44. "Drugs Finance Terror," *Forward,* December 7, 1991.

45. Task Force on Terrorism and Unconventional Warfare, "BCCI and Financing Terrorism," October 4, 1991.

46. Ibid., "BCCI—Between Peru and Washington, DC," September 10, 1991.

47. Agence France Presse in Peru, "A Supreme Court Tribunal Shelves Garcia Case," December 28, 1991.

48. Task Force on Terrorism and Unconventional Warfare, "BCCI—Between Peru and Washington DC," September 10, 1991.

49. See daily newspaper, *El Comercio,* Lima, Peru, June 28, 1990.

50. Ibid., June 18, 1990.

51. Task Force on Terrorism and Unconventional Warfare, "BCCI—Between Peru and Washington, DC," September 10, 1991.

52. Task Force on Terrorism and Unconventional Warfare, "BCCI and the Financing of Terrorism," October 4, 1991.

53. *The Chapter of Allah, The Platform of the Islamic Resistance Movement* (Hamas), translated, interpreted, and annotated by Professor Raphael Israeli, p. 8.

The Colombianization of the United States: Abdicating to the Narcocracy

1. "Narcocracy" was apparently coined by Anthony Henman in an article published in *Latin American Regional Report,* October 5, 1985.

2. Interview, summer 1991, with U.S. Treasury officials who requested to remain anonymous.

3. Bernd Debusmann, "U.S. Crime Statistics Continue to Get Worse," Reuters, June 5, 1991.

4. Hearing of the House Banking, Finance and Urban Affairs Committee: *Operations of Foreign Banks in the US*, Federal News Service, 1991, Federal Information Corporation System, June 11, 1991.

5. Henry B. Gonzalez, in a letter to Alan Greenspan, Chairman of the Federal Reserve, March 14, 1991.

6. Pietro Banas, *Il Mondo*, July 15–22, 1991.

7. James Ring Adams, "Losing the Drug War: Drugs, Banks, and Florida Politics," *American Spectator*, September 1988.

8. Federal Reserve surplus figures as of March 1992.

9. Richard B. Foster, "Strategic Dimensions of the Drug War," paper presented at Freedom House Conference on the Drug Trafficking Threat to Democracy, New York City, September 30, 1988.

10. Richard Berke, "Corruption in Drug Agency Called Crippler of Inquiries and Morale," *New York Times*, December 17, 1989.

11. These figures are the result of a special internal survey by the IRS.

12. "Metropolitan Desk," *New York Times*, May 24, 1983.

13. James Ring Adams, *The Big Fix* (New York: John Wiley & Sons, 1991), p. 34.

14. *Chicago Tribune*, February 9, 1992.

15. Anthony M. DeStefano et al., "Feds Nab Drug Ring Suspects," *Newsday*, November 17, 1989.

16. Associated Press, "From Women's League to Chains," *New York Times*, December 20, 1989.

17. Rachel Ehrenfeld, *Narco-Terrorism* (New York: Basic Books, 1990), pp. 64–65.

18. Ibid., p. 65.

19. John H. Kennedy, "Sixty Percent of Auto Dealers Fail IRS Cash-Reporting Rules," *Boston Globe*, December 3, 1991.

20. Uniform Crime Reports, 1990, FBI; and Associated Press, "The FBI Says Reports on Crime Rose This Year," *New York Times*, October 28, 1991.

21. For a thorough analysis of the development of narco-terrorism in Colombia, see Ehrenfeld, *Narco-Terrorism*, pp. 74–111.

22. *Drugs, Law Enforcement and Foreign Policy: The Cartel, Haiti and Central America.* Hearings of the Subcommittee on Terrorism, Narcotics and International Operations, U.S. Senate, pt. III, U.S. Government Printing Office, Washington, D.C., April 4, 5, 6, and 7, 1988, p. 321.

23. A revealing exposé on Colombia's growing heroin production and sales, "Heroin: The Next Act in the Colombian Drug Drama," by Juan Daniel Jaramillo Ortiz, a Colombian lawyer and economist, was published in *The Wall Street Journal* on December 27, 1991.

24. In 1988, Colombia's drug trade generated approximately $2 billion in profits. Ehrenfeld, *Narco-Terrorism*, p. 105.

25. Robert Grosse, "Colombia's Black Market in Foreign Exchange," International Business and Banking Institute, University of Miami, May 1991.

26. Douglas Farrah, "U.S. and Colombia Focus on Seizing Drug Traffickers' Financial Accounts," *The Washington Post*, December 31, 1991.

27. Ibid.

28. Douglas Farrah, "Jailed Colombian Cartel Leader Offers U.S. Deal on Noriega Evidence," *The Washington Post*, December 18, 1991.

29. *El Tiempo*, January 5, 1992.

30. As quoted by Linda Robinson, "New Target: The Cali Cartel," *U.S. News & World Report*, December 23, 1991.

31. According to the author's conversations with U.S. Treasury Department officials, summer 1991.

32. Anthony Rowley, "Cash Blockage," *The Far Eastern Economic Review*, December 19, 1991.

33. In congressional hearings during 1990 and 1991 government officials and drug-trafficking experts gave various estimates, including these figures.

34. Herman Gold, "Gorge Big Banks, Starve Customers," *The Nation*, December 23, 1991.

35. Ehrenfeld, *Narco-Terrorism*, p. 48.

36. R. T. Naylor, *Hot Money* (London: Unwin Paperbacks, 1987), pp. 167–69.

37. *Latin American Regional Report*, May 29, 1981.

38. Ibid.

39. Stephen Riley, "Can Corrupt Market Forces Be Beat?" *CEO International Strategies*, September–October 1991.

40. In early 1992, Noriega stood trial in the federal courthouse in downtown Miami. Noriega faced a lengthy eleven-count indictment, including charges of drug trafficking and money-laundering.

41. Hearings Before the Subcommittee on Terrorism, Narcotics and International Operations, April 1988.

42. David Adams, "Drug Case Perils Panama's Leader," *San Francisco Chronicle*, December 24, 1991.

43. Tony Walker, "Forged U.S. $100 Bills Flood Banks in Cairo," *Financial Times*, December 4, 1991.

44. Sir Thomas More, *Utopia*.

45. Stephen J. Hedges, "Inside the BCCI Megascandal," *U.S. News & World Report*, August 12, 1991.

Bibliography

Books

Adams, James. *The Financing of Terror*. New York: Simon & Schuster, 1986.

Adams, James Ring. *The Big Fix*. New York: John Wiley & Sons, 1991.

Adams, James Ring, and Frantz, Douglas. *A Full Service Bank*. New York: Pocket Books, 1992.

Clarke, Thurston, and Tigue, John L., Jr. *Dirty Money*. New York: Simon & Schuster, 1975.

Ehrenfeld, Rachel. *Narco-terrorism*. New York: Basic Books, 1990.

Emerson, Steven. *The American House of Saud*. New York: Franklin Watts, 1985.

Erdman, Paul. *The Crash of '79*. New York: Berkeley Books, 1976.

Gugliotta, Guy, and Leen, Jeff. *Kings of Cocaine*. New York: Simon & Schuster, 1989.

Hammer, Richard. *The Vatican Connection*. New York: Holt, Rinehart, Winston, 1982.

Hamas. *The Chapter of Allah, The Platform of the Islamic Resistance Movement.* Translated by Raphael Israeli. Jerusalem, 1988.

Kinsella, W. *Unholy Alliance.* Canada: forthcoming, 1992.

Levitt, Karl, and McIntyre, Alister. *Canada–West Indies Economic Relations.* Toronto: McGill University, The Centre for Developing-Areas Studies, 1967.

Messick, Hank. *Lansky.* New York: G. P. Putnam, 1971.

———. *Secret File.* New York: G. P. Putnam, 1969.

More, Sir Thomas. *Utopia.* New York: Norton, 1976.

Nahas, Gabriel, Jr. *Cocaine: The Great White Plague.* Middlebury, Vt.: Paul S. Eriksson, 1989.

Naylor, R. T. *Hot Money.* New York: Unwin Paperbacks, 1987.

Noonan, John T., Jr. *Bribes.* Berkeley, Calif.: University of California Press, 1987.

Potts, Mark, et al. *Dirty Money.* Washington, D.C.: National Press Books, 1992.

Raviv, Dan, and Melman, Yossi. *Every Spy a Prince.* New York: Houghton Mifflin, 1990.

Shannon, Elaine. *Desperados.* New York: Viking, 1988.

Timmerman, Kenneth R. *The Death Lobby.* New York: Houghton Mifflin, 1991.

Tosches, Nick. *Power on Earth.* New York: Arbor House, 1986.

Periodicals

"Abu Nidal Denies Ties to BCCI." Agence France Presse, August 2, 1991.

Adams, James Ring. "Dingell Ducks Probe into GM's Iraqi Deal." *Forward*, January 24, 1992.

———. "Libya Cash Financing Hate in the U.S." *Forward*, December 20, 1991.

———. "Losing the Drug War: Drugs, Banks, and Florida Politics." *American Spectator*, September 1988.

Anderson, Jack, and Van Atta, Dale. "GOP Loyalty Rewarded." *Washington Post*, November 19, 1989.

"Bahamas Asks for Investigation Head of Drug Probe." Reuters, September 22, 1988.

"Behind Closed Doors." (BCCI) *Financial Times*, November 11, 1991.

Berke, Richard. "Corruption in Drug Agency Called Crippler of Inquiries and Morale." *New York Times*, December 17, 1989.

"Bookkeeper for a Drug Ring Is Given 6½ Years in Prison." *New York Times*, April 17, 1991.

Butler, David, et al. "Khomeini's Victory." *Newsweek*, February 19, 1979.

"Caribbean Closing the Clearing House." *Daily Telegraph* (London), January 11, 1990.

Carmon, Y. "Securing the Future from the Threat of Terrorism." Paper presented, Washington D.C., March 15, 1991.

Damianos, Athena. "New Leader Buoys the Opposition." *Financial Times*, July 10, 1990.

Debusmann, Bernd. "U.S. Crime Statistics Continue to Get Worse." Reuters, June 5, 1991.

DeStefano, Anthony M., et al. "Feds Nab Drug Ring Suspects." *Newsday*, November 17, 1989.

"Drugs Finance Terror." *Forward*, December 7, 1991.

Eddy, Paul, et al. "Paradise Lost." *Sunday Times* (London), September 29, 1985.

Farrah, Douglas. "Jailed Colombian Cartel Leader Offers U.S. Deal on Noriega Evidence." *Washington Post*, December 18, 1991.

———. "U.S. and Colombia Focus on Seizing Drug Traffickers' Financial Accounts." *Washington Post*, December 31, 1991.

"The FBI Says Reports on Crime Rose This Year." *New York Times*, October 28, 1991.

Forrester, James. "Bahamas Outlines Plan to Wipe Out Drug Barons' Cash Hoards." Reuters, October 23, 1989.

Foster, Richard B. "Strategic Dimensions of the Drug War." Paper presented at the Freedom House Conference on the Drug Trafficking Threat to Democracy, New York, September 30, 1988.

Friedman, Alan. "BCCI's Deadly Secrets." *Vanity Fair*, February 1992.

———. "Gokal 'Fronted' in Attempt to Buy U.S. Bank." *Financial Times*, July 24, 1991.

"From Women's League to Chains." *New York Times*, December 20, 1989.

Gerstel, Steve. "Senate Rejects Big Push to Punish Bahamas." UPI, May 11, 1989.

Gold, Herman. "Gorge Big Banks, Starve Customers." *The Nation*, December 23, 1991.

Grosse, Robert. "Colombia's Black Market in Foreign Exchange." International Business and Banking Institute, University of Miami, May 1991.

Hedges, Stephen J. "Inside the BCCI Megascandal." *U.S. News & World Report*, August 12, 1991.

Hiaasen, Carl, and McGee, Jim. "A Nation for Sale. In the Bahamas Smugglers Say Everyone Has a Price." *Miami Herald*, September 23, 1984.

———. "Bimini: Smuggler's Paradise Isle." *Miami Herald*, September 26, 1984.

———. "Corruption in the Bahamas." *Miami Herald*, September 23, 1984.

———. "Pindling's Friend Accused of Accepting Payoff." *Miami Herald*, September 23, 1984.

———. "Probe Ties Key Aide to Money-Laundering." *Miami Herald*, September 27, 1984.

"How Drugs Turned the Tide Against Bahamas' Banks." *Business Week*, May 23, 1988.

Ibrahim, Youssef M. "Algerians, Angry with the Past, Divide over Their Future." *New York Times*, January 19, 1992.

Isikoff, Michael. "Blunt Assessment of Bolivia Ignored." *Washington Post*, March 1, 1990.

———. "Lobbying Firm to Drop Bahamian Account." *Washington Post*, April 6, 1989.

———. "Los Angeles Bank Surplus Linked to Drug Trade." *Washington Post*, March 19, 1990.

———. "U.S. Sues Nine Banks in Drug Money-Laundering." *Washington Post*, March 30, 1989.

Jehl, Douglas. "Bahamas Prime Minister Says U.S. Fails to Back Up Drug-War Pledge." *Los Angeles Times*, September 23, 1989.

Kennedy, John H. "Sixty Percent of Auto Dealers Fail IRS Cash-Reporting Rules." *Boston Globe*, December 3, 1991.

Labaton, Stephen. "Bank in Panama to Forfeit $5 Million in Cocaine Case." *New York Times*, August 15, 1989.

————. "Fighting the Battle of Dirty Money." *New York Times*, August 27, 1989.

Levitt, Karl, and McIntyre, Alister. "Canada-West Indies Economic Relations." McGill University Centre for Developing Area Studies, 1967.

Marsden, William. "How Canadian Banks Are Used to 'Launder' Narcotics Millions: Cash Floods Bahamas Branches." *Montreal Gazette*, December 23, 1985.

————. "Scotiabank Stonewalled U.S. Drug Smuggling Probes." *Montreal Gazette*, December 24, 1985.

Maxwell, Evan Lowell. "Gold, Drugs and Clean Cash." *Los Angeles Times*, February 18, 1980.

McAlary, Mike. "Bill Clinton Banker's BCCI Link." *New York Post*, February 7, 1992.

McGee, Jim. "Bahamian Ex-Official Indicted on Drug-Related Charges." *Washington Post*, March 30, 1989.

Miller, Marjorie. "The Mexico Connection." *Los Angeles Times*, April 13, 1989.

"Money Laundering Case." *Washington Post*, December 29, 1990.

Petzinger, Thomas Jr., and Truell, Peter. "U.K. Audit Points to Large BCCI Role by Two Top U.S. Cable TV Executives." *Wall Street Journal*, January 17, 1992.

"Pindling Cancels 'Today' Interview." *Washington Times*, October 10, 1989.

Riley, Stephen. "Can Corrupt Market Forces Be Beat?" *CEO International Strategies*, September–October 1991.

Robinson, Linda. "New Target: The Cali Cartel." *U.S. News & World Report*, December 23, 1991.

Rowley, Anthony. "Cash Blockage." *Far Eastern Economic Review*, December 19, 1991.

Schanche, Don A. "Bahamas Leader Denies Drug Ties." *Los Angeles Times*, March 5, 1989.

———. "Caribbean States Want U.N. in Drug War." *Los Angeles Times*, October 23, 1989.

Shannon, Elaine. "Why We're Facing a World of Noriegas." *Washington Post*, October 23, 1988.

Shenon, Philip. "Bahamas Leader Calls U.S. Drug Inquiry 'Baseless.'" *New York Times*, September 22, 1988.

Sinai, Joshua. "The Next Stage in Middle Eastern Terrorism." *Défense and Foreign Affairs Strategic Policy*, November 1990.

"A Supreme Court Tribunal Shelves Garcia Case." Agence France Presse (Peru), December 28, 1991.

"Terrorist Tie of Bank Cited in '88." *New York Times*, July 24, 1991.

Thomas, Gray. "Smuggler Says He Bribed Bahamas Prime Minister." Reuters, February 16, 1988.

Walker, Richard. "Extradited Colombian Appears in U.S. Court over Drug Charges." Reuters, September 7, 1989.

Walker, Tony. "Forged U.S. $100 Bills Flood Banks in Cairo." *Financial Times*, December 4, 1991.

Weinstein, Henry. "Two Sisters Cleared in Jewelry District Case." *Los Angeles Times*, December 16, 1990.

Other

Affidavit of Arthur Donelan, Special Agent for the U.S. Customs Service. State and County of New York. March 28, 1989.

Affidavit of Gloria J. Epstein, Barrister & Solicitor. Supreme Court of Ontario. January 1986.

Affidavit of David C. Panek, Special Agent for the U.S. Drug Enforcement Administration. U.S. District Court for the

Northern District of Georgia, Atlanta Division. *United States of America* v. *Pablo Escobar-Gaviria*. April 1, 1990.

A Call for Action. A Personal Rebuttal and Request for Investigation from the Prime Minister of The Bahamas to the U.S. Attorney General, December 13, 1983.

Congressional Record, House. "The Case of Iraq and the Export-Import Bank." February 24, 1990.

Congressional Research Service Issue Brief. "BCCI: Issues for Congress." October 18, 1991.

Correspondence of Henry B. Gonzalez with Alan Greenspan, March 14, 1991.

U.S. District Court for the Central District of California. *United States of America* v. *Nazareth Andonian, et al*. "Trial Memorandum" and bill of indictment, February 1989.

Federal Bureau of Investigation. "Uniform Crime Reports." 1990.

Federal Information Corporation System. "Hearing of the House Banking, Finance and Urban Affairs Committee." Federal News Service. June 11, 1991.

Federal Information Corporation System. "Hearing of the Terrorism, Narcotics and International Operations Subcommittee of the Senate Foreign Relations Committee on Foreign Policy and Narcotics Policy, Implications of BCCI." Federal News Service. August 1, 1991, and October 22, 1991.

Hearings Before the United States Senate Subcommittee on Terrorism, Narcotics and International Communications. "Drugs, Law Enforcement and Foreign Policy: The Cartel, Haiti and Central America." Washington, D.C.: U.S. Government Printing Office, April 4, 5, 6, 7, 1988.

Hearings of Senate Foreign Relations Committee. Federal News Service. April 5, 1989.

Interview with Jean Kawhara, U.S. District Attorney, May 13, 1991.

"NBC Nightly News" transcript. September 5, 1983.

Royal Commission Report. December 1984.

State Department Report on Narcotics. 1986.

State Department Report on Narcotics. "The Bahamas." 1988.

State Department Report on Narcotics. "The Bahamas." 1989.

Task Force on Terrorism and Unconventional Warfare, House Republican Research Committee. "BCCI—An Introduction." September 4, 1991.

Task Force on Terrorism and Unconventional Warfare, House Republican Research Committee. "BCCI—Between Peru and Washington DC." September 10, 1991.

Task Force on Terrorism and Unconventional Warfare, House Republican Research Committee. "BCCI and the Financing of Terrorism." October 4, 1991.

Task Force on Terrorism and Unconventional Warfare, House Republican Research Committee. "BCCI and the Nuclear Question." October 28, 1991.

"Today" interview transcript. September 7, 1983, and September 12, 1983.

Index

Abedi, Agha Hasan, 163–66, 168–70,
        178–80, 185–87, 198, 210
    Carter and, 185
    Clifford and, 183
    Islamic fundamentalism and, 169,
        179
Abu-Bakr, Atif, 207
Abu Dhabi, 164, 167, 210
    BCCI in, 164
Abu Nidal Organization (ANO),
        193–94, 201–204, 206–208
Adderley, Paul, 30
Adham, Kamal, 166, 178, 182
Aeronica, 194
Afghan rebels (mujahadin), 142, 178
Africa, Islamic terrorist groups in,
        199–201
Agca, Mehmet Ali, 133–34
Ahl al-, Bayt, 197
Ahmad, Sani, 183
Airlines, PLO ownership of, 194–95
Airplane manufacturers, 113
Air Zimbabwe, 195
Akbar, Syed Ziauddin, 181
Algeria, 175–77
Ali, Asaf, 205
Altman, Robert, 179, 183
Altun, Dikran, 114, 145, 148, 155
A-Mark Trading Company, 87–90, 96,
        97
American Indian Movement, 189
American International Bank, La Mina
        and, 74
Anderson, Robert B., 219
Andonian, Nazareth and Vahe, 64–68,
        77–83, 85, 88, 89, 91, 119, 120,
        155
    Ferris and, 81–83

prison terms, 60, 118
Vivas and, 96, 97, 100, 102, 103
Anouchian family, 66
Anti-Semitism, 146
Arab countries. See also Bank of Credit
        and Commerce International
        (BCCI); specific countries
    anti-Western sentiment in, 173–76,
        193
    Communist regimes and, 193–95,
        199–203
    corruption in, 175
    Islamic fundamentalism in, 175–77
    nuclear weapons and, 168–69
    oil and, 163
    politics in, 175–77
    terrorism supported by, 176–77
Arboleda-Gonzalez, Jose Duvan, 118
Argin Corporation, 142
Armenians, in California, 65
Arms trade, 163, 202, 242. See also
        Nuclear technology
    drugs-for-arms deals, 242
    Iran-Contra affair, 140, 178
    Peru and, 205
Aruba, 110, 114–16
Atlanta (Georgia)
    DEA's operation in, 104–106,
        110–11, 116
    La Mina in, 70
Azzam, Salem, 196, 197

Bahamas, The
    airstrips, 8–10, 41, 45
    banks in, 37–48
        bribes and, 38
        Canadian, 43–44
        corporate accounts, 39–40

nonresident dollar holdings, 42–43
personal relationships and, 39
secrecy regulations, 37–38
Bay Street Boys in, 7
bribing of officials in, 9, 11–15, 21
Dangerous Drugs Act of 1989, 52
drug consumption in, 20–21
drug trafficking in
arrests and, 41
attempts to control, 50–54
bribes and, 9, 11–13, 21–32, 37, 38, 41
Colombian cartels, 8–14
eviction of local residents, 10, 11, 21
NBC report, 14–19
organized crime and, 33–36
economy, 13–14, 41–43
gambling in, 5, 6
islands involved in drug trafficking, 8–9
Lansky and, 5–8, 38
money-laundering in, 36–49, 51, 53–55
banking secrecy regulations and, 37–38
bribes and, 38
fictitious corporations, 39–40, 45–47
Lansky and, 6
Mutual Legal Assistance Treaty and, 54
personal relationships with bankers and, 39
trust companies and, 45–47
organized crime in, 6–8
police corruption in, 12–13
Royal Commission, 9, 12, 14, 18–25, 27–35, 48, 51, 54
money-laundering and, 45, 47–48
tax laws in, 29, 36–38
U.S. relations with, 15, 51–54
Vesco and, 14, 22–27
Bahamas Central Bank, 42, 46, 48
Bahamas World Airways (BWA), 22
Bahamon, Col. Augusto, 239
Bailey, F. Lee, 17
Banas, Pietro, 215–16
Banca Nazionale del Lavoro (BNL), 155, 184, 215
Banco Ambrosiano, 148–49
Banco Cafetero, 72, 148
Banco de Occidente, 117, 120, 148
La Mina and, 70–72, 88, 105–107, 109, 112, 113

Banco de Santander, 64
Bank Melli, 187
Bank of America (BOA), 121, 164
Bank of Credit and Commerce Canada (BCCC), 187
Bank of Credit and Commerce International (BCCI), 159–210. See also specific people
"Black Network," 172
Canada and, 188–90
Cayman Islands branch, 164–65, 183
CIA and, 168, 177–78
Clifford and, 166, 168, 179, 183
Clinton and, 180
corporate structure of, 165
drug trafficking and, 202–208
establishment of, 164
FGB takeover and, 166
First American Bank and, 166, 181, 183–84, 189
Hussein and, 184, 185
ideological origins of, 169–71, 178–79
Iran and, 190–91
Iran-Contra affair and, 178
Islamic fundamentalism and, 169–71, 176–79, 193
Kopp affair and, 155–56
La Mina and, 91, 113, 115
Lance and, 179
Latin America operations, 203–208
Libya and, 184–92
Operation C-Chase and, 70
Pharaon and, 179
political leaders' endorsement of, 179–82, 184–86
shell game transactions, 171–72
shutting down of, 163, 174, 178, 209–10
as anti-Islamic action, 169
Sierra Leone operations and, 201
tactics of, 183–84
Tampa case, 91
terrorist organizations and, 171, 177–79
Abu Nidal, 201–204, 206–208
in Europe, 186–88
PLO, 194–95
Shining Path, 203–208
Third World and, 168–72
collapse and, 174–75
special services, 168–69, 171–73
unrecorded deposits, 171
U.S. operations, 166–68, 188–90
lack of official interest, 190

Bank of Credit (cont.)
  weapons technology and equipment
      transfer and, 168–69, 172–73,
      184, 187, 190–94, 202–203, 205
  Young and, 179, 185–86
Bank of England, BCCI shut down by,
    209
Bank of Luxembourg, La Mina and, 70
Bank of Nova Scotia, 24–25, 39, 43–44
Bank of the Commonwealth, 168
Banks (banking industry). See also
    specific banks and other topics
  arms trade and, 163
  in The Bahamas, 37–48
    bribes and, 37–48
    Canadian banks, 43–45
    corporate accounts, 39–40
    nonresident dollar holdings, 42–43
    personal relationships and, 39
    secrecy regulations, 37–38
  Canadian, 43–45
  cash deposits and, 62–94
  in Florida, 216, 241–42
  Islamic, 170n
  La Mina and, 64, 67–70, 72, 74, 77,
      88, 91, 98, 105–107, 109–10,
      112–16, 119–21
  Medellín cartel and, 64, 72
  regulatory system, 210–15
  Swiss. See Switzerland
  in Uruguay, 115
Bank Sepah Iran, 187
Banna, Sabri al-, 202
Bannister, Everette, 21–23, 29–31, 36
Banque Arabe Internationale
    d'Investissements, 181
Banque de Commerce et de Placements
    (BCP), 155, 198
Barbie, Klaus, 243
Barbouti, Ishan, 184
Barclay's Bank, 26
Barco, Virgilio, 116, 117, 234
Baron, George William, 41
Barrow, William Dean "Wig," 218–19
Batista, Fulgencio, 7
Bay Street Boys, 7
BCCI. See Bank of Credit and
    Commerce International
Bekir, Celenk, 133
Beshlian, Harout, 80–81
Betancur, Belisario, 234
Bhutto, Zulfikar Ali, 163, 191
Bimini (Bahamas), 8–9, 21, 37, 41–42,
    45
Blandon, José, 244

Boeing Company, 168
Bolivia, 243–44
Bonner, Robert, 63
Bouzidi, Hussein, 207
Bowe, Nigel, 9, 40–41
Brady, Frank, 44
Brandt, Willy, 180
Brown, Jimmy (John Featherly),
    103–111, 114–16
Brown and Carrera, 103–18
Brumlik, Timothy, 218
Bulgaria, 202
  drug trafficking in, 133, 141–45, 150
Bush, George, 61
Bush, George, Jr., 180

Cabal, Tomas, 245
Cable television, BCCI and, 182
Caledonian Airlines, 194
Cali cartel, 239
  cooperation between Medellín cartel
      and, 119
California. See also Los Angeles
  Armenians in, 65
  rise in cash deposits in, 62–64
Callaghan, James Lord, 180, 185
Calvi, Roberto, 149
Cambio Italia, 70, 71, 93–95, 98
Canada
  banks, in the Caribbean, 43–44
  BCCI and, 188–90
  Pindling's suit and, 17–18
Canadian Imperial Bank (CIB), 44
Capcom Financial Services, Ltd., 182
Car dealerships, 226
Caribbean Development Bank, 185
Carrera, Alex (Cesar Diaz), 103–10,
    114–16
Carter, Jimmy, 180, 185
Carter, Lynda, 179
Caruana, Salvatore Michael, 227
  Bahamas operations of, 33–36
Cash, Sir Gerald, 19
Castro, Fidel, 5–7, 232
Cayman Islands, BCCI branch in,
    164–65, 183
Central Bank of New York, La Mina
    and, 98
Central Intelligence Agency (CIA)
  BCCI and, 168, 177–78
  Kopp affair and, 130–31, 138
Centrust Bank, 181
Chahinian, Krikor, 79
Chase Manhattan Bank, 95, 105
  La Mina funds and, 88

Chelsea National Bank, 183
Chemical Bank, 64
Chepe, Don. *See* Moncada, Geraldo
China, 192, 202
Citibank, 218
Citizens Bank, 119, 121
  La Mina and, 105
Clifford, Clark, 166, 168, 179, 183
Clinton, Bill, 180
Colombia
  crackdown on drug trafficking in,
    116–17
  drug trafficking in, 230–40, 247. *See
    also* Colombian drug cartels
    arrests and, 239
    constitution and, 231
    economic effects, 233–34
    extradition laws, 231, 234, 235,
      237, 238
    revenue from, 237
  extradition laws, 118
  terrorist organizations in, 232–36
Colombian drug cartels. *See also* Cali
    cartel; Lehder, Carlos; Medellín
    cartel
  Bahamas operations of, 8–15, 20, 21
    bribing of officials by, 9, 11–14
  cooperation between, 119
  new drug-running routes, 53
  organized crime and, 120
  Vesco and, 14, 26
Columbus Trust Company, 45–47
Comerci, Eduardo, 97–98
Commercial Exchange Bank and Trust,
    219
Commonwealth Bank, 26
Continental Bank International, 64
  La Mina and, 109
Continental Illinois National Bank, La
    Mina and, 109
Conyers, John, Jr., 229
Corporations, fictitious, 39–40, 45–47,
    113
Corruption in Arab countries, 175
Countryman, Wayne, 223
Crédit Suisse, 114, 136, 138, 140–42,
    147, 148
  Pizza Connection and, 141
Cronkite, Walter, 10
Cuba, 5, 6, 27, 202, 242
Çukurova, 155
Customs Service, U.S. *See also*
    Operation Polar Cap
  La Mina and, 69, 85–86
Czechoslovakia, 202

Dahabi, Celal, 147
DAIWA Bank, 64
Damouri, Mohamad, 226
Dangasian, Vagram Marion (Tio), 97,
    98
Dar-al-Maaral Islami, 170
Dar-al-Mal-al-Islam (DMI), 196
Davidson, Ian, 47
DeLorean, John Z., 218
Democratic Senatorial Campaign
    Committee (DSCC), 181
Deng Xiaoping, 185
Desoretz, Carlos, 85, 87, 88, 90–91,
    95, 100
de Soto, Hernando, 208
Diaz, Cesar. *See* Carrera, Alex
Dobriansky, Lev E., 15
Dollars, U.S., 240–41, 245–46
Donelan, Arthur, 269*n*
Drogoul, Christopher, 184
Drug Enforcement Agency (DEA), U.S.,
    63. *See also* Operation Polar Cap
  Bahamian drug trafficking and,
    11–13
  Bulgarian Government and, 144
  Kopp affair and, 129, 130, 138
  La Mina and, 69, 73, 77–81, 84, 85,
    102
  Brown and Carrera, 103–18
Drugs-for-arms deals, 242
Drug trafficking. *See also* Colombian
    drug cartels
  BCCI and, 202–208
  in Colombia, 230–40, 247. *See also*
    Colombian drug cartels
    arrests and, 239
    constitution and, 231
    economic effects, 233–34
    extradition laws, 231, 234, 235,
      237, 238
    revenue from, 237
  greed as motive for, 247
  Peru and, 203–208
  political influence and, 241–42
  as political warfare, 242
  terrorist organizations and
    in Colombia, 232–36
    Shining Path (Peru), 203–207
  Turkish-Bulgarian connection,
    133–34, 141–44, 149, 150
Dubai Islamic Bank, 196

Eastern Europe, Arab terrorist
    organizations and, 193–95,
    199–203

East Germany, 202
  Arab terrorist organizations and, 194, 195, 202
Eddy, Paul, 11
Ellicott, Robert J., 19
Endara, Guillermo, 245
Erdman, Paul, 163
Ernst, Rudei, 131
Escobar, Carlos Ossa, 238
Escobar-Gaviria, Pablo, 10–11, 26–27, 70, 110, 228, 237–39
Europe
  Iranian terrorists in, 186–88
  Islamic fundamentalism in, 195–99
  terrorist activities, 197–98

Fadlallah, Ayatollah Mohammed Hussayn, 197
Fadlallah, Mohammed Bakir Sayid, 197
Faisal, King, 166–67
Faisal al-Saud, Prince Mohammed bin-, 170
Faisal Islamic Bank, 170, 196
Falcon, Augusto, 245
Farach, Antonio, 242
Farah, Liala, 225
Farrakhan, Louis, 189
Faruq, Mian, 192
Favret, Rémi, 226
Featherly, John (Jimmy Brown), 103–11, 114–16
Federal Bureau of Investigation (FBI).
    See also Operation Polar Cap
  La Mina and, 69, 74–77, 84, 85, 101, 102
Federal Reserve Bank, 216
  La Mina and, 74
Ferris, Richard, 81–83, 85–91, 95, 96
Financial General Bankshares (FGB), 166, 183
First American Bank, 166, 181, 183–84, 189
First Arabian Corporation, 168
Florida. See also Miami
  banks in, 216, 241–42
  South Florida Drug Task Force, 15, 61
Florida/Caribbean Drug Enforcement Task Force, 216
France, Islamic terrorist groups in, 197–98
Franjiyeh, Soliman, 225, 226
Frappier, Robert L., 23, 25

Fuerzas Armadas Revolucionaries de Colombia (FARC), 231, 232
Fujimori, Alberto, 207–208
Fulani, Lenora, 189

Gacha, José Gonzalo Rodriguez, 27, 70, 229, 235–36
Galán, Luís Carlos, 235
Gallina, Jorge, 100
Gamble, Fred, 218
Gambling, in The Bahamas, 5, 6
Gandhi, Indira, 180
García, Alan, 180, 203–205
Garcia, Darnell, 223–24
Garcia de Paredes, Clara, 107, 109
Gargil Metals, 81–83
Gaviria, César, 234–37
Gemayal, Bashir, 225
Gerber, Rudolf, 136–37, 151–52
Ghorbanifar, Manucher, 178
Giulietti, Nicola, 149
Globus, 144
Gokal, Hussein, 169, 183, 187
Gokal, Mustafa, 169, 183, 187–88
Goldstein, Richard, 91
Goldstein family, 71, 86, 89–91
Gold trade. See La Mina
Gomez, Lt. Col. Luis Arce, 243
Gomez, Right Rev. Drexel W., 19, 30–32
Gomez, Roberto Suarez, 243
Gonzalez, Henry, 215
Goruh Zarbat, 186
Grand Bahamas Development Company, 28
Great Britain, Islamic terrorist groups in, 198–99
Greenspan, Alan, 215
Griffin, Bruce, 40–41
Gross, Delmus "Bunt," 222
Guarantee International Bank (GIB), 98
Guardian Trust Company, Ltd., 47
Guarin-Pulencio, William, 107
Gulam Ishaq Research Institute, 169
Gulf Shipping Lines, 187
Gulf states, 164, 177
Gulf War, 173–74, 208–209
Gutman, Wilton, 92, 93

Halens, Christoph, 190
Hallak, George, 194
Hallett, Carol Boyd, 51
Hamad, Mustaffah, 186
Hammud, Mohammed, 186–87, 198

Hammud family, 198
Hanna, Marann, 225
Haq, Brig. Inam ul-, 173
Harken Energy, 180
Hartmann, Alfred, 155
Hashemi, Mehdi, 197–202
Hasson Ichab, Yaacov, 207
Hatch, Orrin, 186
Hawamdah, Mussa, 186
Hayward, Jack, 28
Heilbrunn, Richard and Paul, 224
Heritage Loan and Investment Bank,
    118–19
HizbAllah, 187, 196–99, 209
Hochman, Sergio, 91–97, 100–102, 119
    arrest of, 101–102
Hungary, 202
Hurley, Edmund, 227
Hussein, Saddam, 173–74, 215
    BCCI and, 184, 186

Independence Bank of Encino, 77, 168,
    181
Inter-American Development Bank,
    185
Internal Revenue Service, U.S. See also
    Operation Polar Cap
    La Mina and, 69, 85
International Metro, 198–99
International Monetary Fund, 183, 205,
    240
International Precious Metals Institute
    (IPMI), 87
Investors Overseas Services (IOS), 14,
    25–26
Iran, 177, 192. See also Islamic
    fundamentalism
    BCCI and, 190
    drugs-for-arms deals and, 150
Iran-Contra affair, 140
    BCCI and, 178
Iraq, 177. See also Hussein, Saddam
    nuclear and chemical weapons
        programs of, 184–85
Ishizaki, Frankie T., 79–80
Islamic banks, 170–71
"Islamic bomb," 168, 190, 191
Islamic Conference, 196
Islamic Development Bank (IDB), 196
Islamic fundamentalism, 176–77. See
    also Shiite Muslims
    agenda of, 210
    Communist regimes and, 193, 195,
        199–203

    in Europe, 195–99
        terrorist activities, 197–99
    HizbAllah and, 187
    jihad and, 177
    politics and, 175–77
Islamic Holding Company, 196
Islamic nations. See Arab countries
Israel, 187
    Kalmanovitch and, 200–201

Jackson, John, 223, 224
John Paul II, Pope, 134
Jordanian-Islamic Bank, 196

Kaeslin, Jacques-André, 150
Kalmanovitch, Shabtai, 200
Kane, Barry, 9
Kapital Beratung, A.G., 132–33
Karachi Textile Mills, 193
Karamehmet, Mehmet Emin, 155
Katz, Arnold, 34–35
Kenya, PLO and, 194
Kenya Airways, 195
Kerr, Richard, 177–78
Kerry, John, 181–82
KGB, Sierra Leone operations and,
    200–201
Khan, Abdul Qader, 168–69, 172
Khan, Anwar, 188
Khashoggi, Adnan, 178
Khawaloujian, Chanes, 79–80
Khomeini, Ayatollah, 176, 179, 185,
    195
Kilhefner, Jack, 67
Kinsella, Warren, 188
Kintex, 144
Kopp, Elizabeth, 126–28, 130, 136–37
    Jewishness of, 130
    phone call to husband by, 126,
        134–35, 136–37, 150
    resignation of, 126, 128
Kopp, Hans, 126–37, 150, 151
    BCCI and, 156
    conspiracy theory of, 130, 133, 138
    investigations involving, 131–33
    media and, 131–33
Kopp affair, 126–51
    alleged U.S. objectives and, 128–29
    BCCI and, 155–56
    drugs-for-arms deals and, 150
    Kopp's conspiracy theory and, 131,
        133, 138
    Marty and, 146, 149

Kopp affair (*cont.*)
  Switzerland and, 127–29, 135–36, 140–46, 155–56
  Turkish-Bulgarian connection and, 133, 142, 144–45, 149, 150
Korekom, 144
Kouyoumjian, Raffi, 76–77, 83
Kouyoumjian, Simon, 76, 97
Koyomejian, Wanis, 66, 74, 75, 83–85, 88, 95–97, 113, 151, 153
Koyomejian family, 66, 83–85, 103

Lacey, Robert, 259*n*
Lakhani, Moe, 87–88
La Mina, 61–118
  Andonian brothers and, 60, 64–68, 77–83, 85
  Atlanta operations of, 70–71
  banks involved in, 64, 67–70, 72, 74, 77, 88, 91, 98, 105–107, 109–10, 112–16, 119–21
  Brown and Carrera and, 103–18
  circular flow of gold and, 85, 87–88
  closed-circuit television and, 78–80, 101
  description of operation, 111–13, 115–16
  Ferris and, 81–83, 85–91, 95, 96
  Hochman and, 91–97, 100–102, 119
  Kennedy Airport seizure and, 102
  Koyomejian family and, 75–80, 83–85
  Letra, S.A., and, 70, 71, 88–91, 94, 95, 98
  Loren Industries and, 71, 86–91
  Martinez and, 105–18
  Ronel and, 78, 81–91, 95–97, 100
  Ropex and, 66, 68–69, 74–77, 79–80, 83, 95–97, 120, 151
  South American gold and, 86–91
  telephone and fax taps and bugs, 80–84, 102
  trash collection and, 75–78
  Vivas and, 71, 93–103, 119, 120
  Wells Fargo investigation and, 67–69
Lance, Bert, 168, 179, 180, 183, 185
Lansky, Meyer, 5–8, 38
LaRouche, Lyndon, 145
Latin America, BCCI and, 203–208
Latouf, Michael, 225
Leary, Linda, 224
Lebanon Connection. *See* Kopp affair
Lehder, Carlos, 233
  Bahamas operations of, 9–15, 21
    Vesco and, 14

money-laundering by, 47–48
  trial and conviction of, 41, 48–50
Leshay, Randy, 87
Letra, S.A., 70, 71, 88–91, 94, 95, 98
Leung Yu Hung, 173
LIAT, 200–201
Libya, 177
  BCCI and, 184–93
  nuclear and chemical weapons programs of, 184
Liman, Arthur, 178
Lloyds Bank International, 64
Loomis Armored Transport Company, 68–69, 74, 76, 77, 102
López, José O., 222
Loren Industries, Inc., 71, 86–91
Los Angeles. *See also* La Mina
  as drug-trafficking center, 61–62
  Hill Street jewelry district, 65–66, 72–73, 95–96
  immigrants in, 61, 65

Mafia. *See* Organized crime
Magdaloyo, Nellie, 73–74
Magharian, Jean and Barkev, 113–14, 127, 140–55, 157
  indictments of, 148
  Iran-Contra affair and, 140
Magluta, Salvador, 245
Magness, Robert, 182
Maldive Airways, 194
Manara Travel Agency, Inc., 188–90
Mandel, Rita and Arnold, 173
Manfra, Tordella, and Brooks, 98
Manley, Michael, 50
Manual, Phillip, 259*n*
Marcos, Ferdinand, 185
Markle, Dennis, 46
Marsden, William, 23, 39, 40
Martinez, Pedro, 93, 100–101
Martinez Romero, Eduardo, 61, 70, 71
  Brown and Carrera and, 105–12
Marty, Dick, 146, 149, 150
Masihy, Jorge, 93, 100
Matiyow, Randy, 84
Maxwell, Evan Lowell, 72–73
Medellín cartel, 182
  airplane manufacturers and, 113
  Bahamas operations of, 9–11, 27
  banks used by, 64
  Brown and Carrera and, 103–18
  Colombian crackdown on, 116–17
  cooperation between Cali cartel and, 119
  demise of, 239

Kopp affair and, 148
La Mina and, 60, 71
Martinez and, 107–110
Operation Polar Cap and, 70
Vesco and, 26–27
Vivas and, 94, 97
Mejia, Mauricio, 93
Menem, Carlos, 180
Merkel, Robert, 13
Merkin, Celio, 101
Merkle, Robert, 50
Mexico, Colombian cartels and, 54
Meza, Gen. Garcia, 243
Miami (Florida), 8–9
banks in, 241–42
drug trade in, 12–13
money-laundering in, 62–64
Miami Herald, 34–35, 42
Mickens, Thomas, 219–20
Minnig, Timothy, 23–25, 27, 38–39
Mirza, Haci, 133, 149, 150
Mollicone, Joseph, Jr., 118–19
Momdijian, Joyce, 118
Momdijian family, 66
Momoh, Joseph, 200
Moncada, Geraldo, 70, 72, 110, 119
Money-laundering
amount laundered annually, 240–41
in The Bahamas, 36–49, 51, 53–55
banking secrecy regulations and,
37–38
bribes and, 38
fictitious corporations, 39–40,
45–47
Lansky and, 6
Mutual Legal Assistance Treaty
and, 54
personal relationships with bankers
and, 39
trust companies and, 46–48
bids on, 63
U.S. dollar supply and, 240–41,
245–46
U.S. laws on, 36–37
Moon, Rev. Sun Myung, 243, 219
Morgan Guarantee Trust, 64
Morgenthau, Robert M., 165, 166, 174,
180
Moroyan, Sepur, 118
Moroyan family, 66
Movimiento 19 de Abril (M-19), 231,
232, 234, 236
Murphy, Adm. Daniel, 15
Muslim Brotherhood, 196
Musullulu, Yasar, 133, 139

Mutual Legal Assistance Treaty
(MLAT), 53–54

Najmeddin, Saamir, 199–200
Naqvi, Swaleh, 166
Narachan, Mohammad Reza, 198
National Bank (Panama), 244–45
National Bank of Georgia, 168, 181,
183, 186
National Broadcasting Company (NBC),
"The Navy and The Bahamas"
report and, 14–18, 20
National Republic Bank, 146, 152
National Security Council, BCCI and,
178
Nation of Islam, 189
Neutron International Trading Co., 190
New Alliance Party, 189
New Providence Island (Bahamas), 8–9
New York Intermaritime Bank, 184
Nicaragua, 202, 242
PLO and, 194
Nidal, Abu, 172, 177, 199–200
Nigeria, PLO and, 194–95
Nigeria Airways, 194–95
Noriega, Gen. Manuel, 54–55, 107,
140, 244
BCCI and, 180, 185
Martinez and, 116
Norman's Cay (Bahamas), Lehder's base
on, 10–14, 21, 47, 50
North Korea, 202
nuclear program of, 192
Nottage, Kendal, 15, 28, 33–36, 45–46,
49, 227–28
Nottage, Rubie, 33–36, 227–28
Nuclear technology, BCCI and transfer
of, 168–69, 171–72
Nyerere, Julius, 180

Oba, Tomomitsu, 240
Ochoa Vasquez, Fabio, 26–27
Ochoa Vasquez, Jorge, 10–13, 27, 70,
110
Oftah Brothers, 173
Oil, 163
as political weapon, 164
Old Stone Bank, 119
Operation C-Chase, 69–70, 72, 85
Operation Polar Cap, 69–73
arrests and indictments and, 120,
145, 149–50
closed-circuit television and, 78–80,
101
convictions and, 117–18

Operation Polar Cap (*cont.*)
cooperation between government
agencies and, 69, 72
indictments and, 120
organized crime and, 120
Swiss operations, 151–52
telephone and fax taps and bugs,
80–84, 102
trash collection and, 74–78
undercover agents, 72–74
Brown and Carrera, 103–17
Organization of American States, 185
Organized crime
Bahamas operations of, 6–8, 33–36
Bulgarian, 141–42
Colombian drug cartels and, 120
Cuntrera-Caruana clan, 33
drug trade in, 33
Operation Polar Cap and, 120
Patriarca family, 70
Turkish, 133–34
"Orofe," 87–89, 95
Orosio Corporation, 75, 76, 97
Orozco-Prada, Eduardo, 217–18

Pakistan. *See also* Bank of Credit and
Commerce International (BCCI)
drug and arms traffic in, 165
nuclear program of, 168–69, 172,
191
Palestine Liberation Organization (PLO),
164, 173
airlines and duty-free stores owned
by, 194–95
BCCI and, 194
Panama, 114–15, 244–45. *See also*
Noriega, Gen. Manuel
banks, 38–39, 120, 244–45
BCCI and, 204–205
La Mina and, 105, 109, 112, 113
busts in, 116
corporate shells and, 40
Pan-Arabism, 177
Paredes, Clara Garcia de, 107, 109
Patriarca, Raymond, 33
Patriarca family, 70
Paul, David, 181
Pauley, Jane, 15, 17
Paunov, Stoyan, 144
People's Committee for Libyan
Students, 189
Pérez de Cuéllar, Javiér, 180
Perlowin, Bruce, 220–21
Peru, BCCI and, 203–208

Pervez, Ashad, 173
Pharaon, Ghaith, 77, 168, 179–83
Pindling, Lynden Oscar, 7–8, 11–33
alleged American conspiracy against,
18, 50
antidrug campaign of, 50–51
bribes and, 8, 12–13, 23–32, 41
Lansky and, 7
Lehder's testimony and, 48–50
NBC report and, 14–18, 19
Norman's Cay raid, 11–13
Royal Commission and, 18–25
Somoza and, 30
Vesco and, 15, 23–25, 27
Pineda, Carlos, 148
Pinto-Buitrago, Luis Alfonso, 228–29
Pizza Connection, 141
Poland, 202
Arab terrorist organizations and,
193–95, 202
Political influence, drug trafficking and,
241–42
Price Waterhouse, 174
Priscolin, Ruben, 94
Prosegur, Inc., 84, 88, 89, 96, 97
Pryce-Jones, David, 175

Qaddafi, Col. Muammar, 188, 190–92
Qassar brothers, 202–203
Qassem, Ghassem, 177
Qirtas Conserve Company, 186

Rahman, Masihur, 180–81
RAOF, 94, 95
Ravelo-Renedo, Fernando, 232
Reagan, Ronald, 15
Reber, Alfred, 137
Republic National Bank, 64
La Mina and, 70, 98, 105
Resorts International, 22
Rhode Island, banks in, 118, 119, 121
Rhode Island Hospital Trust, 119
Rich, Bruce, 91
Richter, Frank, 19, 27–29
Riggs National Bank, 189
Roll, John J., 29–30
Romania, 202
Romrell, Larry, 182
Ronel Refining Company, 71, 78,
81–91, 95–97, 100
South American gold and, 86–91
Ropex Corporation, 66, 68–69, 74–77,
79–80, 83, 95–97, 120, 151

Ross, Brian, 14–17, 20
  Pindling and, 15–17
Rossi, Tuto, 147
Royal Bank of Canada, 42, 44
Royal Canadian Mounted Police
      (RCMP), 19, 75–76, 113, 229

Saccoccia, Donna, 118
Saccoccia, Stephen A., 118, 121
Sadar, Immam Mussa, 187
Sadat, Anwar, 167
Safra, Edmund, 146
St. George, Edward, 28
Sakhia, Abdur, 165, 170, 184
SAMED, 193
Saudi Arabia, 166–68, 177, 179, 181,
      196, 209–210
  BCCI and, 164–65, 168–70, 172
SAVAMA, 198–99
Savings and loan scandal, 181, 214,
      229
Sawyer, Eric, 24–25, 39
Schoop, Kathrina, 126, 130, 136
Schroeder International Bank, 113, 142
Schwob, Renate, 136–38
Scotiabank, 41
Secord, Richard, 178
Security Pacific International Bank, 64
Security Pacific National Bank, 222
Serrano, Francisco, 70–71
Shahabadi, Ayatollah, 198
Shakarchi, Mahmoud Kassen, 149
Shakarchi, Mohamed, 113–14, 127,
      132–35, 139–53
  BCCI and, 155–56
  Bulgarian Government and, 144–45
  Iran-Contra affair and, 140
  negative publicity and, 143
  subpoena of, 152
  U.S. government and, 142
Shakarchi Trading Company, 126–27,
      131, 134–41, 149, 152
Sharir, Aharon, 120–21
Shiachadin, Sheik Hussayn, 199–201
Shiite Muslims, 186–88, 209
  in Africa, 199–201
  in Europe, 195–99
Shining Path, BCCI and, 203–208
Sierra Leone, Islamic terrorist groups in,
      199–201
Silverman, Ira, 19
Slomovitz, Barry, 121
Smith, George, 21–23, 49
Smith, Howard, 12–13

Smith, Sir James A., 19
Smith, William French, 18
So, Richard and Nancy, 222–23
Société de Banque Suisse (SBS), 140
Somoza, Anastasio, 29
Southern Bank, La Mina and, 105
South Florida Drug Task Force, 15,
      61
Stephens, Bruce R., 75–76, 79–80
Stephens, Jackson, 180
Stockley, David, 19
Suarez, Blanca, 228
Suarez, Jorge Roca, 228
Sunni Muslims, 196
Swiss Banking Corporation (SBC), 64,
      139, 142, 147–48
Switzerland, 113. See also Kopp affair
  anti-American feelings in, 128–29
  anti-drug money-laundering laws in,
      127–30, 135–36, 153, 155–56
  anti-Semitism in, 145–46
  Kopp affair and, 128–29, 135–36,
      140–43, 145–46, 155–56
  media of, 131, 132
  Passport Control in, 153
  as police state, 127–28
  Ticino, 147–49
Syria, 177, 192, 242

Tankazyan, Arutyun, 98
Tankazyan, Mario, 98, 102
Tankazyan, Vagram, 79
Taqwa Bank of Algeria, 196
Task Force on Terrorism and
      Unconventional Warfare,
      199–200, 203
TeleCommunications, Inc. (TCI), 182
Terrorist organizations
  BCCI and, 171–72, 176–79
    Abu Nidal, 201–202, 207–210
    in Europe, 186–88
    PLO, 194–95
    Shining Path, 203–208
  Communist regimes and, 193–95,
      198–203
  drug trafficking and,
    in Colombia, 232–36
    Shining Path, 202–206
  in Europe, 186–88, 197–99
  support of, 176
Third World, BCCI and, 167, 169–72
Thornburgh, Richard, 49, 69
Ticino (Switzerland), 147–49
Tochkov, Ivanoff, 144

Tokaltian, Avetis, 97–98
Trans-K-B Investment Company, 131
Trust companies, Bahamian, 45–48
Tunisia, 177
Turabi, Hassan al-, 194
Turkey, 143–44, 150
 organized crime in, 133–34
Turkish drug traffickers, La Mina and,
  60

Union Bank of Switzerland (UBS), 64,
  114, 140, 147–48
United Bank, Ltd., 163
United Nations (UN)
 antidrug armed force proposed for,
  50–51
 Convention Against Illicit Traffic in
  Narcotic Drugs and Psychotropic
  Substances, 52
United States. See also Operation Polar
  Cap; and specific U.S.
  Government agencies
 antidrug actions of, 243–44
 The Bahamas and, 15, 51–54
 BCCI's operations in. See Bank of
  Credit and Commerce
  International (BCCI)
 certification law, 53
 Colombian extradition treaty and,
  231, 234, 235, 237, 238
 currency supply, 240–41, 245–46
 drug use in, 214–15, 230, 247
 money-laundering in, 214–30,
  246–48. See also Bank of Credit
  and Commerce International
  (BCCI); La Mina
  crime rate and, 214–15, 230
  fear of investigating, 214
  foreign banks and, 215–16
  laws, 36–37
  motives for, 247
  sample cases, 217–30
 Shakarchi's claims and, 142–43
Uruguay, 92–93
 banks in, 115

Vasquez, Fabio Ochoa, 26–27
Vasquez, Jorge Ochoa, 10–13, 27, 70,
  110
Vesco, Robert
 Bahamas operations of, 14, 22–27,
  45–46
 Colombian drug cartels and, 14,
  26–27
Vivas, Raoul, 70–71, 93–103, 119, 120
 false imports and, 99
 Houston operation of, 100, 101
 New York operation of, 100
 prison terms, 60, 118
von Raab, William, 241–42, 246–47
Von Wedel, Paul, 184

Wade, Robert, 44
Ward, Edward, 21–23, 27
Ward, Mrs. Edward, 22, 30
Waridel, Paul, 133, 139
Wells, Andrew, 19
Wells Fargo bank, La Mina and,
  67–69
Willes, Edwin, 19
Winn, Philip, 142
Wolff, Antonis Navarro, 236–37
World Bank, 183
Worthen National Bank, 180
Wright, Jim, 53, 219
Wrobleski, Ann, 264n

Yemen, 177
Yldirim, Mehmet, 147
Young, Andrew, 179–80, 185–86
Yugoslavia, 202

Zarouk, Carlos, 194
Zayed bin Sultan al-Nahayan, Sheik,
  164, 166–67, 169–70
Zhao Ziyang, 185
Zia -ul-Haq, Mohammad, 180, 186–87,
  191
Zimbabwe, PLO and, 195
Zuazo, Hernan Siles, 243

About The Author

Rachel Ehrenfeld's *Evil Money* was first published by Harper Collins in 1992. Her previous book, *Narco-Terrorism*, published in 1990 by Basic Books, was reissued in paperback in 1992.

Terrorism Against
The United States

SPI
BOOKS

☐ **Terror! The Inside Story of the Terrorist Conspiracy in America** *by Yossef Bodansky.* America and Israel are facing a wave of violent terrorist attacks that may turn US cities into versions of Beirut and Belfast! Federal agents managed to prevent the destruction of New York City's tunnels and bridges, but Islamic terrorists from Iran, Sudan, Pakistan and Syria have billions of dollars and thousands of trained saboteurs poised to wreak havoc on America "The Great Satan" and Israel "the Little Satan." The author of *Target America: Terrorism in the U.S. Today* here exposes the inner workings of the group behind the World Trade Center bombing. With inside information on terrorist tactics, resources and motives—that will not emerge in the terrorist's trials—*TERROR!* will convince unwary Americans we are at war. (ISBN 1-56171-301-5) $5.99 U.S.

☐ **Target America: Terrorism in the U.S. Today** *by Yossef Bodansky. Intro by Congressman Bill McCallum (R-FL)* The World Trade Center bombing was only the beginning. International terrorists from Iran, Iraq, Libya, Syria and successor states from the former Yugoslavia are plotting against not only Israel, but also against America, the world's remaining superpower. Now for the first time, Yossef Bodansky, Director of the Republican Congressional Task Force on Terrorism and Unconventional Warfare and Terror documents these new sources of terror and how they have set up powerful and widespread networks to strike at targets in Israel, as well as here in the U.S. and Canada. (ISBN 1-56171-269-8) $5.99 U.S.

SPECIAL: BOTH BOOKS FOR $10.00

To order in North America, please sent this coupon to:
S.P.I. Books •136 W 22nd St. • New York, NY 10011
Tel: 212/633-2022 • Fax: 212/633-2123

Please send European orders with £ payment to:
Bookpoint Ltd. • 39 Milton Park • Abingdon Oxon OX14 4TD • England
Tel: (0235) 8335001 • Fax: (0235) 861038

Please send _____ books. I have enclosed check or money order for $/£
(please add $1.95 U.S./£ for first book for postage/handling & 50¢/50p. for each
additional book). Make dollar checks drawn on U.S. branches payable to **S.P.I.
Books**; Sterling checks to **Bookpoint Ltd.** Allow 2 to 3 weeks for delivery.
☐MC ☐ Visa # _____ Exp. date _____
Name _____
Address _____